PERSPECTIVES IN SOCIOLOGY
Herman R. Lantz, *General Editor*

Sociology and the Twilight of Man

Homocentrism and Discourse in Sociological Theory

By Charles C. Lemert

Southern Illinois University Press *Carbondale and Edwardsville*

Feffer & Simons, Inc. *London and Amsterdam*

Library of Congress Cataloging in Publication Data

Lemert, Charles C   1937-
   Sociology and the twilight of man.

   (Perspectives in sociology)
   Bibliography: p.
   Includes index.
   1. Sociology—Addresses, essays, lectures. I. Title.
II. Series.
HM24.L435 1978   301   78-17146
ISBN 0-8093-0851-7

For Matthew,

qui, pendant l'écriture de ce livre,
luttait, comme son père, avec l'espace
difficile entre la voix et le texte.

Contents

Preface

It is often said that theoreticians are too theoretical which is a way of saying that a great deal of theoretical writing seems unrelated to empirical research. Those who hold this opinion are, undoubtedly, even more disgusted by the rise of a theoretical subspecialty that concerns itself with metatheory, the theory of theory. The present book is one of the latter and thereby may contribute to the consternation of some sociologists.

I share at least an element of this concern though from a different perspective. It must be agreed that sociology will make its way only as an empirical science. However, this book has been written in part out of the conviction that sociologists are not now (any more than they ever have been) very clear on what constitutes the so-called empirical world. I believe that it is in recognition of this confusion that theoretical and metatheoretical studies find their justifications. Whatever else theory can be, there is a place for theory as the orderly sorting out of problems surrounding empirical work, even when this sort of theorizing does not directly result in numbers and propositions.

The problem, of course, is how to achieve this goal. I am also convinced that most recent sociological theory and metatheory do not achieve their own goals much less the one I define. Therefore, I attempt here to suggest an alternative to popular opinion and current practices in American sociological theory.

Having made this daring announcement, I wish immediately to efface the personal pronoun "I" in which, one has reason to believe, is contained much of the explanation for the inadequacy of current sociological work. The alternative here employed has been selected, not invented. The author is eccentric to this study.

This book has been written from an alternative that, by the standards of many recent intellectual fads, is already reasonably well aged. One hesitates to give the approach a name because the most accurate labels are not common in the United States and the one that is known has been grotesquely deformed by misunderstanding. But, since the latter will inevitably come to many minds, I mention it once (and once only) in the hope that its brief appearance will be a sufficient cathartic to expel it. In Europe (especially, France, Italy, and, increasingly, Great Britain) *structuralism* has proliferated in so many directions and undergone so many transformations that the term is no longer used without qualifying adjectives. Those who require a label are better off talking of *semiotics, poetics, grammatology* or *intellectual archaeology*.

The most important sources for the following text have been the principal writings of Michel Foucault and Jacques Derrida; in particular, the former's *The Archaeology of Knowledge* and *The Order of Things*. Other texts have been important, including those of Althusser, Culler, Saussure, Eco, Lévi-Strauss, though in a less explicit manner.

One of the ideas to be inferred from these texts is that theoretical analysis properly includes a consideration of the mundane facts (cost of paper, book market prices, and so forth) which are codeterminants of the final shape of any published text. Such material factors as these required that this text be much shorter than its original version. Consequently, this book lacks a long methodological chapter which described my use of Foucault, Derrida, and others. I have, however, included a brief summary of the position taken, supplied ample notes to background and methodological resources, and throughout simply used this type of discursive analysis (occasionally in an overstated manner in order to signal that what was being done was being done intentionally). The omission of a complete methodological statement is partially excused by the existence in English of good discussions of various aspects and versions of the position within which I have worked. Of these, the best are those by Jonathan Culler (1975, 1976), Umberto Eco (1976), Edward Said (1975), Guilio Lepschy (1970), Macksey and Donato (1970), Fredric Jameson (1972), and Dominique Lecourt (1974).

Four further points are worth the printing expense.

1) In what some will inevitably call the "substantive" chapters (2–8) I write about *written* theories, not complete sociological statements. Though I would deny that the two are ultimately separable, I am not embarrassed to write a theory of theory. Where appropriate, I have offered illustrations from the empirical work of the authors examined. However, in several cases (Blalock, Habermas, Schutz) this type of illustration is either sparse or a bit awkward because the authors themselves have not provided the material. This in itself is an important fact, as in the case of Habermas who has, at least for the time being, turned critical theory away from empirical writing to epistemology and social ethics.

2) Some will be disturbed by the representative figures chosen; for example, the choice of Cicourel to represent ethnomethodology. I have tried to justify this and other choices at the beginning of each chapter and in the notes. Also, it should be noted that the criterion for selection was discursive, not statistical. "Who speaks well for ethnomethodology or . . . ?" Not: "Who is most often cited?"

3) First person pronouns (I, my, we, ours, and so forth) have been omitted out of theoretical conviction, not personal or stylistic preference. One can hardly write a book on the decline of homocentrism in the first person. The exceptions to this rule are in this preface and several places where I seek specifically to connote something thereby (as in chapter 6 where the "I" functions as an illustration of phenomenologists' talk). One may take these occasional lapses as

signs of the author's own rootedness in homocentrism and, equally, as an indication that one is not here intentionally sponsoring an antihumanistic ideology. One cannot be sure whether to cry or rejoice at the death of man.

4) The approach taken here looks at theory as discourse. Among other things, this provides a different perspective on acknowledgments. It is a little observed fact that the style of acknowledgments varies dichotomously according to two types of theory. Dialogic theories see the written text as a product of meaningful interaction with special others and, therefore, are often accompanied by tender expressions of human love for those others "without whom the book could not have been." Monologic theories believe that the text is a result of the author's heroic mastery of a serious problem and often are prefaced by polite and/or clever thanksgivings which, in the end, admit that "the author alone is responsible."

If, however, theory is discourse then what is written is the product neither of dialogues nor monologues alone, but of a complex, largely anonymous formation of discursive conditions in respect to which the author is neither a simple beneficiary nor the central force. Both gratitude and heroism, therefore, have a real but more modest place. Thus, I hope that those whom I sincerely acknowledge here will understand that it is out of theoretical consistency that I refrain from an excessive public display of sentiment.

Herman Lantz, editor of the Southern Illinois University Press Perspectives in Sociology series, helped make the book much more readable and less obscure. He also continued to support the book even after reading several rather bizarre early drafts. My several departmental directors and deans—especially: Charles Snyder, John Hayward, Jerry Gaston, and Lon Shelby—skillfully worked the institutional papers that gave me time for writing. Both the Graduate School and the College of Liberal Arts at Southern Illinois University at Carbondale provided funds for travel and other assistance. The National Endowment for the Humanities supported the trip to Paris during which the project was begun. Carol Cox did most of the typing. In France, the *Centre Universitaire International* of the University of Paris and the *Centre d'Etudes Sociologiques* were very generous in giving me work space and other crucial types of help during three trips to Paris. Garth Gillan helped me talk through many of my ideas. Nicolas Mullins read the entire manuscript and offered sound criticism. Sang Jin Han, my research assistant for three terms, did much of the dreary library work. Most of these people were paid to do what they did, but the proof that the materiality of discourse is more than economic is that many of them would have done it anyhow and several did it for nothing.

Charles C. Lemert

Carbondale, Illinois
January 1978

Sociology and the Twilight of Man

1

Homocentrism and Sociological Discourse

Theoretical Pluralism?

It is probable that the most important theoretical problem in sociology is theory itself. The new glamour field in sociology is metatheory, the theory of theory. Even those who reject metatheory as speculation can often be heard, in conversation, giving their opinion of basic changes taking place in sociology. Indeed it is difficult to talk to any sociologist for very long without hearing the name "Thomas Kuhn" and the terms "paradigm" or "scientific revolution."

Most sociologists seem to believe that sociologists are thinking differently than they did in the past. Of course, one would not find so many respectable and otherwise cautious intellectuals speaking about "paradigm shifts" without good reasons. The most apparent of these good reasons are: the many philosophical studies of sociological theory (for example, Habermas 1971a, Emmet and MacIntyre 1970, Filmer et al. 1972, O'Neill 1972); the large number of sociologies of sociology recently published (for example, Gouldner 1970, Mullins 1973, Friedrichs 1972a, Warshay 1975, Curtis 1972); the many attempts to develop fundamentally new theories; and, of course, the fact that Thomas Kuhn's book (1962) has itself become a textbook (Kuhn 1962:10) for sociologists thinking about sociology (for example, Ritzer 1975, Friedrichs 1972a, Wilson 1970). One cannot fail to agree that—on the surface, at least—the present state of sociological theory does seem to correspond to Kuhn's symptoms of a collapse in normal science: "The proliferation of competing articulations, the willingness to try anything, the expression of explicit discontent, the recourse to philosophy, and the debate over fundamentals, all of these are symptoms of a transition from normal to extraordinary research" (Kuhn 1962:90).

Perhaps the most popular belief to emerge from this metatheoretical extravaganza is that recent sociological theory has become pluralistic (for example, Shils 1970, McKinney and Tiryakian 1970, Ritzer 1975, Rex 1974:3–22). Some seem to think that this pluralism is a good thing (for example, Warshay 1975:165, Friedrichs 1972a:325). For better or worse, most accept theoretical pluralism as a fact to be lived with.

This idea owes mostly to the two books which, in the early 1970s, initiated this metatheoretical moment in sociology: Robert Friedrichs' *A Sociology of Sociology* and Alvin Gouldner's *The Coming Crisis in Western Sociology*. Friedrich's argument is that the recent interest in phenomenological-type theory constitutes a new dialectical paradigm within sociology. Because this new model presumably accounts for both social order and social change, Friedrichs believes that the dialectical paradigm is itself pluralistic in that it expresses both conservative and "humanistic" sociological ideas. It is, thus, a pluralistic paradigm for a pluralistic discipline in a pluralistic society (see Friedrichs 1972a: 325; compare 1972b, 1972c). Gouldner's view is similar (1970:159). In American academic sociology, the earlier dominance of Talcott Parsons is now being replaced by more open, less structural theories such as those of Homans, Garfinkel, and Goffman. At the same time, in the rest of the world, Marxism (the major non-American sociological force) has also become polycentric as Maoism, Castroism, and various other neo-Marxisms have become important theoretical influences.

The success of the pluralism hypothesis owes largely to

the fact that writers like Friedrichs and Gouldner have pointed to something most sociologists already knew even though they had no metatheory to explain it. Since the early 1960s a tremendous number of apparently new theories have arisen: conflict theory, phenomenological sociology, reflexive sociology, ethnomethodology, sociological "naturalism," exchange theory, critical theory, theory constructionism—to mention only a few of the best known. To sociologists accustomed to defining theory by the works of Weber, Durkheim, Parsons, Mead, Merton (and their interpreters), this panoply of theories with new names and new programs surely must have appeared to be a paradigm shift, a new pluralism, the beginning of an extraordinary science.

There is only one problem with the pluralism hypothesis. It could be that the enthusiasm for Kuhn and the liberal appeal of the notion of pluralism has swept sociological metatheory off its feet and prevented it from reading the same set of facts in a different way.

It is entirely possible to look at recent sociology and see not pluralism, but unity. To be sure the unity would not be that of the 1950s when Parsons dominated sociology in the United States. But one can see behind all this pluralism and polycentrism traces of a very traditional sociological urge toward solidification, synthesis, and the past.

At that very moment when Parsons' was supposed to have been replaced by these theoretical inventions one can see that the new theories were in fact very, very Parsonsian, at least methodologically. Though often critical of Parsons, many seem to have shared his approach of defining theoretical work as the synthesis of classical philosophical and sociological ideas. Homans' (1964b) famous ASA presidential address was a landmark in the emergency of modern exchange theory and yet it was based upon a consolidation of elementary themes from classical economics and behavioral psychology. Berger and Luckmann's (1967) *Social Construction of Reality* was, for a while, read as the great advance in humanistic sociology, yet basically it was little more than a creative synthesis of Schutz, Sartre, Mead, Weber, and Durkheim. At the same time, Tiryakian (1965) attracted a lot of attention to phenomenological theory by his claim that all classical sociology could be consolidated as phenomenology. And how different really was this than Kingsley Davis' (1959) earlier claim that all was functionalism; or Denzin's (1969) later claim that there were no real differences between ethnomethodology and symbolic interactionism; or Pierre L. van den Berghe's (1963) argument that functional and dialectical theories can be integrated?

Activities such as these are, undoubtedly, new in some sense. But are they new paradigms? The question becomes all the more pertinent when one examines that period in both cultural and sociological history when one would expect to find the greatest amount of pluralism: the late 1960s. In sociology what one finds is that between 1966 and 1969 the classical texts in these presumably new paradigms were published and that they shared two common features: all were synthetic works and all relied heavily on rather classical ideas. In addition to Berger and Luckmann (1967) and Homans (1964a; but see 1967), one finds the following: Garfinkel's *Studies in Ethnomethodology* (1967) announced a new sociology, but one largely inspired by Alfred Schutz. Walter Buckley's *Sociology and Modern Systems Theory* (1967) was, in a parallel fashion, dependent on elementary information and systems theory. Arthur Stinchcombe's *Constructing Social Theories* (1968) quickly became a basic text in the new field of theory constructionism, yet its principal theoretical resources were formal logic and, again, information theory; moreover, it included the grand synthetic argument that there is no basic difference between historicist, functional, and demographic methods. Juergen Habermas' *Knowledge and Human Interests* (1971a) was hailed as the new advance in Marxian critical theory, yet it turned out to be the first step toward reverting Marxian theory to themes in Freudian and pragmatist social philosophies. And, within the pragmatist tradition, one also finds Bruyn's (1966) basic statement of the participant observational technique and the definitive collection of Herbert Blumer's (1969) theoretical and methodological essays. Neither Bruyn nor

Blumer did anything more than consolidate the classical ideas of symbolic interactionism.

The argument to be made is not that there is nothing new here; nor that there is no pluralism. The only question is whether or not theories so reliant on tradition and so similar methodologically to Parsons' synthetic method can be claimed to have reconstituted sociology as a multiparadigm science. Whatever else was going on in the late 1960s, it was not a polycentric orgy of daring new theories. It is possible that what really took place was marginal diversification within a traditional paradigm.

Metatheory, Theory, and Text

To question the pluralism thesis is, first of all, to question sociological metatheory itself. Its detractors are correct on at least one point. Metatheory can be, and often is, highly speculative. Whenever one tries to go beyond or behind or beneath the surface meanings of theoretical texts, it is easy to slip away from evidence into overly general and careless concepts. No better illustration is the term "paradigm." Among the sociologists who use the term, it is difficult to find a careful and critical examination of its technical methodological status. For the most part, it has been taken over, uncritically, from Kuhn with only modest qualifications (for example, Ritzer 1975, Effrat 1972, Friedrichs 1972a). The problem is that Kuhn himself was not very clear on the meaning of paradigm. Originally (Kuhn 1962) there were twenty-one different uses of the concept. It was not until some time later that, with the help of Masterman (1970), he was able to settle on three basic paradigms (see T. Kuhn 1969). But even three is a lot and most sociological discussions do not reflect this remaining ambiguity.

An illustration is easily given. When Friedrichs (1972a) describes his new dialectical paradigm he is making two metatheoretical judgments: one, that this new paradigm can be read in the texts of writers such as Berger and Luckmann (1967); two, that there is extratextual evidence to verify the dialectical nature of these texts. In other words, people are assumed to be interested in dialectical writings such as *The Social Construction of Reality* because they live in a dialectical (active, pluralistic, changing, differentiated) society. Since it would be strange to argue that Berger and Luckmann caused this type of society, what the analysis comes to is that this dialectical paradigm is somehow a distinctive feature of complex, volatile societies which engender dialectical texts. The fatal weakness of this method is that it is, at best, analogical. It assumes that certain texts "look like" certain social conditions. The concept *dialectical paradigm*, thereby, functions as a general name for this similarity.

At this point *paradigm* begins to bear the burdens of all other analogic concepts (domain assumption, ethos, world view, *zeitgeist*). When used in sociological reasoning, analogies of this sort do little more than destroy the primacy of whatever evidence is at hand by attempting to explain with reference to undocumentable characterizations summarizing causal "forces" "behind" the facts. Evidence is replaced by appealing mysteries with no explanatory value.

This problem is inherent in all meta-studies, but especially those that attempt to make meta-sociological judgments about theoretical texts. This is what the pluralism hypothesis does in claiming that the new texts with different names are in fact the result of a new multiparadigm sociology. Though often unstated, the reasoning is that a pluralistic ethos is causing a pluralism in sociological theorizing. By referring oneself back to an ethos or a paradigm, attention is drawn away from the theoretical texts themselves.

This is the chief difficulty. If there is pluralism in sociological theory, one must be able to demonstrate that pluralism with respect to actual published texts. There is no other evidence. Any method which ignores these texts may be properly accused of speculation. At this point it is clear that the methodological difficulty is not sociological alone.

Metatheory cannot avoid becoming comparative literature. In the simplest of terms, all literary theory involves the same dilemma. Presumably texts are similar or different because they possess similar or different meanings. But how does one determine the meaning of a text? If, on the one hand, it is claimed that the meaning is found *in* the text then how is one to decipher that text when it is well known that language is a social convention susceptible to tremendous variation. Different words may have similar meanings, and the same words may have different meanings in different contexts. On the other hand, if one attempts to get at the motivations which cause this variation in language, one is tempted to go *outside* the text to its social environment (its ethos) or the psychological intentions of its author (its paradigm). In the former case one risks reducing metatheory to linguistics, in the latter case one risks turning it into theology.

Of these two risks, the former is the better to take. It has the tremendous advantage of modesty insofar as it keeps one close to texts, to the evidence. At the same time its dangers are avoidable. Work with texts need not involve linguistic reductionism. On the contrary to define metatheoretical work as a species of literary theory can be understood as a proper sociological conclusion, in the following respect. Whatever else a theory is, a *scientific* theory is always and unavoidably something written and published. *Publi*cation and *object*-ification are inseparable in science inasmuch as the most basic and material meaning of objectivity is that scientific ideas must be made into *public objects*. Whether publication is formal (books, journal articles) or informal (letters, preprints, conference papers) there can be no scientific objectivity without published texts. Thus it follows that any metatheoretical attempt to compare the meaning of theories must examine scientific texts first and foremost. Otherwise, one cannot speak about the meaning of a scientific theory and all the well-intended talk of paradigms and ethoi will be totally lacking in foundation.

Theory as a Discursive Event

To base metatheory on the text is to treat theories superficially. More accurately put: it is to study theory at the point of its surface appearance as a material, public object. This methodological starting point is used here in order to counteract the tendency of most metatheory to be unjustifiably "profound." It is to provide an alternative to most paradigm searches which, by looking for "deeper" meanings, ignore the theory.

To take this approach is, of course, to risk what in some quarters is the most damning of accusations: positivism! It is admitted that to concern oneself with surface appearance is a positive approach, but this is not the positivism usually attacked in sociological circles. It is not "positivistic" in the sense that it naively holds that social facts make themselves positively available for harvesting by social scientists' surveys, experiments, or observations. It is positive in the sense that, given the relative inaccessibility of social facts, it insists that social science is better off rejecting hermeneutical mysteries and working with the only observable, given evidence a social scientist ever has: the materially concrete events produced in practiced discourse (see Foucault 1972b:234).[1]

Discursive analysis, thus defined, is a general sociological strategy. Even though, in this book, it will be applied strictly to sociology's discursive events (published theories), it is understood as an approach to everyday life social phenomena as well. Though some might view this as a type of reductionism, it is actually a rather mundane realism. Sociology—whether theoretical or metatheoretical—has only discourse to begin with and is only discourse in the end. Sociology has no choice but to start any research with discursive facts (oral interviews, written questionnaires, jotted field notes, printed demographic reports, collected historical documents, published reports on economic conditions, and so forth). In the end, sociology appears as a public object only by rewriting other people's discourse, becoming thereby a collection of texts on texts: verbal interpretations of mathematical formulae which are themselves (often) rewritings of computerly printed-out numbers which are coded rewritings of written or oral reports of somebody's talk about what has been happening. All of sociology moves, without exception, from text to text to text, usually beginning in talk and finishing in writing. The great mistake that is sometimes made is to assume that the people (along with their paradigms and ethoi) who "originate" the talk and, eventually, "finalize" published texts are more important, *sociologically*, than the texts themselves. When it is made, this mistake undoubtedly comes from the liberal humanistic idea that the human spirit suffers some kind of spiritual deprivation when it is read through its most visible and sophisticated products: its talk and writing. In contrast to such romanticism, the discursive analysis used here holds that sociology ought to be a positive science of the product of human discursive labor. To be so requires no necessary attachment to anything extratextual—be it paradigms or, even, the human spirit itself.

Though there is not sufficient space to fully develop the explanation and justification for this approach,[2] it is possible to explain what kind of theory of discourse leads to this methodology.

Discourse, most simply defined, is language-used. Language-in-use is always indexical; that is: talk always, without exception, functions by referring to other talk (Garfinkel and Sacks 1970), just as writing works with reference to other texts. Because discourse is thereby *con-texted* it may be understood as text-producing labor (Eco 1976, Derrida 1976, Foucault 1972a). This means that discourse is at least three things: 1) a social practice, 2) a material event, 3) a product resulting from social conditions.

First, it is a social practice in that texts are not epiphanies of the transcendent mind of an author. Authors cannot write without language and language is a social convention (Saussure 1959, Culler 1975). Discourse is an effective use of language only because it obeys the socially defined, normal rules for talking and writing. Discourse is, thus, a regulated social practice.

Secondly, as a social practice, discourse is a public event. It is material and concrete. Discourse resulting in texts leaves traces, especially in the case of scientific texts which are, by definition, written (compare Derrida 1976). Here is the positivity of the texts (Foucault 1972a). Public events cannot be hidden in the spiritual mysteries of paradigms and ethoi. This means that the regularities governing discourse are discoverable only through specific events, in roughly the same manner whereby the grammars of ancient, forgotten languages have been reconstructed by readings of (usually imperfect) hieroglyphic fragments and papyrus scraps.

However, thirdly, this positivity of the text is not easily arrived at because texts are products of social conditions. Their *contextedness* makes their reading difficult. Here one notes the eccentric relationship of discourse to language. To the extent that discourse is the practice of *language* it is a universal human activity. But, to the extent that it is a *practice*, an *event*, any particular discourse is found only in a particular and unique *context*. Whereas the rules of language are relatively general, the rules of discourse are relatively particular in that they are the socially determined rules governing normal discourse at a moment, in a place.[3] The social mechanisms governing the production of texts are, sociologically viewed, the social mechanisms permitting and obligating normal discourse. They include: grammar instruction in lower schools; parental modeling of "good speech"; classification procedures in mental hospitals, elementary schools, and prisons; school detentions for speaking "out of turn"; the national spelling bee; editorial review boards for defining "scholarly" writing; and so forth. Taken together, these mechanisms are the social conditions necessary to a given discursive formation and one cannot accurately read any particular text (theoretical or everyday life) without, at least to some extent, entering into an analysis of its discursive formation (Foucault 1972a, Kristeva

1974). This, then, is the only possible sense in which one can read theories extratextually. Instead of paradigms one reads con-texts defined as a discursive formation. Strictly speaking this is not an extratextual activity at all because it amounts, purely and simply, to an act of inter-textuality. That is to say: one reads the given theoretical texts over against those *con-texts* upon which are inscribed the social conditions for permissible talk and writing in a given discursive formation.

In simpler terms, discursive analysis in sociological theory compares two texts with respect to their literary value, not their spiritual implications. Faced with theoretical texts to be compared, discursive analysis refrains from asking such questions as: Who is the author? What kind of a thinker was he? Who influenced him? What was his social ethos? Instead, discursive analysis would ask: To whom is the author writing? What textual form (article, book, essay, letter, note) is used? Is the theoretical content determined by the textual form? Is the style conversational or formal? Is the author visible or invisible in the text? Is the corpus within which his/her text is found repetitive ("circular") or is it relatively nonrepetitive ("linear")? Who published the text and why and when? What economic factors determined the condition of its publication? What institutional authority does the author presuppose in order to legitimate the text or, even, the audacity of writing at all? Is the text written for fellow scientists, for students, or for general audiences? What does the text expect of the reader? Is the reader excluded, intimidated, threatened or included, comforted, persuaded? Is the language connotative or denotative? Though not all these questions are posed in each instance and, in some instances, others will arise, what should be known is that discursive analysis is confined to relevant permutations of a single problem: Why has this been *said* and not something else? (See Foucault 1972a:27 et passim; 1972b.)

Homocentrism in Sociology

Among the differences between a search for paradigms and a discursive analysis is the fact that the former is organized around a transcendent center. When a paradigm search is a search for the idea, puzzle solution (T. Kuhn 1969:191–210), domain assumption, ethos, principle, or whatever which lies "behind" the theory as its metatheoretical explanation or its meaning, the method requires the assumption that thought is centered. Centered thought is that in which ideas are, directly or indirectly, referred ultimately to some organizing principle which serves to limit the free play of the thought system (Derrida 1970). In this regard, most sociological studies of paradigms are metaphysical, insofar as metaphysics is the attempt to reduce reality to its central universal essences.[4]

By contrast, discursive analysis is necessarily decentered and antimetaphysical because it is the positive study of material products. Scientific discourse, as noted, is material because it is science only by being public and it is public only by being published, and written/printed things leave material traces which occupy space. Theories of science which ignore this fact are idealistically metaphysical because they believe that science exists in ideas, not ink and paper. If, in the one case, a theory is seen as an idea then it is naturally centered in some sort of mind—an author or an ethos. If, in the other case, a theory is print and paper then it cannot be summarized, collapsed, drawn up into any single, transcendent center. Print, ink, and paper can only be dispersed, not centered, in space. This distinction between centered and decentered views of theory is important because it leads to the first superficial signs that contemporary sociology is not very pluralistic.

If modern sociological discourse were truly pluralistic, then—at the least—one would expect that it not be centered; that it not be discourse searching constantly for some kind (it makes no difference which kind) of central idea, axiom, principle, or force to explain itself; in other words, that it not be so traditional.[5] What this book will show is that all of the major alternatives within recent sociological theory are, in fact, centered; and, furthermore, that they are centered in a particular and common fashion. There is evidence to demonstrate that even the most recent of presumed sociological "inventions" are *homocentric*.[6] One way or another, they all return to the peculiarly nineteenth-century idea which holds that *man* is the measure of all things (Foucault 1973:chs. 8, 9, 10). They are homocentric in that *man* is the condition which permits them to be written as they are.

The first, most superficial, evidence for this proposition is already contained in the fact that current metasociology has relied on so centered and metaphysical a tool as *paradigm* and its cognates. Were there genuinely new alternatives within sociology, the first place one would hope to find them would be in the metatheory used to interpret sociology. Since *paradigm* is used so traditionally, then one does not have much reason for confidence that it could describe anything new. In other words, from the point of view of a traditional, nineteenth-century metatheory, relatively minor variations in theory itself could appear to be much more important than they truly are.

The second, still superficial, evidence is that made available by the very idea that a material product such as discourse can and should be the primary topic of sociological talk. Why should this idea have occurred first to non-sociologists such as Foucault, Derrida, Barthes, and others in France and been totally ignored by sociologists? After all, were sociology so pluralistic as it is claimed, could not one reasonably expect language and its use to be given at least some serious attention by someone?

To be sure, language has always been discussed by sociologists, even from the beginning. Mead (1962:142), Cooley (1964:92), Durkheim (1965:94), Weber (1964:138), among others—all had something to say about language. But, in these cases, language was never taken seriously as discourse, as the product of a social practice. More often, language was seen as a sign of something else, usually *man*.

Mead is a clear example: "I know of no other form of behavior than the linguistic in which the individual is an object to himself" (Mead 1962:142). With Mead language points to man, just as with Durkheim *collective representations* point to the *collective consciousness*, with Weber *understanding* all but totally swallows up the discourse by which it is achieved, and with Parsons language remains a mere *medium* of exchanges. Sociology has never produced a forthright theory of language-practiced, of discourse. This is even true, as will be shown below in chapters 7 and 8, of the two most significant recent sociological attempts at discursive theory—ethnomethodology and Habermas' critical theory.

The explanation for this awkward gap in sociological writing may well be that a centered theory is incapable of treating a decentered phenomenon. In other words, a homocentric sociology may not be able to talk about so dispersed and eccentric a thing as discourse. The corollary of this is the hypothesis that when one examines current sociology as discourse what one will find is not pluralism but simply marginally diversified attempts to organize sociological talk homocentrically. This is the idea to be examined in what follows.

But first one must ask: *Homocentrism? What is it? Where does it come from?* [7] Homocentrism is a way of describing the dominant discursive mode during that period (usually called the "nineteenth century") which extended in western thought from the last quarter of the 1700s (with the publication of Kant's *Critique of Pure Reason* [1781] and Adam Smith's *Wealth of Nations* [1776]) through the first third of the 1900s (when Freud and relativity theory decisively began to rearrange our way of thinking). One is tempted to equate homocentrism with *liberalism* or *humanism* or even *historicism*. This is not entirely wrong, if it is kept in mind that homocentrism does not here refer to an ideal but to a condition permitting a certain type of discourse. Very very roughly put, one can mark the discursive terrain of homocentrism by noting that it is a space opened by Kant's *Critique of Pure Reason* in which man is, simultaneously, condemned to a finitude of phenomena alone and released as the principal agent in a subjective world of consciousness. It is, likewise, the discursive space that was then enlarged by the great economic and naturalistic texts of the nineteenth century—Smith's *Wealth of Nations*, Darwin's *The Descent of Man*, and Marx's *Capital*—in which man is situated within histories defining the place of the finite subject. Finally, homocentrism reaches its limits in Husserl wherein the phenomenological subjectivism Kant invented achieves an extreme form.

It may seem strange for us to speak this way about man because we, especially those who are sociologists, are so accustomed to thinking of man as a given. But the fact is that it was only in the nineteenth century that man thrived as a condition for intellectual talk. "Man is an invention of recent date. And one perhaps nearing its end" (Foucault 1973:387). Unfortunately, the economic conditions governing the production of the text you are now reading do not permit even a minimally adequate explanation of this fact and its implications. Fortunately, you can consult Michel Foucault's *The Order of Things* for a complete discussion of homocentrism.

What can be noted is that sociology with its origins in such nineteenth-century writers as Weber, Durkheim, Marx, Dilthey, and Dewey can be expected to have originally participated in homocentrism. Even the most superficial reflection suggests the probability of this relationship. Did not Durkheim seek to relate both the substance and method of sociology to the organizing power of man's collective consciousness? And, likewise, did not Weber base everything on the central idea of man as a rational creator of understandable meanings? And was not everything sociological in Mead derived from the assumption that society evolved from the human self's ability to represent himself to himself? It is a relatively easy matter to find, among the original sociologists, homocentric texts: "Social things are actualized only through men; they are the product of human activity" (Durkheim 1938:17). "'Culture' is a finite segment of the meaningless infinity of the world process, a segment on which human beings confer meaning and significance" (Weber 1949:81). Though these passing references cannot secure an argument they do suggest what most sociologists already know, even if it is not normally phrased in this way: Sociology began as one of the many nineteenth-century human sciences made possible by the discovery of man as a finite subject who creates a meaningful history.

However, the important fact is quite independent even of proof of its appearance in classical sociology. Homocentrism is unique to the nineteenth century. Prior to this period, thought was centered in more explicitly metaphysical objects—*logos, ousia,* God, *arché* (Derrida 1970:249). After the nineteenth century, theoretical talk was of relationships, not centers. In fact the nineteenth century, as a discursive space, is defined by *man*, its birth and decline as a condition for talk. Thus, it can be reasonably argued that, if modern sociological theory is in fact pluralistic in some fundamental way, pluralism must exhibit fundamentally new, post-nineteenth-century, discursive features. Conversely, if it can be shown that even current sociological theory remains strongly homocentric then it makes little sense to talk about sociology as a pluralistic science.

Strictly defined, *homocentrism is that discursive formation which centers itself upon man as a finite subject who dominates his own history. Finitude, subjectivity,* and *historicism*—these nineteenth-century inventions are the marks of man as a center.

Finitude. It is not too far wrong to say that Kant invented the nineteenth century by the curious tactic of demonstrating man's total incapacity to possess knowledge of the external world. By a stern subjectivity in which man was denied sure knowledge of the natural world, Kant made knowledge the practical product of a finite creature. Though there are more explicit nineteenth-century statements of the distinction, Kant's epistemology made necessary the divorce between culture and nature. With him man's finitude was his inability to grasp nature and its things. However, the consequence of this finitude is ironic. Man, though shriveled back into subjective consciousness, was nonetheless granted the subjective categories of understanding by which he then became the center of all knowledge.

Subjectivity. As seen from the case of Kant, finitude engenders and requires subjectivity. If knowledge was no longer a given of the natural mind in the natural world, then there was no place else for it to be located but in the subject. With subjectivity one can see the range of homocentrism insofar as the thinking of the nineteenth-century economists is precisely parallel to that of Kant. With Adam Smith, David Ricardo, and Thomas Malthus one finds—their mutual differences notwithstanding—finitude engendering subjectivity. Among the economists, man was trapped within the limits of natural market conditions. Particularly with Ricardo and Malthus one found the natural laws of the economy leading inexorably to overpopulation, scarcity, and death. With Malthus, for example, nature was death to man: "Famine seems to be the last, the most dreadful recourse of nature. The power of population is so superior to the power of the earth to provide subsistence . . . that premature death must in some shape or other visit the human race." Gloomy though they were, Ricardo and Malthus did not reject Smith's classical liberal theory of economic value wherein value was the product of human labor. With Smith, value was the creative product of a self-interested subject.

Of course, the third pillar of this formulation is in the evolutionary thinking of the nineteenth century in which man was the progressive subject made possible by Darwin's attempt to describe his peculiarly central place at the limits of nature. The words with which Darwin closes *The Descent of Man* are a particularly clear testimony to the necessary relationship between finitude and human subjectivity.

Man may be excused for feeling some pride at having risen, though not through his own exertions, to the very summit of the organic scale, and the fact of his having thus risen, instead of having been aboriginally placed there, may give him hope for a still higher destiny in the distant future. . . . We must, however, acknowledge as it seems to me, that man with all his noble qualities, . . . still bears in his bodily frame the indelible stamp of his lowly origin.

Historicity. The finite subject would have remained an abstraction were it not for history. In the nineteenth century, man-expelled-from-nature was given history as the place of which he became the central principle. But this was no arbitrary assignment. History was a necessity. With Kant's destruction of classical metaphysics and his invention of the finite of knowledge the following problem arose: What is thought to do if it cannot prove God, lodge itself in Being, or even perceive naturally occurring things in themselves? It must, of necessity, retreat to that which it can legitimately think. As a result, modern thought was forced to think itself. Thence arose a second problem. If thought thinks itself, how is it to extend itself? How is thought to be anything more than pure self-reflection? If the subject of thought is the foundation of knowledge, how does one move from his own subjectivity to that of the Other? Since Nature and Being are now removed as a basis for knowledge, one could no longer assume that some inherent principle of identity linked self with Other. Under the analytic of finitude the self was potentially against the Other. Yet without this Other thought would have no content, nothing to think but itself.

The solution to this problem was in the transformation of history from an external chronicle of events to a place for the human subject. Thought came to think the Other by conceiving of it as a difference to which self is united by placement in a series; that is, in historical time. Self and Other—though, in this scheme, still separated by differences projected along the movement of time—had access to each other by means of analogy. Analogy was thought's only access to that which forever succeeds or precedes it in the flow of time. But in what was that analogy grounded? This was a crucial question because, once begun, analogous thought can extend itself virtually infinitely. It must have a beginning in order to limit its free play, in order to allow man to function as its center. That beginning was also its telos: the human subject. Therefore, the analogic thought of history was that which commenced with a knowledge of the Other; that is, with the kind of self-knowledge that derives from self-reflection. Thought thinking itself is the basis for its thinking the Other. Man then became the subject of knowledge who was projected, analogically, forward through this succession of differences.

Thus, all of the great ideas of the nineteenth century—Kant's practical reason, the liberal theory of value, natural selection and evolutionism—were all historicist in the sense that knowledge, value, and life were saved from the doom of finitude by *history* understood as the realm of successions and analogies in which man created a meaningful human world over against nature. Beginning as the subject of knowledge, value, and life, man was permitted to expand himself as that presence which constituted the entire realm created by the new division with the universe between natural and historical things.

Man, the finite subject of history.   If there is novelty, invention, and pluralism in recent sociological theory one should not find this nineteenth-century discursive rule. The fact that it continues to condition sociological discourse is the subject of what follows and the good reason for doubting that sociology is pluralistic. Even more, it is the reason for suspecting that sociology is still very uncomfortable with the uniquely twentieth-century notion that we are now living in the twilight of man.

Varieties of Sociological Homocentrism

In order to examine the place of homocentrism in sociological theory it is necessary to characterize the important types of sociology in which sociologists believe. Were it the case that no significant differences could be identified, then no problem would exist for there would be no basis for the pluralism thesis. But, obviously, those who believe in sociological pluralism are not naive. There are certainly some kinds of differences of sufficient plausibility to persuade sociologists that a classification of theory types is necessary. The only question is whether or not these differences are fundamental or marginal. Thus, these beliefs in diversity cannot be dismissed out of hand.

However, neither can one accept uncritically the schemes in use because this would be an a priori admission that what has been said to this point is without worth. It has been argued here that the metatheoretical study of sociology must begin by treating scientific theory for what it is in its most specific and empirical sense: discourse. Previous sociological metatheory has not done this, so to employ existing classifications would cripple the present project from the outset.

On the other hand, it is not acceptable to invent a classificatory scheme that has nothing at all in common with what sociologists themselves recognize as a plausible account of what is going on in sociology. This strategy would be properly liable to the charge that it is an argument by definition. Therefore, one must set forth a classificatory scheme which does the following: 1) allows one to treat sociological theory as a discursive practice; 2) fairly represents the divisions that sociologists seem to think exist; 3) does not depend so heavily on its own inner logic that it draws attention away from the texts examined. In short the scheme must be *discursive, empirical*, and *simple*.

Therefore, sociological theory shall be subdivided according to which aspect of discursive practice the various types emphasize. The *first* is a type of sociological discourse which places emphasis upon the definition, specification, manipulation, and clarification of technical terms. It shall be called *lexical sociology*. Others have called it positive (Wagner 1963), priestly (Friedrichs 1972a), absolutistic (Douglas 1971), normative (Wilson 1970), or strict (Habermas 1971a, Schroyer 1971).

A *second* approach to sociology is that which emphasizes the meaning of empirical events in the social world. Ironically, it seldom pays strict attention to the meaning of terms used by sociologists and often even denies that this is possible. This type of sociology self-consciously sets itself off from the first approach and makes an issue of reducing the dominance of sociological language over human events that sociologists study. These are sociologists whose discourse seeks an interpretation of meaning which is taken as the essential quality by which man is differentiated from animals and things. This shall be called *semantical sociology*. Others have called it interpretative (Wagner, Wilson), prophetic (Friedrichs), naturalistic (Douglas), and hermeneutical (Habermas, Schroyer).

The *third* basic subgroup within sociology is that which is usually taken as the residual approach. One text, for example, defines this group as "those authors [who] neither consider nor actually treat sociology as a positive or interpretative science" (Wagner 1963:738). When it is defined substantively, the reference is, of course, to Marxian, neo-Marxian, radical, or critical sociological theories. That is, roughly, to those approaches that give primary attention to the normative basis of social science and which develop sociological theory with reference to explicitly stated values. It shall be called here *syntactical sociology* because, from the point of view of its discursive regularity, it concentrates on the normative rules that govern both sociological talk and social life.

The use of these labels—*lexical, semantical, syntactical*—must be cautious. There is no intention here of reducing sociological theory to linguistics. However, terms normally used in linguistics are here used to focus attention on the discursive nature of sociological theory. This is not to say that these theories will be analyzed linguistically, though it is to say that these discursive functions will be considered the best way to characterize the most important types of sociological speaking and writing. One is not being playful or coy in the use of these terms. They should be taken in the sense that some would like to call literal, as opposed to metaphorical. If a metaphorical usage is one in which the terms picture a phenomenon by reference to some similar, but different, phenomenon ("George Washington is the father of our country") and a "literal" expression is one that claims to represent directly the phenomenon itself, then this usage may be considered literal. One is not here looking for the root metaphors in sociological thought, but for what has actually been *said* by sociologists. Thus, the claim is that a certain large group of sociologists write in a way that emphasizes the *lexicality* of social phenomena, others write so as to call attention to the *semanticality* of social phenomena, and others write with an interest in the *syntacticality* of society. Accordingly, discursive practice and substance are not considered separable.

2

Axiomatic
Explanation:

George Homans

Lexicality in Sociological Discourse

Texts brought together under the label *lexicality* speak
of sociology as a definitional task. These texts vary widely
according to the type of definition used. Some are verbal,
others are mathematical; some are "analytical," others are
strictly logical; some are formed inductively, others deduc-
tively. These differences will be discussed below. What is
important now is that all texts in the lexical category place
the definition of terms at the center of sociological work.
This methodological style naturally reflects the more general assumption that the social world is amenable to definition. It is believed that the only obstacles to the creation of
a precise sociological lexicon are technical. The "problem"
of sociological work is merely that of improving sociology's
technical skills in logic, mathematics, reasoning, computer-
use and so forth. There is considerable faith here that if
sociologists were sufficiently committed to this task, it
could be accomplished. It is *not* assumed that the nature of
things stands in the way of lexical sociology. Reality is
understood as a *surmountable* obstacle. The social world
is not absurd or chaotic. In other words, the two most general assumptions of lexical sociology are these: 1) that the
task of sociology is definitional;   2) that the social world

lends itself to definitions. "As a science advances, it progressively redefines its concepts until they accurately represent the phenomena of the world" (Stinchcombe 1968: 40; compare Parsons 1954:352; Blalock 1969:6; Homans 1964b:818).

If one were to follow the custom of calling this type of sociology "positivism" one would be left with a vague, overly general label. By contrast, to describe this approach as *lexical* is specifically to limit analysis to the empirical facts of a discursive practice. In this case particularly one immediately discovers a feature of this type of sociology that is nearly always overlooked: lexicalists are extremely self-conscious about their own discourse. This is a conclusion contrary to the usual criticism in which "positivists" are attacked for being unreflective or uncritical. To be sure, lexical sociologists are often oblivious to many important problems sociologists should worry about. But, when one looks at lexicality as a discursive practice, it must be insisted that this type of writing is, in fact, very critical of sociological language. Indeed, its major purpose is tied to this discursive self-consciousness.

How lexical sociologists use their terms once they are defined is another matter. Here there is some considerable variance. There are two major types of lexical sociologists. Often they are at odds with each other. Many would not group these writers together. But the convictions they share are more important than their differences. The differences have to do with how they develop and use the terms in their lexicons, not with the basic fact of their lexicality. One of these points of view is that which insists that sociology should form clearly stated propositions. These propositions are seen as the content of theory. "A theory is a point of view and requires an assertion. . . . Substantive theory, in short, is propositional. Its propositions are assertions about society. Its concepts have referents in the empirical world. . . . Its conclusions have truth claims. And it is the ultimate goal of sociological inquiry" (Bierstedt 1959:141). Writers who hold this point of view include: Paul Lazarsfeld, Hubert Blalock, Arthur Stinchcombe, Paul Reynolds, Jack Gibbs,

James Coleman. Many of these are sometimes called *theory constructionists.*

The other major type of lexical sociology differs insofar as it is less concerned to develop terms and concepts that are *strictly* related (or relatable) to empirical events. Thus, the terms they use typically are not formulated into propositions. Instead this group is satisfied to employ defined terms within conceptual schemes which attempt to organize concepts in an analytic and systematic fashion. This group is often falsely and superficially criticized for paying little heed to the data. Strictly speaking, this accusation is not accurate insofar as the conceptual schemes are usually illustrated with reference to empirical studies and developed in response to empirical information. This group includes such writers as Talcott Parsons, Marion Levy, Neil Smelser, and Walter Buckley.

Therefore, the distinction between these subgroups is not between empiricists and "grand theoreticians." While there are differences, it will be shown that they are relatively unimportant when one examines their common interest in writing sociology around a lexicon. Even authors as apparently different as Talcott Parsons and Hubert Blalock are quite in accord that sociology can only become a mature science when it makes its theoretical vocabulary precise (Blalock 1973:2, 1969:3; Parsons 1954:350; 1951a:3). For all lexicalists scientific research is the manipulation of theoretical terms in an attempt to get them to reflect the social world.

It is at this point that homocentrism appears. What is the force behind these lexical duties? Who defines? Who manipulates the lexical items? Who presumes to catch the data of the world in the nets of formal concepts? It is none other than man. That same man who was born and lived in the nineteenth century. The homocentrism of lexical sociologists is found in the presence and dominance of *man the sociologist.* As will be seen, this is a man who in his own way acknowledges the finitude in which social phenomena are trapped. At the same time, lexical man lives confidently with the confinements of history; in this case the history of the terms, propositions, concepts and schemes that are accumulated to constitute, for him, the body of sociology.

This will sound strange to some. Blalock and Parsons as "humanists"? Impossible! Think of all the ink spilt to show that lexical sociology is the product of "hardhearted," "absolutists," "conservatives," "grand theorists," and so forth. Is it not common to treat these sociologists as the very antithesis of everything personal, radical, and human? Yes. And it is wrong. It is the intention of chapters 2, 3, and 4 to show that lexical sociology is no less homocentric than those other sociologies that talk openly about "humanism," "liberation," "freedom" and the like.

Theory Is Explanation

George Homans is a particularly interesting figure in the lexical group of writers because his published writings contain themes that are similar to both lexical subgroups. While consistently maintaining a concern for propositional statements, he has done so in a way that betrays a stylistic sympathy for those who work with conceptual schemes. He cannot, therefore, be strictly associated with the new theory constructionist movement of Blalock, Stinchcombe, Mullins, Gibbs, Reynolds, and others, even though it is to these writers that his manifest intents are most similar. At the same time, Homans has always been a "theorist" in the sense that Parsons is often disparagingly labelled; that is, one who does theory without doing "original empirical research." Homans' most important books and articles are not founded upon empirical research. They are secondary analyses of the work of other researchers and, more important, they have as their goal the development of the elemental principles of sociology. The best examples here are his earliest important book, *The Human Group*, and, later, his *Social Behavior*. Even though these books are different in a crucial methodological respect, they share the goal of attempting to define the necessary concepts for adequate sociological thinking. It is here that Homans differs from other propositional lexicalists. For example, neither Hubert Blalock nor Arthur Stinchcombe have sought to establish agreement on specific substantive propositions. Instead they have been more interested in educating their colleagues in the methods of theory construction. Therefore this examination of the texts of Homans will serve primarily as an introduction to the propositional approach to lexical discourse. Secondarily, it will serve to indicate the general discursive characteristics of the entire range of lexical sociology.

In order to get at the regularities which govern Homans' sociological discourse, one may first look at what he has said with respect to the nature of theory. On this topic, his position was very clearly stated because, in many ways, Homans' work has been almost exclusively metatheoretical. That is, he has sought to explain how theory ought to be done in sociology.[1]

What then is Homans' theory of theory? The answer is found in a single phrase that repeats itself again and again. *Theory is explanation.* This is the statement which has governed all of Homans' literary work (see 1962:1–49). On the one hand, the phrase is used to demonstrate what Homans takes to be his distance from standard practice in sociology: the idea that theory can serve useful scientific purposes even though it may only be a general description bound in a series or system of concepts. His straw man, in this respect, is Talcott Parsons, though he does not spare others in the functionalist tradition—Durkheim, Radcliffe-Brown, Malinowski, Neil Smelser, and Kinsley Davis (see Homans 1962, 1964a, 1964b, 1967). What is wrong with functionalism and, for that matter, most sociological theory is that it can explain nothing; or, at best, when it explains something it does so accidentally.

Therefore, *theory is explanation* is Homans' affirmation of what is needed. What does he mean? "Explanation is the deduction of empirical propositions from more general ones" (1967:31). The three elements in Homans' scientific strategy are here: "deduction," "empirical," and "propositions."

First of all, theory can only advance if it is part of a *deductive system*. This is a crucial point to Homans, one that he came to in reflecting on his book, *The Human Group* (1951). This earlier study of small groups was self-consciously inductive. There he looked at case studies of various human groups and sought to derive generalizations with respect to group behavior. He found four classes of behavior: sentiments, activities, interactions, and norms. Homans then developed a number of general propositions by testing lower-level hypotheses as he moved from case to case. The problem, he concluded at the beginning of his later book, *Social Behavior*, was that *The Human Group* did not explain much at all about these classes of behavior (Homans, 1961:8–12).[2] Why not? Homans is not entirely clear. But the chief reason seems to be that generalizations cannot explain unless they are placed within a deductive system. Only then can they be precisely used to evaluate and explain the findings of empirical research.

This leads to the second element. Science—social science included—must work from a body of well-ordered general propositions that are systematically applied to *empirical research* and, thus, tested against the data. But how is this done? Homans does not favor empirical research for the sake of empirical research. Empirical study is disciplined, in two senses: it is undertaken *with* discipline (that is, self-restrained care governed by rules); and it occurs *within* a discipline (that is, by and between a group of scientists who define and redefine theories in order to test and retest them). He objects that much of sociological research has been undisciplined in these respects. "We adventurers reach more and more 'exciting' findings; foundations give us more and more money to advance the 'growing edge' of our fields, but behind the growing edge the intellectual work that would organize the findings remains largely undone" (1967:109). Therefore, while he argues against a kind of general theory that is unrelated to ongoing empirical research, he also opposes research that is not governed by disciplined theorizing—that is, explaining.

Thus, thirdly, propositions of a certain kind are essential: "A theory of a phenomenon consists of a series of propositions, each stating a relationship between properties of nature" (Homans 1964b:811). The series of propositions of which theory is constituted must form a deductive system. Scientific research must possess certain general propositions which have the force of being axioms; axial principles to which everything else in the system is related. Where do these axioms come from? Here Homans places great confidence in the scientist. The general propositions, upon which everything else rests, may be either invented or borrowed (1961:9, 1964a:975). Simply put, the process goes like this: one scans the literature for findings (for data) in the area under investigation. The propositions discovered there are borrowed. One then attempts to make them more general. How can they be rewritten so as to express even more general statements? "When you have reduced your set of propositions as far as you dare, ask what propositions of a higher level of generality still your set might in turn be derived from" (Homans 1964a:975).[3] Thus by working thoughtfully up and down the line from findings to the most general discoverable set of propositions one eventually polishes the deductive system which is then ready for testing against further research. Homans succinctly summarizes the process in the following description of his own work style:

A lower-order proposition in the theory represented an empirical finding. It could be deduced from higher-order ones under specified given conditions, and the deduction might make use of the rules of logic and mathematics. When the lower-order proposition was so deduced, it was said to be explained, so that a theory was also an explanation. From the higher-order propositions, under different givens, a number of other lower-order propositions could likewise be derived. . . . [T]he highest-order propositions were logically independent of one another. If any lower-order proposition, derivable from the theory under specified givens, repeatedly failed to represent the observed facts, the theory was liable sooner or later to be modified. . . . [Homans 1962:43–44]

Throughout this process it is clear that the scientist is guided primarily by the rules of formal logic, but not to the exclusion of disciplined imagination: "Invent the higher propositions if you must" (1964a:975). Clearly, considerable trust is placed in the rational capacities of the working theorist insofar as explanation is created by the hard work of the theorist. The two movements of explanation are interrelated. The general propositions are induced by intellectual creativity; then checked, clarified, and made precise by deduction which is governed by the rules of formal logic (1961:10). "Deductive theories are inductively arrived at" (1962:46).[4]

The actual deductive system that Homans has set forth is known as an exchange theory (1958, 1961). It rests on the assumption that the most general feature of human interaction is the exchange of material *and* nonmaterial goods (1958:115). It is worthwhile to look at one instance of Homans' exchange theorizing in order to illustrate his manner of speaking of theory as explanation.

Going back to the earliest of his major publications, *English Villagers in the Thirteenth Century* (1941), Homans has consistently maintained that one of the universal classes of human behavior is interaction. (Others are sentiment and activity.)[5] In his study of small groups, *The Human Group*, Homans developed a lower-order proposition with respect to interaction. It went like this: "If the frequency of interaction between two or more persons increases, the degree of their liking for one another will increase, and vice versa" (1951:112). This proposition was originally arrived at inductively. Homans drew it from his analysis of the famous Bank Wiring Observation Room study of workers in the Hawthorne Western Electric Plant (F. J. Roethlisberger and W. J. Dickson 1939). In other words, he took what he considered to be useful empirical findings and invented this proposition. The proposition, as stated, involves two of his universal classes of human behavior: interaction and sentiment. The sentiment is "liking."

This is a good example of the type of proposition Homans has sought to construct. It is not vague. (Such as: "Interaction is a function of liking, and vice versa.") Nor is it overly precise. (Such as: "Interaction varies with liking according to an 'n-' proportionality constant.") Clearly he would have preferred the more precise type of statement, but the middle range form was all that was possible with the data at hand (1961:51). In *The Human Group* he did relate this proposition to others that were developed from it on the basis of analysis of his data (1951:112–13). But these propositions did not take the form of a deductive system.

The exact same proposition appears in his later book, *Social Behavior: Its Elemental Forms*, wherein he employs his version of deductive theorizing. But here it is in quite a different theoretical and textual setting. First of all, in *Social Behavior* it is expressed as a proposition that can be deduced from other more general propositions, one of which is: "The more valuable to Person a unit of activity Other gives him, the more often he will emit activity, including sentiment, rewarded by Other's activity" (1961:181). This higher-order proposition, in combination with others of comparable generality, are used to explain the original lower-order statement. Before illustrating Homans' exact deductive explanation, it is necessary to explain how Homans got these higher-order propositions in the first place.

As noted earlier, Homans believes that higher-order propositions may be either invented or borrowed. His, he admits (1961:12), were borrowed from two sources: the behavioral psychology of B. F. Skinner and what he calls "elementary economics." The former source is clearly the more important (1962:47). Why? What compelled Homans to lean so heavily on behavioral psychology? There are, it seems, at least four reasons. Its principles are well-grounded in the findings of experimental research (1961:12). They appeal to common sense (1958:115). They are, of all the propositions used in the social sciences, the most general (1967:43). And, fourth, they work; that is, in his opinion they explain better than other general propositions.

The fourth of these justifications reveals a good deal about Homans' theoretical methodology. He is not content to borrow blindly or superficially. His strategy seems to be this: if the principles of behavioral psychology are going to be used for explanation in social science, their explanatory power must be demonstrated. Therefore, he is careful to attempt to show the excellence of what he is borrowing by demonstrating that historical, anthropological, economic, and social psychological explanations can all be reduced to these psychological principles (1967:43, 55; 1964a; 1971). They are borrowed, yes; but also defended. These defenses depend consistently on the agility of Homans' own reasoning, on the capacity of the theoretician to develop his own arguments. As a result his defense of behavioral doctrine has led him to take positions that many consider to be quite audacious, such as his claim that one can explain the fact that William the Conquerer did not invade Scotland by a series of propositions that go back to the simple behavioral assertion that "the greater the value of a reward to a person, the more likely he is to take action to get that reward" (1967:44). In this same connection, it is interesting to note the particular literary device he employs in his most careful presentation of these general principles. It is nothing less than an imaginary parable of a simple exchange relationship between two office workers (1961:31 f.). While drawn loosely upon Peter Blau's *Dynamics of Bureaucracy*, this little fiction (which guides the entire presentation of his basic terms and propositions) is strikingly close to a technique that is seldom associated with lexical-type sociologists: the ideal-type! Homans, in spite of his concern with the rules of formal logic and the findings of empirical research, is willing to place an overwhelming amount of confidence in the intellectual intuition and imagination of the scientific theoretician.

Returning now to the general propositions themselves, there are five in all:

1) If in the past the occurrence of a particular stimulus-situation has been the occasion on which a man's activity has been rewarded, then the more similar the present stimulus-situation is to the past one, the more likely he is to emit the activity, or some similar activity, now. [1961:53]

2) The more often within a given period of time a man's activity rewards the activity of another, the more often the other will emit the activity. [1961:54]

3) The more valuable to a man a unit of the activity another gives him, the more often he will emit activity rewarded by the activity of the other. [1961:55]

4) The more often a man has in the recent past received a rewarding activity from another, the less valuable any further unit of that activity becomes to him. [1961:55]

5) The more to a man's disadvantage the rule of distributive justice fails of realization, the more likely he is to display the emotional behavior we call anger. [1961:75]

In each of these one can see the translations of B. F. Skinner's principles in the importance given to reward and stimulus.[6] This is the mark of Homans' curious definition of the term *induction* as borrowing and invention (1961:10). However, one may also see the evidence of the more traditional, commonsense type of induction which refers to generalizing from data. For here are those three classes of human behavior that Homans first began to discover in his empirical study of medieval England (1941): activities, sentiments ("anger"), and interactions. This is what he means in saying that deductive theories are inductively arrived at (1962:46).

So, now, it is possible to return to and explain that lower-order proposition with which this illustration began: "If the

frequency of interaction between two or more persons increases, the degree of their liking for one another will
increase." The problem, of course, is how to link this lower-order proposition with any or all of the most general,
higher-order propositions we have just looked at. This is the
task of deduction, which is accomplished by the derivation
of three "connective" propositions:

a) The more valuable to Person a unit of activity Other gives
him, the more often he will emit activity, including sentiment,
rewarded by Other's activity. [1961:181]

b) Now one of the activities Person may give to Other is the
generalized reinforcer called social approval; and . . . the more
valuable to Person is the activity Other gives him, the more valuable is the approval or liking Person gives Other. [1961:182]

c) The more valuable to Person the activity Other gives him,
the more valuable the approval he gives Other and the more often
he emits activity, including sentiment, to Other. [1961:182]

What exactly are the connections? It is important to remember that the relationship among propositions must be
explanatory. It goes like this: Propositions (a) and (b) are
deduced from the general propositions (1), (2), and (3). The
deduction depends entirely upon Homans' operational definition of the crucial term, value. Following Skinner, value
is defined simply as the amount of reinforcement or punishment a person gets from a unit of activity given to him by
an other (1961:40). One measures value historically; that is,
by observing the history of the person in question. These
observations reveal that the person values a unit of activity,
such as help in completing a difficult task, if that person
considers help a reward (a reinforcer). How is this determined? Simply by observing the person's behavior on those
occasions when he/she is given help. If, on these occasions,
he/she exchanges some other unit of activity (such as, giving to the helper praise or some other expression of social
approval), then the help is considered to be valuable to the

person. In other words, help is valuable to the person who is observed giving to someone else units of social approval in order that he/she may receive the reward of help. Given this understanding of the lexical item *value*, then we can see that propositions (a) and (b) are merely a rephrasing of the general propositions (1), (2), and (3). The rephrasing depends entirely upon the operational definition applied to the term value.

Once propositions (a) and (b) are thus established, the proposition (c) follows as a consequence. It is this third proposition (c) that is finally used to explain the lower-order proposition which states that liking and the frequency of interaction vary directly with one another. The theory of the empirical observation that liking and frequency of interaction vary directly with each other is the complete system of explanations Homans has created.

Now, it is important to note that Homans does not rest his case here. In the chapter in *Social Behavior* in which this argument is presented, Homans immediately returns the reader to a review of empirical findings which support the explained low-order proposition (1961:182–86). Then, he introduces an important qualification. He notes that there are many situations in which people interact even though they do not like each other. Most of us, at some time or another, have been forced to work with persons whom we did not like. In these cases frequency of interaction is totally unrelated to the sentiment liking. Here the other person's activity is not a reward but a punishment. How is this to be explained? Homans is forced to introduce other considerations such as situations in which persons are not free to ignore each other and the effect of the esteem of the other. With this the deductive process is started over. A new set of explanations is set forth (including, for example, new propositions such as the higher the esteem in which Other is held, the greater the amount of interaction he receives). These are then related back to the more general propositions and then tested against available data (1961:186–202).

In summary the process goes like this. Observations are

made. Classes of behavior are sorted out. Lower-order propositions representing the relationships between empirical instances of these classes of behavior are stated. A general scheme of propositions is invented or borrowed. Lower-order propositions are deduced from these, by a process that relies heavily on the definition of working terms. The deductive system pertinent to the problem at hand is established. It is checked against available data. If problems are encountered, the explanations are reworked and the system reestablished to account for the difficulties. The final product, in Homans' case, is a book like *Social Behavior* which is a complex web of logically interconnected explanatory propositions. This matrix of explanations is what Homans calls sociological theory.

Homans' Explanatory Lexicality

Now, in what sense is this view of theory lexical? An objection could be raised. Why not call this propositional sociology? Do not the texts of Homans carry more references to propositions than to terms? Does not the idea of a deductive system depend on the logical formulations of these propositions? This objection is met by reference to the methodology explained in the previous chapter. The issue here is the discursive regularity that governs the texts. This is not a statistical problem. It is not of interest that the word "proposition" appears frequently in Homans' corpus and the word "lexical" appears only occasionally disguised in certain cognates ("definition," "concept," and so forth). What is important is how what appears on the material surfaces of the texts reveals the crucial manner of speaking, and, thereby, permits one to see a regularity in the actual discursive events.

An examination of Homans' most complete theoretical statement, *Social Behavior*, shows that the chapter headings read exactly as a lexicon. Following the introductory portion, Homans' chapter titles include: "Influence," "Conformity," "Competition," "Esteem," "Interaction," and so forth. His earlier article on exchange theory follows exactly the same format (Homans, 1958).

More significant is the fact that it is these terms listed in *Social Behavior* and others that Homans carefully defines that make his texts work. It is terms which allow him to speak in his sociological manner. What does this mean? Just this: one must ask what it is that allows Homans' texts to make sense to sociologists. It is clearly not his commitment to deductive science, to formal logic, or to the logic of explanation. Were he simply to have written books and articles on these subjects using sociological illustrations then we would find, under the name Homans, popularizations of a certain point of view in the philosophy of science. His texts would not be read widely by sociologists. He would not have access to the platforms of Harvard's Sociology Department or the journals of the American Sociological Association. Therefore, what makes his texts sociological is not a philosophy of scientific explanation but the manner in which this brand of philosophy is applied to sociological topics. This is what makes them *work* for sociologists. Remember that the analysis is of a discursive *practice*.

Viewed in this way it can be seen that the sociological effectiveness of Homans' discourse depends entirely upon what he does with his lexical material. We have already seen a clear example of this in his discussion of interaction. How was Homans able to make a connection between the general propositions drawn from Skinner and the lower-order proposition induced from data? It was only by his treatment of the crucial term value. By making explicit his working definitions of value and providing it with sufficient explanatory and illustrative text (1961:39–49), he was then able to deduce a middle-level proposition ("The more valuable to Person a unit of activity Other gives him, the more often he will emit activity rewarded by Other's activity" [1961:181]) from the general proposition ("The more often within a given period of time a man's activity rewards the activity of another, the more often the other will emit the activity" [1961:54; see above]). The general proposition dealt with the problem of the relationship between frequency of interaction and reward. The middle-level proposition included a more explicit account of the value of activity. It then became applicable to the lowest-order proposition (that frequency of interaction and liking vary positively with each other). The steps depended entirely upon a stated definition of the term value, its relationship to another crucial lexical item, reward, and then its specification to the explained proposition.

Thus Homans' sociological work is not the defense and use of propositions nearly so much as the sociological use of various lexical items. This is why the first two methodological chapters in *Social Behavior* (1961:chs. 2, 3) are exclusively devoted to the crucial terms: reinforcer (1961:18), deprivation and satiation (1961:19, 20), stimuli (1961:22), cost (1961:26), quantity (1961:36 f.), value (1961:29 f.). The propositions of Homans would be utterly meaningless to sociologists were it not for the primary attention Homans gives to these terms. Thus, it can be said, *Social Behavior* is only a web of interrelated propositions because it is first a careful lexicon of technical terms applied to sociological topics.

Sociological Man and the Lexicon

Having now shown what is different about Homans one returns to the larger question. Is the difference sufficient to interpret Homans' exchange theory as a separate "paradigm"? The answer is no because it can be demonstrated that Homans' lexical theory is also profoundly homocentric.

So much of that which horrifies Homans' humanist opponents seems to suggest that whatever he has done the least seems to be placing a human presence at the center of his sociology. Does not all this talk of propositions, definitions, and data create the image of a cold, objective scientist? Does not a devotion to formal logic and deductive systems suggest a very archaic, at best traditional, scholastic approach to human behavior? Is not behaviorism, with its emphasis on the observation of external behavior, an outright denial of the "freedom" and "inner meaning" of human life?

It must be remembered that homocentrism is not an ideology or a way of life. Humanism and the discursive practice called homocentrism are related but not the same. They have the same origin in the nineteenth-century discovery of man, but have taken on quite different functions. Therefore, the consideration of Homans as a homocentrist must be made on technical grounds with reference to the four characteristics of this discursive regularity that have already been described: finitude, subjectivity, historicism, and the centrality of man.

1) Even though Homans states no formal epistemology, it is apparent that he does not believe in the absoluteness of human knowledge. Homans does not believe that knowledge is given in the structures of natural order. Note, for example, the following: "As we move towards more and more general propositions, we reach, at any given time in the history of science, propositions that cannot themselves be explained" (1967:26). Homans' axioms are not laws of nature. While he claims that his five axioms are nearly universal in human behavior, he does not admit that they can be proved as natural principles. If he were an epistemological absolutist, believing that knowledge is given in the structures of being, then this would be, for him, a still higher-order proposition which could be used to explain their universality. And everyone can rest assured that if Homans—of all people—believed that there were such still higher-order explanations to be had, he would have grasped them immediately. His theoretical program is exceedingly bold. In its assertion of general explanatory axioms, it is— in its own way—every bit as cosmic as the schemes of Parsons. But it is not so bold as to reach for explanations that Homans obviously does not think are there.

This is even more solidly documented by Homans' theoretical methodology. The reference here is to his assertion that the crucial higher-order propositions must be borrowed or invented. His propositions are not deduced from natural laws as in scholastic thought which comes to mind as a pure illustration of classical deductive reasoning. *Propositions must be invented or borrowed from someone else who invented them.* Since they are not given in the nature of reality, they are not implanted in the mind of the scientist. They are, at some point or another, invented by scientists who are attempting to know what is "out there" and doing what they can to invent explanations for an alien reality. Scientific knowledge does bear the mark of man's finitude. Homans, bold though he is, is nevertheless not interested in circumventing what almost every serious epistemologist since Kant has been saying. At no place is this more apparent than in his explanation for the poor record of the social sciences. Why have they not developed more cumulative knowledge? Not, he says (1967:89), because social scientists are stupid; nor because the discipline is new. It is because that which they study is so difficult to grasp. "The human mind is not altogether a free agent. It is subdued to the material on which it works" (1967:89).

2) This leads to the second element in homocentric scientific discourse, subjectivism. The extent to which lexical sociologists—Homans included—are prepared to introduce their own subjective presence into their writings is almost always overlooked. The silliness with which the opponents of lexical sociologists have sought to isolate them as violators of the human spirit has, once again, blinded many to the facts. Talcott Parsons responds to theoretical problems by restating them in terms of his own intellectual history (Parsons 1970b). Arthur Stinchcombe and Hubert Blalock often write in a strongly active first person singular which has the effect of locating their texts relative to their own personal convictions and sentiments. Homans is no exception. In 1962 Homans published a collection of his essays. The texts treated exceedingly diverse subjects. On the first page of this book he acknowledges his responsibility to provide some sort of principle of unification. What does he decide to do? He explains this varied collection with reference to his own biography:

I have indeed scattered my shots, and the best thing I can do by way of introduction to these essays is to take advantage of this very deficiency by explaining it. Few of us social scientists have tried to write our intellectual autobiographies and to tell as best we could why we got interested in the subjects we have worked on and why influences have played upon us as we worked. Without trying to analyze the deeper and less conscious influences, I shall explain the scattering of my subjects by giving, as well as I can at this late date, the more obvious reasons why I took them up and why I pursued them as I did. [1962:1–2]

This very interesting essay then proceeds to lay out his major work (prior to 1962, of course) with respect to the influences of his good friends Lawrence Henderson, B. F. Skinner, Conrad Arensberg, Bernard DeVoto, William Allen White (and others) and the controversies engendered by other good friends and personal acquaintances such as Talcott Parsons, Clyde Kluckhohn, and Radcliffe-Brown. The essay reads from a central, profound conviction that, for the thirty years he discusses, all that was important to social science was within the body of Harvard University at whose breast he nursed. One could discount this observation as a peculiarity of Harvard; or as a necessity in autobiographical discourse. But this is too easy. Whatever the place of these factors, it remains evident that Homans freely accepted them, and for a self-conscious puritan (1962:49) this fact cannot be casually dismissed.

The more definitive sign of Homans' subjectivity is his literary style. It is overwhelmingly personal. Even in those texts which are not overtly autobiographical, one cannot avoid the presence of Homans' forceful first-person prose. The reader must either contend with a Homans in the first person *singular* who unrelentingly states his personal case or with a Homans in the first person *plural* who seeks to seduce the reader along a journey into the inner workings of his mind. *Social Behavior*, for example, shifts from the former to the latter as he begins his substantive argument:

"At this point I give up the competitive 'I' and we, my readers and myself, assume the collaborative 'we'" (Homans 1961:16). The personal pronoun can be used either neutrally or personally. With Homans there is little neutrality. The reader is forced to concede the point, or argue it, or feel like a fool for not having seen it before. The sentence with which Homans concludes his famous and controversial presidential address to the American Sociological Association (an address which began with the admission that he was, therein, going to speak "ex cathedra" 1964b:809) is typical of this literary quality: "I must acknowledge freely that everything I have said seems to me obvious. But why cannot we take the obvious seriously?" (Homans 1964b:818).

These intimations of a subjectivism are further supported by a critical reading of the texts. As seen above, Homans' deductive system is, on the surface, rational and tightly closed. But, on closer examination, it gives the crucial place to his own intuitions. The deductive first principles must be invented and borrowed and this is left up to the scientist himself. There are no natural rules to guide this step without which nothing at all could be said. The power of the first person in his literary style is not accidental. It goes hand in glove with Homans' most important methodological conviction.

This makes clear the basis of lexical sociology's homocentrism. It is a type of sociology in which all of the social world is drawn up into the subjectivity of the scientist. To be sure this is done subtly. It is simply a way of speaking that appears perfectly sensible to this type of sociologist. Its subtlety is protected by the careful suppression of all affective and normative elements, by which tactic the aura of objectivism is conveyed. Thus it is no wonder that tendentious critics of lexical sociology are unable to detect the central importance of its epistemological subjectivism. This, of course, is a corollary of the analytic of finitude accepted by this school. Having accepted as given the unbridgeable gap between the knower and the known, lexical sociologists such as Homans, reintroduce epistemological faith by over-affirming the capacity of the subjective mind of the knower. Thus, what is lost to the intractability of the world which is "out there" is made up by the confidence placed in the reasonableness of the scientist. To put it simply, one might ask: where does the social world to be studied *exist* for lexicalists? In the mind of the scientist!

But surely someone will say this is a ridiculous observation. Ask any lexical sociologist, Homans included, whether the world is real and he will say yes. Homans himself has denied that he is a nominalist (for example, 1967:61, 74). The issue, let it be remembered, is not to classify according to epistemological theories but as to what appears in the text itself as its effective rules. When this is done lexicalists such as Homans, whatever they may themselves argue about nominalism and epistemology in general, are able to speak only because they have placed themselves at the center of the discursive process. The substance of this approach lies entirely in the assumption that the sociologist is the one who defines the properties of nature, who elongates an adequate lexicon, who manipulates lexical items into logical propositions and, finally, permits that world "out there" to serve as a test for his carefully crafted scheme.

Thus, the claim that people like Homans are crude empiricists is ridiculous, if empiricism means the belief that the world contains facts which give themselves as the basis of scientific theory. Whatever Homans may believe philosophically, it is clear that what he has written makes sense only when one understands that the scientist gives to the world its definitions and thus constitutes it for scientific work. The "world" appearing in Homans' writings subsists in the minds of the inventors and borrowers of axioms. And here one sees a further irony in the criticisms of the humanists who complain so sincerely about the absolutism of lexical sociology. For, while there are criticisms to be made, it is not that this school manipulates the world under investigation. It is the humanists who have the supreme confidence in an outer world that speaks to them. What the lexicalists manipulate is their own definitions of that world. They work with lexical items they have themselves intentionally defined. One may note, in support of this point, that lexicalists are the ones who have so little regard for quality control over the data they use. Who else but the lexicalist is so willing to jump headlong into census data or to borrow, as they say, "data" from a survey taken years before by God knows whom. One sees this in Homans, who is so fastidious in caring for his own logic, but so sloppy in applying that logic to other people's data, data (such as the Hawthorne studies) which are susceptible to all manner of questions for their validity. The tendency is to borrow "findings" from any which place may be in error, but that error is not that of taking the world too seriously. It is rather the mark of a type of thought that considers the world a necessary but troublesome guest at the seminar table. The point of confidence is subjective, the mind of the scientist wherein the representations of that outer world are constituted as the primary objects of sociological discourse.

The clearest example of this in Homans' writings is his defense of what many call his psychological reductionism. Briefly, the criticism is that Homans' exchange theory is so intentionally psychological that it ignores the reality of large-scale social institutions which in their very complexity seem to take on characteristics that are not explainable by reference to individual exchange behavior. One version of this argument is that bureaucratic organizations often possess an autonomy of their own whereby decisions are made without reference to individual needs or values, but according to institutional imperatives. Homans' defense takes the form of what is called "methodological individualism" (1967:61). He concedes that scientific explanations operate on two levels: those of individuals and those of social aggregates (1967:80–81). Homans' methodological individualism insists that it is scientifically uninteresting to argue about the reality of the external social world, whether it is "social" or "individual" or some combination of the two (1967:2). Thus the question of reality is set aside. Sociology is to be governed entirely by what works in its attempt to explain. The decisive factor, therefore, is within the subjective realm of scientific reasoning. One must settle upon the exchange activity of individuals because it is only here that one can discover propositions that are sufficiently general to explain anything. Put differently, this conclusion seems to have been arrived at in the following manner. The social world seems to exist in the behavior of individuals and in social institutions. Science must be guided by explanation. We must use only general propositions that explain the evidence we have. Only psychology possesses these general propositions. Therefore, for methodological reasons, the individual is considered the conclusive level for sociological investigation. In other words, Homans is not concerned to enter the debate over the true features of the external social world. This problem is completely subordinated to a sociological pragmatism wherein all such matters are drawn up into that subjective realm in which what really matters is not things but words; not reality as such, but its representations; not data, but their lexical definition and organization.

3) Historicism? Again, potent questions arise. Is not this rationality, this determinism, this infatuation with formal logic the very antithesis of the historicism of homocentric discourse? Does not this drawing up of everything into the subjectivism of the scientist negate everything that is commonly associated with historicism? Curiously enough, it is with respect to his methodological individualism that Homans launches his discussion of the historicist nature of social science (1967:90–104).

The question now is why, in social science, there should be such a gap between our general propositions, which are psychological and refer to individuals, and our propositions about aggregates, which are either of limited scope or of low explanatory power. One reason is obvious. *Implied in the psychological propositions themselves is a strong element of historicity:* past history combined with present circumstances determines behavior. Many of our propositions are limited by the variety of special historical circumstances in which they hold good. [1967:90; emphasis added]

It must be remembered that the homocentric perspective requires historicism in order to account for the welter of differences created when everything is drawn back up into subjective consciousness. Homans is remarkably clear on this point. He notes (1967:93–94) that the problem with explanation in sociology is *not* that there are so many variables nor that the many variables are difficult to control. Instead the problem lies "in the historical or . . . the genetic character of our explanations" (1967:94). Methodologically the problem is this. At the highest level in a deductive system there are general propositions that make some kind of universal-type claim. At the lower levels are the simpler propositions based upon empirical observations. The latter are, therefore, based upon the activities of different men. How can the general and these particular differences be combined? This is a special problem in any system such as Homans' wherein there is no claim that the general propositions are given in the nature of things. Since these axioms are necessarily interdependent with the differing values contained in the lower-order propositions, they are constantly threatened by relativity. Invented by the scientist, these axioms cannot be assumed to possess a built-in identity with empirical events in the external world. There is, therefore, no choice but to view the scientific process as existing within a history; that is, an elongation over time which unifies these differences by giving them the protective shelter of successive analogy.

For Homans, this historicism occurs at three interrelated levels. First, at the level of the community of scientists, one finds that Homans (as with all lexical sociologists) places great emphasis on the accumulation of theory and data, an accumulation that can only take place when terms are clearly defined (1967:109). Second, at the level of scientific discourse itself, there is the point that the substance of a science is in the history of its lexicon, that is, the way in which increasingly standardized terms are variously manipulated in differing propositions. Third, and most important, at the level of any specific scientific explanation, sociology is forced to employ genetic explanations (1967:94–99). What does this mean? If the sociologist is trying to explain the relationship between interaction and liking, this requires certain basic terms (as seen above). One of them, for example, is value. The general propositions cannot be applied to this particular sociological problem without a notion of value. So value is operationally defined in terms of that which attracts reward-seeking behavior. But how is value measured? There is only one way. It is measured historically, that is, from the point of view of observations of persons exchanging interactions and liking. As noted above, one can only know that the sentiment liking is a value (a reward) to a person by observing historically that other persons treat it as such. The same process is in effect for the definition of all of Homans' basic terms. Therefore, we can now see why four of his five universal axioms are stated with reference to a line of historical development. For example: "The more often a man has *in the recent past* received a rewarding activity from another, the less valuable any *further* unit of that activity becomes to him" (1961:55; emphasis added).

The effect of this reasoning is to say that the explanation of human behavior depends upon the recognition that human creatures have a history. And, since the propositions (including even the most general ones) cannot possibly be formed without reference to this history, they too are caught up in this history. Homans is not simpleminded about this. He recognizes that these "genetic chains . . . become terribly long and complex, and, unless cut off at some arbitrary point, lead back to the very beginnings of written history in the West" (1967:99). The requirement that sociology give this kind of historical explanation (genetic) is also what creates its chief difficulties. History makes for enormous complexity in the study of social phenomena. If one takes a strict and narrow "historical" attitude it is always possible to observe the ongoing behavior of a given group or individual and find an exception to a proposition. It is not too difficult to find persons who do not value the sentiment liking, for example. But Homans finds a way out. It is to establish the meaning of terms and the content of propositions with reference to the species, that is, by observing aggregates of individuals over time. This is the phenomenon of convergence in history (1967:99–104). Here we discover an important reversal. Those very social aggregates that were pushed to the background by Homans' methodological individualism are now dramatically reintroduced. Aggregated social behavior now forms the very foundation for establishing the central concepts of the deductive system. This is to say that the complex social whole is brought back to life by the discovery of the historicism of the individuals who are the central objects in sociological research. It is the history of man which both allows for the necessity of genetic explanations and permits Homans' system of thought to maintain a viable contact with the transpsychological aspect of social creatures.

Therefore, it should now be no surprise that when Homans gets around to comparing sociological explanation with that of the other sciences—physics, biology, history—it is to the last mentioned that he finds sociology most comparable. Thus, it is clear that Homans in his own way, accepts the historicist distinction between nature and culture (1967:21–22, 73). In spite of all the apparent confidence in the protocols of natural science and all the behavioristic allusions to similarities between pigeons and men (1961), when it comes to applying these to the problems of sociology he freely allows for the uniqueness and troublesomeness of man, the historical creature, who possesses special problems by his very historicity. Historicity has its role to play in the other sciences, even in physics (1967:94), but it is only in the social sciences that the problem cannot be gotten around. "In most of the social sciences . . . historicity either in individuals or in groups is a problem right from the beginning, and the scientists are rarely able to neutralize it" (1967:95–96).

While his historicism is not that of Dilthey and nine-teenth-century historicism in Germany, it is quite obviously that of other great nineteenth-century figures. This is the connection to be made to the fact that Homans, perhaps more self-consciously than any other contemporary sociol-ogist, has borrowed his crucial ideas from the classics of the century of history. What, after all, is the intellectual source of Skinner's behaviorism if it is not nineteenth-century util-itarianism? And what is this mysterious "elementary eco-nomics" from which he has also borrowed (1961:12)? Is it not also the economics of these same figures? Is not the uni-fying theme in these sources the idea that the self-interested actions of laboring and exchanging persons create the his-tory of the market? This is Homans' historicism.

4) Finally, it is now evident that Homans follows homo-centric practice by placing man at the center of this history. But it is important to make this point carefully. In Homans' lexical sociology the man who is most emphatically at the center is not the man of objective history. Homans' thought is a homocentrism of the scientist. The crucial history is the history of the lexicon and the proposition. And the vital force in that history is the sociologist. This is the sense in which it is true that lexical sociologists are reflexive and self-critical. What is primary in Homans' lexicality is socio-logical discourse. It is this discourse—at the level of spe-cific explanations, at the level of the discipline's lexicon, at the level of intersociologist discourse—which constitutes the substance of sociology. The coherence of this discourse is not rigidly superimposed, nor is it given in the nature of things. It is entirely a practiced coherence, a coherence created in the practical concerns of speaking sociologically. It is, therefore, necessarily spread out over history so that the history of the sociological "community" is, ideally, cumulative. That is, sociologists write and speak for and to each other over time. The history of the sociological lexicon is the interlinking, over time, of specified and tested propositions. The history of explanation is genetic, locating present observations in respect to prior behaviors. And, for Homans, none of this can possibly work without the forceful presence of the sociologist himself. This man is the presence who defines the lexicon, manipulates its terms, invents and borrows general axioms. Without him there would be nothing, certainly nothing that would speak to sociologists.

This is not to say that Homans expels man from the history of the world "out there." It is well known that he has been concerned to bring man back in to sociological discourse: "If a serious effort is made to construct theories that will even begin to explain social phenomena, it turns out that their general propositions are not about the equilibrium of societies but about the behavior of men" (1964b: 818). It is also true, as shown above, that for Homans man is the special object of sociological studies who, because of his similarity to the scientist himself, creates certain unique difficulties for sociology (1967:72). But, for Homans, this man of the external world of fact is part rhetorical, part derivative. He is at times the rhetorical device used against functionalism (1958). At other times, he is the object that must be considered because of his likeness to the sociologist (1967). What is more fundamental to Homans' homocentrism is man the social scientist. The man whose knowledge is finite, whose subjective rationality empowers a lexicon, whose history as definer of terms is the history of sociology. He is the man whose discourse creates that privileged kingdom wherein one must reside in order to speak sociologically.

3

Theory Constructionism:

Hubert Blalock

George Homans looks to a group of younger scholars for his faith in the history of man the sociologist: "I have great faith in the generation of sociologists next below my own, men like Ted Blalock, Jim Coleman, Bob Hamblin, Arthur Stinchcombe, Harrison White, and Hans Zetterberg, men who are innoculated against the nonsense about theory that bemused my generation and who are much better trained technically" (Homans 1969). The sociologists mentioned all share Homans' concern to state theory formally. However, they differ from Homans in a way that goes beyond simply being "better trained technically." Those cited by Homans form the nucleus of a large and influential group of lexical sociologists whose formal approach to sociological theory is guided by considerable consensus over the rules for sociological research. This point of view may be described as *theory constructionism*. It shares with Homans a concern for formal theory, explanation, and axiomatic approaches. It differs to the extent that its adherents are far more explicit in their understanding of how such theories are constructed.

The temptation is strong to label these writings mathematical sociology. But, as shall be seen, this is too narrow.

While all are mathematical in the sense that they favor mathematical over verbal theories (where appropriate), many substantive writings are largely verbal (for example, Stinchcombe 1968). Theory constructionists are not, therefore, theory reductionists; they simply take mathematics as that language which most efficiently and precisely is able to state the terms and propositions of theory.

An important qualification should be introduced immediately. It is not strictly accurate to imply that the consensus among theory constructionists is complete. There are indeed many differences of opinion. Roughly, these differences are with respect to two issues. 1) What shall be the final test of adequacy for a theory? Some, such as Hubert Blalock, insist that a theory is adequate only if it describes causal processes. Others are close to Homans requirement of explanation, in a deductive sense. And still others (for example, Gibbs 1972) are satisfied if a theory has proven predictive power. 2) What shall be the emphasis given to mathematics in theory construction? Some, such as Blalock, emphasize an instrumental attitude toward mathematics. The statistical procedures involved are often quite sophisticated and, thus, require considerable mathematical skill. But, this tendency does not often use mathematics as a primary source of sociological theory. At the other extreme are those, such as James Coleman, who give considerable autonomy to mathematical laws as a positive source of sociological axioms. An example of the latter is James Coleman's use of the mathematically established differential equations for the rate of diffusion with reference to the rate at which a new drug is adopted by physicians (Coleman 1964:41–46). The basic equations here represent a mathematical law equally applicable to population growth, the development of biological organisms, the rate of interest growth in finance, as well as the transmission of information in a network of physicians. In this case mathematics, quite independent of any sociological theory, offers an effective model applicable to a social process.

Moreover, this is a movement which has had its own inner history over the past twenty-five years, a history that has taken several different paths. Two figures stand out as classical leaders. One is Paul Lazarsfeld who, through his teaching at Columbia University, has been responsible for important developments in the application of statistical techniques to sociological research. The other is less well known to the general sociological community, but he has been as forceful an influence amongst those primarily concerned with mathematical modeling in sociology as Lazarsfeld has been amongst social statisticians. This is Herbert Simon, whose most widely cited book is a collection of his essays in mathematical sociology, *Models of Man: Social and Rational* (1957).

From the middle of the 1960s Hubert Blalock and James Coleman have arisen as major leaders in this group. More recently, Arthur Stinchcombe has joined these two. There is now a list of introductory texts to the approach. The first, and best known, was Hans Zetterberg's *On Theory and Verification* (1963). To this a number of others have been added: Dubin (1969), Gibbs (1972), Stinchcombe (1968), Blalock (1969), Reynolds (1971), Mullins (1971). While these texts have served to introduce theory constructionism to a wide audience, they have also accentuated differences of opinion. Blalock and Stinchcombe think in terms of causal processes (with the aid of concepts borrowed from elementary information theory), Zetterberg emphasizes the deductive approach, and Gibbs seeks to establish predictiveness as a more general and adequate criterion for theory construction. The movement is by no means single-minded.

In spite of the differences noted, it remains a fact that by the middle of the 1970s a more or less coherent theory group has been established around a set of practices that can best be called theory constructionism. Sociology departments now advertise for staff members who specialize in theory construction—not methodology, not theory, but theory construction. For this type of sociologist the writings of Lazarsfeld, Simon, Coleman, Blalock, and Stinchcombe are primary sources, in spite of the fact that not all of these writers would necessarily label themselves theory constructionists. Some (Mullins 1973) prefer to call this movement "causal process" sociology. Here the more general designation is preferred because it more accurately describes a discursive practice; a practice which is roughly consistent with respect to its intention to speak in formal (and where possible mathematical) language.

In the following discussion, primary attention will be paid to several of the crucial texts of Hubert Blalock. This is justified by the fact that his texts are more widely known than any other in the theory constructionist perspective (with the possible exception of Arthur Stinchcombe's *Constructing Social Theories*). Moreover they serve a wide range of readerships. Some are introductory texts (1960, 1970a); others are for technical readers only (for example, 1971b); some are more like intermediate introductions to various problems of theory construction (1964, 1969, 1970b). At least one is an attempt at substantive theory (1967). Blalock, furthermore, has been recognized by his colleagues as a primary influence in the profession. He was the first recipient of the American Sociological Association's Samuel A. Stouffer award for excellence in the advancement of the methodology of sociological research. His writings are thoroughly known by theory constructionists. At the same time, they are known—on some level or another—by virtually every literate sociologist. Thus, his writings can be taken as being reasonably central to and representative of the discursive field of theory constructionism.

The Construction of Formal Theory

Blalock's position takes shape in texts that appear from the mid-sixties until 1970. *Causal Inferences in Nonexperimental Research* (1964) sets forth proposals for solving the technical and theoretical problems that create the "gap between the languages of theory and research" (1964:5). Here is found one of his earliest introductions to problems of causal modeling. Appearing in 1967, *Toward a Theory of*

Minority Group Relations is his major attempt at substantive theory. It is entirely a setting forth of a deductive theory in propositional form, without detailed reference to technical questions. His theory constructionist strategy is explicitly stated in 1968 in an essay, "The Formalization of Sociological Theory" (1970b). The last mentioned is a particularly good source for an understanding of Blalock's strategy because it contains the essentials in what he considers to be their most simplified form (1970b:273). It is especially interesting for the present discussion because of its discursive origin. It is published in the book *Theoretical Sociology* (McKinney and Tiryakian 1970) which includes papers originally given in 1968 at a Duke University conference at which leading sociological theorists of differing points of view summarized their own approaches to theory. Papers by Parsons, Garfinkel, Lazarsfeld, Bottomore, and others are included. In short this book and the conference upon which it was founded represent a discursive occasion at which Blalock may be assumed to have tried to explain his point of view in its clearest, yet technically fundamental sense. It will be the basis for the discussion that immediately follows.

There are three problems with which Blalock is preoccupied: 1) model construction, 2) the "identification problem," and 3) auxiliary theory.

Model construction. For Blalock, model means formal model, one that can eventually be expressed in mathematical language by means of a careful and difficult process. Model construction begins with existing verbal theories which serve to stimulate one's thinking. For Blalock, sociological thinking focuses on one topic above all else: *variables.* Theory construction begins by sorting out variables from concepts. If a concept is any mental image of an object of thought, then a variable is such an image expressed in a form that allows it to be of use in scientific work. Stinchcombe gives a nice description of the difference: "A 'variable' in science is a concept which can have *various values,* and which is defined in such a way that *one can tell by means of observations which value it has in a particular* occurrence" (1968:28; compare Lazarsfeld 1970:303). In verbal theories, the actual expression of a variable may be exactly the same as that of its concept; or it can be quite different. In fact one of the principal disputes within this branch of lexical sociology is over the relationship between concepts and variables. For example, discrimination is a concept that makes sense even in commonsense discourse. It is sometimes used as a variable. But is the latter a legitimate usage? Do we know precisely enough what discrimination is that it may appear in formal theory? (See Brown 1973; Blalock 1971a.) Blalock is aware of this difficulty but he does not permit it to diminish his confidence, at least at the early stages of model construction.

The first thing one does with variables is to distinguish them from each other. This is done by drawing a simple diagram of the variables in a given theory. The surfaces of theory constructionist texts are replete with pictures, diagrams, and graphs. Since the goal is to formalize verbal theories, one of the best ways to reduce the excesses of verbal statements is to get rid of ambiguous verbs, unnecessary adjectives, troublesome adverbs, and so forth. A good, simple diagram does this efficiently. Therefore, if one is interested in discrimination, the most general statement of a theory might be "that discrimination is influenced by personality characteristics, specific prejudices toward the minority, various situational factors, and the behavior of the minority itself" (1970b:275). Even in this most general theoretical statement there are problems. What is the direction, strength, and nature of the "influence" of these variables on discrimination? What is included in "various" situational factors or "specific" prejudices and so forth? At this stage what Blalock does is to ignore these subtleties by setting them up in a neat diagram, such as the one on page 57.[1] The ambiguous verb in the verbal theory is, in fact, no less ambiguous here, but visually it takes on the aura of far greater precision. The "influences" are pictured by the arrows linking the various variables to each other and to discrimination itself. Likewise, adjectives are kept to a minimum.

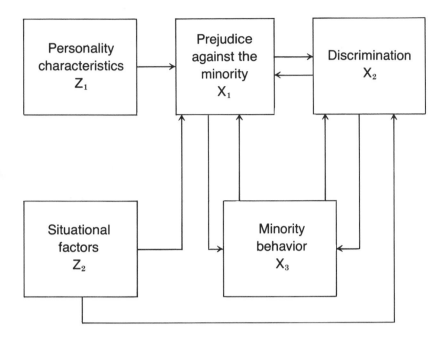

Terms appear clearly. Without cumbersome words one can say something that seems to be quite strong, at least about directions of influence and the basic variable terms.

The chief gain in this step is that the variables are blocked off from each other. But note the consequences. Do we not know from practical experience that it is at least possible that situational factors influence personality characteristics? Is there not something about life in a black urban ghetto that is likely to produce different personality characteristics from life in a white, middle-class suburb? Blalock admits that this is likely. In fact he repeatedly concedes that reality is far more complex than anything that can be put into such a diagram and, thereby, into any formal theory.

If one allows for the possibility that every variable affects every other variable, there will be too many unknowns in the system for empirical tests or for estimation of parameters. Though such a theory may represent reality more adequately than a simple one, it may not imply any testable predictions; its utility would thus be destroyed. [1970b:276]

This is a very important statement. It says in effect that reality must be made subservient to the technical requirements of formal theory. In other words, the scientific ideal of formal precision is more important than the scientific ideal of empirical accuracy, at least at this stage. This is so important that Blalock, because of the goals of formal theory, submits himself to the indignity of saying things which are all but absolutely certain to be wrong. For example, reflecting on the diagram shown in this chapter, he says: "Neither general personality characteristics, nor situational factors are affected by discrimination, minority behavior, or prejudice" (1970b:277). Even if the statement is blatantly wrong, Blalock must make it for the sake of his theory.

What is expressed by such a diagram is not, of course, a theory in any final sense. Blalock calls it a theoretical checklist. It is necessary, however, to the next step which is to specify the variables *within* each of the blocks of the diagram. One of the main reasons for this is to clarify the relationships proposed at the beginning. Here Blalock reveals the dialectical quality of his strategy. One must constantly reflect back on the theory and attempt to clarify imprecise statements. It is a matter of thinking things through, a purely theoretical task. For example, Blalock proposes (1970b: 277) several possible components of the variable *situational factors*, including: relative size of the minority, political variables, environmental influences. It could be argued that, in the short run, such a variable as *size of the minority* might not influence *discrimination*. But once this subvariable is isolated one can begin to think about it. Then another possibility appears. What if, over a long period of time (say three to five years), there is a change within another of the blocks in the diagram, *minority behavior*. In particular, what if there is an increase in migration by a certain minority group, such as a gradual but significant increase in the number of blacks living in a certain city. Here, immediately, is a circumstance in which the original diagram must be modified. Now a variable within *minority behavior* (migration) has influenced a variable within *situation factors* (size of the minority). A new arrow must be drawn. Furthermore, the increase in the size of the minority is now likely to have an effect on the *discrimination*. Insurance companies may in this case change their policy with respect to underwriting home insurance in a black neighborhood when that population becomes significantly larger, for example. This means that one should probably draw an arrow from *discrimination* back to *situational factors*.

There is a second, equally important, reason for considering these variables within variables. This is the question of measurement. Even at this early stage the theory constructionist worries about measurement. What data can be gathered to test the theory? Clearly it is difficult to measure the most abstract variables. What is an indicator of *discrimination* or *minority behavior*? Typically, it is only when one examines the variables *within* these blocks that possible empirical indicators suggest themselves. For example, among the variables within *discrimination* Blalock includes *residential exclusion* which he defines as "the denial of access to certain residential areas to the minority" (1970b:279). Such a definition begins to suggest things that can be observed: zoning laws, proportions of minorities in given neighborhoods, insurance rates, new home construction starts, and so forth. At this stage there is still much to be done to develop valid indicators even of *residential exclusion*, but it is possible now to see where the answers might lie.

What is accomplished, by this point, is the establishment of a theoretical system. The general system diagramed above contains two kinds of variables. First, there are those that are called *endogenous*. These are: *prejudice, discrimination,* and *minority behavior*. They are, so to speak, the guts of the system in that these are the variables that are influenced by other variables within the system. *Discrimination* influences *minority behavior* and *prejudice*. At the same time it is influenced by these others. But note that the remaining two variables are different in this theoretical system. Neither personality characteristics nor situational factors are assumed to be influenced by any other variable within this system. They are, therefore, *exogenous* because they are partially left outside of the main system. The same reasoning of course applies to any subsystem created within each of the major variables appearing in blocks.

Identification problem. Once a theoretical system is established in this way one is lead to the next stage in formalization. Now theory is expressed mathematically in order to increase the precision of the theoretical system. Mathematical statements have the capacity to tell Blalock many things about the theoretical system of which not even empirical data can speak helpfully (1969:50; 1970b:282). This involves what is known as the identification problem, which is the second of Blalock's three major problems in theory construction.

It is very important to note that the identification problem is entirely a mathematical question. It can only be diagnosed after the theory has been expressed mathematically. It is entirely apart from the data. Unless it is solved the data cannot make sense. In its most general form, the identification problem can be described as the problem of having so many hypothetical causal relationships and so many unknowns to a theoretical system that it becomes theoretically impossible to identify any particular relationship (1969:48–75; 1970b:281–86). This arises because theoretical systems that are too general (try to account for too many causal relationships) in effect generate too many data. At best what one might be able to show is that all of the variables are correlated with each other. But this would be only a statistical fact. It would possess little or no explanatory power. Statistical correlations do not, in themselves, say anything about the strength and direction of causal relationships.

It can be shown that if one allows for the possibility that everything causes everything else, with unspecified parameters, then there will be an infinite number of sets of parameter values, all of which will be consistent with the same set of data. This implies that theorists can talk past one another, each arguing that a particular set of variables is "more important" than another, without there being any conceivable way of resolving the dispute by purely empirical means. [1970b:282]

The most important thing to realize for the present discussion is that Blalock believes one can only identify exact relationships with the aid of mathematical procedures.

This is an excellent example of the value theory constructionists place on mathematical language. It is also important to understand that, in this respect, the mathematical formulation is entirely a theoretical step, quite apart from the analysis of actual data.

It is not necessary to present Blalock's complete technical argument here. What it amounts to is this: in order to be able to explain causal relationships, theoretical systems must be written so that there is a certain balance between endogenous and exogenous variables. The latter are essential to any theory. They serve as the boundaries which constitute the system. "The exogenous variables are the 'givens' or the starting points of the theory" (Blalock 1969:61). In the diagram shown, *personality characteristics* and *situational factors*—the exogenous variables—are the points beyond which the present theory will not attempt to go.

This is not so arbitrary as some might think. There are certain mathematical laws which require it. These boundary variables are therefore exogenous but not extraneous. It makes a major difference how they are related to the endogenous system. This difference is determined entirely on mathematical grounds. The example Blalock gives (1970b:282–86) takes the form of the simplest type of mathematical expression for otherwise complex theories. This is called a linear additive relationship, which involves putting each endogenous variable in the system into a simultaneous equation which in turn represents the relationship of that variable to all others in the system. For the sake of simplicity (and in spite of the fact that it would never be done), one can imagine such a statement for the general theory above. It would first be necessary to make mathematical definitions.[2]

Prejudice (P) $= X_1 = b_{12}X_2 + b_{13}X_3 + c_{11}Z_1 + c_{21}Z_2 + U_1$

Discrimination (D) $= X_2 = b_{21}X_2 + b_{23}X_3 + c_{22}Z_2 + U_2$

Minority Behavior (B) $= X_3 = b_{13}X_1 + b_{23}X_2 + U_3$

Now, one of the properties of simultaneous equations is that it is permissible to multiply the equations by any arbitrary constant adding the results as one goes through the series. This is in fact a standard mathematical device for solving for unknowns. However, the potential effect of such a step is chaos. For example, one could multiply each of the above equations by any number of constants, adding results as one proceeds with the following effect. The equations generated would be *mathematically* equivalent to the original equations but, depending on the value assigned to the constant, the values of the variables would differ over a tremendous— virtually infinite—range of possibilities. What this means is that were one to attempt to solve such equations as these by an elementary rule of simultaneous equations one could not determine the effects of one variable upon another. This leads to a statement that some will surely find startling: "The values of the structural parameters, which provide us with a mathematical explanation of the empirical relationships, *cannot be determined from the data alone*" (Blalock 1970b:284; emphasis added).

However, for simple relationships (recursive, with one-way causation) there is an answer. This too is mathematical. It takes the following form. All endogenous variables are represented in linear additive equations. (This is what was done in the hypothetical, mathematical definitions above.) One counts the number of endogenous variables—in this case three. The rule then applies that, whatever the total number of endogenous variables, this number minus one must be left out of any equation one is attempting to identify. For example, in the equation for *minority behavior*, all three endogenous variables are included. The rule requires that three minus one (that is, two) of the endogenous variables be left out. Therefore, on these theoretical grounds Blalock would conclude that this equation for the variable *minority behavior* could be distinguished from either of the other two (1969:65). In order to achieve this balance one must add exogenous variables to the original theoretical system, which involves revising the original theory, inventing new exogenous variables, and restating the equations. For example, on might—on the basis of a theoretical analysis of variables within the *minority behavior* block—decide to separate out migratory behavior from other minority behaviors and state this as an exogenous variable. Something like this would have to be done for all the variables in the entire theoretical system, until all equations met the mathematical rule governing this type of equation.[3]

It is important to see exactly what has gone on here. The mathematical requirements of the theoretical system have demanded a restatement of the theory without the least regard to anything at all having to do with data. The empirical world bears no relevance to the effect of the mathematical theory upon the original verbal theory. ("[I]f we wish to build *theories* we cannot rest contented with simple empirical relationships" [Blalock, 1969:58].) To state it simply, this is a case of one theoretical language acting back upon the very language from which its own terms were originally drawn. Blalock uses mathematics for greater precision, and the mathematics forces him to restate his original verbal theory. In the process, whatever might be true in the real world is totally and unashamedly ignored. Moreover, it is a process that relies entirely upon the theoretical inventions of the theorist.

Auxiliary theory. This leads to a third major step, one that may well be most representative of Blalock's approach. Most of what has been discussed to this point is recognizable as an abstract theory. However, for Blalock, theory does not stop here, even if the mathematical formulations are carefully checked and cross-checked. It is necessary to add to this what Blalock calls auxiliary theory. Its use is defended in the following way:

Assumptions about disturbing influences affecting error terms, the exact forms of one's equations, and possible measurement errors are not commonly included in discussions of theory, but in a very real sense they are just as important in connection with the verification process as are the various propositions contained in the theory proper. [Blalock 1970b:289; compare 1968a]

Auxiliary theory is, in effect, a theory of measurement. It is the kind of thing that many are fond of dismissing as "technical considerations" and, thereby, divorcing totally from theoretical work. Blalock plainly believes that this is ill-advised. This view derives in large part from his conviction that all actual measurement of variable behavior is necessarily indirect (Blalock 1968a; 1971a). It is unlikely that there can ever be a one-to-one correspondence between a variable such as *discrimination* and any indicator by which it is measured. The point he makes is that the problem of auxiliary theory is unavoidable because it is nothing less than the problem of the relationship between theory and these indirect measures. One is foolish, therefore, to pretend that there are no implications for theory in the decisions made with respect to measurement. Whatever might be chosen as an indicator of *discrimination*—perhaps *residential exclusion* which in turn has its own indicator—the choice necessarily involves a strategic theoretical decision. "It is important to note that no main body of deductive theory can ever be tested without the use of some such auxiliary theory, whether explicit or not" (Blalock, 1968a:25).

Among the problems involved in auxiliary theory are the following. One stems directly from the identification problem. If there are requirements that certain variables be left out, what are the implications of these exclusions? At the very least it is likely that the omission of any variable originally thought to have been important might produce serious errors in actual empirical testing (1970b:291).

Another type of error is called specification error. This involves errors in estimating either the exact relationships in the theoretical system or the strength of those relationships. It is possible that data may show that the original theory is wrong; that, for example, linear additive relationships cannot be used and that multiplicative models must replace them (1970b:294).

Other problems have to do with the linking of indicators with concepts. One might wish to measure discrimination through such sub-variables as *occupational, educational,* or *residential discrimination* (1970b:278–81). To this end one might hope to set up *occupational inequalities, educational inequalities,* and *residential segregation* as indicators. But immediately it is clear (from the theory itself) that inequality is influenced by *minority behavior* as well as by *discrimination.* Thus measures of types of *minority behavior* must be added to those of *inequality* (1970b:295, 296). This is only the beginning in even so apparently straightforward a theory as the example given. The complexity quickly becomes enormous. Thus, the theory constructionist must constantly balance the need for maximum simplicity against the requirement of maximum empirical accuracy. Unfortunately, 'the cost of greater simplicity is . . . the sacrifice of realism" (1970b:296).

In the kind of work Blalock wishes to do these difficulties cannot be avoided. One can only choose between treating them openly or postponing (or otherwise neglecting) their consideration. In his opinion there is little wisdom to the latter tactic. Therefore, for Blalock the decisions made with respect to measurement constitute the auxiliary theory which must be explicitly incorporated in the process of formal theory construction. A formal theory of discrimination includes an explicit theory of the measures of discrimination.

Blalock's Radical Lexicality

There is much to indicate that Blalock is very largely preoccupied with language problems.

The careful reworking of *verbal* theories is undoubtedly one of the most challenging tasks confronting us. The major portion of this enterprise will undoubtedly consist of clarifying concepts, eliminating or consolidating variables, *translating* existing *verbal* theories into *common languages*, searching the *literature* for *propositions*, and looking for implicit assumptions connecting the major *propositions* in important theoretical works. The final *translation* into formal mathematics, and the actual use of mathematical reasoning would seem to be a relatively simpler task that can be performed by a smaller group of specialists. [1969:27; emphasis added]

This passage clearly shows that Blalock believes that the primary goal of sociology ought to be translation. Due to the imprecision of verbal theories, sociology can only become a mature science by translating them into propositions, then formal theories and, finally, into mathematical statements. In short, sociological work is language work. The crucial intellectual decisions are at the points of translation into increasingly more formal terms. As anyone who has worked with a second language knows, successful translation involves, above all else, lexical competence. Knowledge of grammar is useless, without a knowledge of standard definitions.

Thus, the basic work of theory construction is definitional. Concepts must be defined, then redefined as variables. Variables must be continually examined and often defined again as one invents subvariables within a general theory system and then searches for indicators. Furthermore, in both theory proper and auxiliary theory, variables and indicators must be redefined in mathematical terms. What, after all, is "Residential exclusion $(R) = X_1 = f_1(E, O, P) = f_1(X_2, X_3, X_4) \ldots = b_{12}X_2 + b_{13}X_3 + b_{14}X_4 + e_1$" (Blalock 1970b:283)? It is a definition of a term in a series of equations and, as such, is the same type of lexical thing as: "$R =$ residential exclusion; or the denial of access to certain residential areas to the minority" (Blalock 1970b:279). The only difference is that the same term is defined in two different kinds of languages.

What is the distinctively sociological aspect of Blalock's theoretical approach? It is *not* the goal of formalization. Nor is it a commitment to operationalization (1968a). Nor mathematical formalization. Nor the ideal of deductive theory. Other scientists and philosophers of science use and understand these things. What is sociological is the definitions that are created and employed. It is such sociological concepts as *discrimination*; the idea that it has something to do with minority groups, occupations, place of residence, migratory behavior, and so forth. It is the way in which the defined term is related to other definitions. It is the way in which blocks are drawn in preliminary causal models (what is put into a block is a verbal/graphic definition). It is the way in which propositions are stated around these definitions. It is the definitions made when equations are written to express verbal terms. Each of these steps involves theory in a definitional problem, above all else. To be sure, there are grammatical type considerations (the form of equations), stylistic problems (the drawing of diagrams), and punctuation requirements (is there properly a period beyond the list of exogenous variables, or should it be a comma?). But, as in all translation work, the substance of freshly put statements is in the definition of otherwise incomprehensible lexical items. In fact, in Blalock's case, this is a strictly lexical problem. He is not *primarily* interested in the semantical question of the meaning of terms, or in their ability to represent an objective reality. For Blalock, the lexical terms can be quite arbitrary [as when "$f_1 (X_2, X_3, X_4)$" is used as a definition]. Lexical terms do not necessarily "mean" anything, they just fit into a lexical system.

Blalock's lexicality can best be seen in his discussion of the problem of operational definitions (1968a). Though he obviously believes in operational definitions, Blalock is not an "operationalist." Strict operationalism (usually associated with Percy Bridgman, the physicist, and with George Lundberg in sociology) holds that measurement is definition. The indices by which variables are measured are the basic definitions involved in the theory. If one is measuring the mass of an object, the pointer readings of an instrument are what mass is! Or, intelligence is what an IQ test measures (Blalock 1968a:8).

Blalock strenuously objects to this kind of simple empiricism (1968a:9–13). In his view the result of such an approach is confusion. There can be no confident generality in the long run, because one would be required always to know all of the exact details of any particular measurement. Moreover, there would be little encouragement to improve measurement techniques because Scientist B would be required to use the exact same instrument as Scientist A used it when checking a previous study. Recent controversy over the validity of standard IQ tests in measuring the intelligence of nonwhite, lower-class persons illustrates the importance of freedom to improve measurement devices. The problem comes down to the place of replication in science. If science is objective knowledge, it must therefore be intersubjective knowledge. Two different investigators must be able to get the same or nearly the same results in testing a given theory. All theories must, at least in principle, be replicable. Operationalism permits this only under the narrowest of conditions. This form of empiricism is impossible in Blalock's mind.

Blalock's way out of this dilemma is based upon the notion of "epistemic correlations," which he borrows from F. S. C. Northrop (1947). An epistemic correlation is: "a relation joining an unobserved component of anything designated by a concept by postulation to its directly inspected component denoted by a concept by intuition" (Northrop 1947:119). A concept by postulation is a concept included in a deductive theoretical statement; a concept by intuition is one that is created with reference to direct observations. Roughly put, the former is "theoretical"; the latter is "experiential." In the example given above, *discrimination* is a postulated concept (part of a deductive theory); *residential exclusion* (observed in terms of the proportion of minority persons in a neighborhood) is an intuitive concept. Or, to state it with reference to Blalock's own idea of theory, the former is a part of the abstract, theoretical system; the latter is a part of the auxiliary theory.

The effect of this distinction is to keep the two kinds of theories—abstract and auxiliary—separate without divorcing them. This is required by Blalock's conviction that in a truly deductive formal theory the variables are never directly testable (1968a:11; 1971a). This is so because they were invented at a high level of abstraction by means of the formal rules of deductive reasoning. We have seen this clearly illustrated in the discussion of Blalock's approach to theory construction. The theory of discrimination must first meet the conditions of logical and mathematical adequacy (as for example in the case of the identification problem). As seen above, the only way that a deductive theory can be tested is by means of an explicit auxiliary theory of measurement. The concepts (and their variable equivalents) in one cannot be confused with those in the other because they are different sorts of concepts. *Discrimination* is not the same thing as *residential exclusion* any more than the latter is the same thing as "percent minorities denied housing in a neighborhood." To pretend that they are the same is to open up the difficulties of operationalism and, more seriously, to imply a degree of empirical accuracy that formal deductive theory simply does not and cannot possess.

The implication of this position for Blalock's lexicality is that the precision of the definitions in the theoretical system is maintained. They remain, in a sense, pure and uncorrupted by careless intermingling with empirically besmudged operational terms. In other words, the most distinctive feature of Blalock's view of theory construction —the auxiliary theory—depends entirely upon his particular attitude toward the lexical items by which that theory is constructed. There must be two types of concepts (postulated and intuitive) and, accordingly, two types of variables (deductive and auxiliary). If they are confused there is no hope for authentic generality in the deductive theory. The deductive theory would be overwhelmed by too much unanalyzable information from the empirical world. Thus the special difficulty social scientists have with replication (1968a: 17, 1970a: 26–29) is overcome not by greater technical finesse in measurement, but by greater theoretical control over the sociological lexicon.

Of course, Blalock's lexicality does differ from that of Homans. To the extent that is mathematical, it is more formal. As a result the defined lexical terms are manipulated more freely. Abstract symbols and equations are more easily erased, displaced, and rewritten than are words and verbal propositions. As a result, Blalock is able to take up a position of far greater control over his lexical items. When reading Homans, one is struck by the text itself—the clarity of the prose, the power of the argumentation, the choice of words, the integrity of the total document. None of these ever impress one in reading Blalock. The difference is not merely a matter of inferior literary style (though Blalock's is decidedly inferior). In the case of a more radical lexicalist, such as Blalock, the eye is drawn to the formal statements— graphs, equations, diagrams, tables—around which the text is written. The distinctive feature of formal terms is that they tend to be standardized. Indeed, this is precisely their intent. Individual style does enter at such points as: the way in which causal arrows are drawn in diagrams, the way in which variables are put into equations, the explanatory text in which formal expressions are embedded, and so forth. But here style is secondary; the substance of the sociological material is represented in the formal lexicon and its manipulations. In reading Blalock one is seldom drawn into the idiosyncracies of his writing or thinking. In fact, one must work very hard to discover what exactly is distinctive of Blalock (while one is immediately aware of Homans' special biases and perspectives).

Thus, when reading theory constructionist texts one is first of all attracted to the diagrams, abstract symbols, tables, and equations. The prose texts remain, in the end, as commentary drawing out the nuances of the formal terms. The effect is that the *critical* reader finds himself examining in detail the abstract translated terms and their manipulations. Serious study of constructionists texts almost inevitably involves the copying and redrawing of the basic diagrams (Can the causal relationships be defined differently?) or the writing out of the essential equations (How was equation I.12 derived from equation I.1? Was it done correctly? Could it have been done differently?). These requirements for critical reading depend entirely upon the reader's own inventiveness; on his or her own ability to apply rules of formal reasoning (logical and mathematical). This is required, be-

cause what counts is the success of the lexical manipulations: Have the terms been defined (carved out) properly?
Have they been linked plausibly? What happens to the link-
ages if the definitions are changed? What happens to the
definitions when the terms are manipulated mathematically? Rules govern a good bit of this reasoning (for example,
the rules for handling simultaneous equations), but in the
final analysis the key to theory construction is the intellectual prowess of the theorist.

Theoretical Man As Inventor

The theory constructionist is, above all else, a constructor
of theories. The emphasis is on inventiveness, that is, the
power of the individual scientist to create, define, manipulate, check, redefine, and manipulate again the basic lexical terms. In other words, man the sociologist stands at the
center of this sociological enterprise. In this respect Blalock
does not differ from Homans, except to the degree that he is
more nakedly homocentric.

1) The place of finitude in Blalock's scheme is suggested
by a passage previously quoted: "The cost of greater simplicity is the sacrifice of realism" (1970b:296; compare
1964:9). Theory poses a dilemma. On the one hand, it must
be precise and simple. This is the role of formality. On the
other hand, its main purpose is to represent the real world.
Both cannot be gained simultaneously to the same degree.
An increase in simplicity (that is, refinement of the abstract
statement) is inversely related to the capacity of formal
statements to describe reality *fully*. A choice must be made
and Blalock clearly makes it on the side of precision. Reduce "reality" to verbal statements, verbal statements to
propositions, propositions to diagrams, diagrams to abstract
symbols, abstract symbols to mathematical definitions. The
further one moves through this process, the more one is

committed to a language that is unable to incorporate the nuances of the empirical world. Blalock is troubled by the dilemma, but his choice in favor of simplicity and precision is clear. In other words, Blalock places a stern limitation on the ability of theory to reach out and grasp the reality of the world out there.

From another angle, one sees this in his attitude with respect to that world. Time and time again, he describes the world sociologists study as "complex" (1973, 1969:4, 1970a:5, 1970b:272, 1968a:6). Virtually every discussion of theory construction begins with a reference to this complexity. Even though Blalock never fully explains this complexity, it clearly has an important impact upon his understanding of theory. Obviously, he believes that because social forces are complex and historical, they cannot be easily controlled and, thus, are not amenable to pure experimental procedures (1973). This is to be seen in his conclusion that the effect of the complexity of reality is in the damage it does to the sociologist's ability to replicate previous studies. In other words, the effect is upon the theory of measurement and in turn upon the theory itself. Faced with complexity, Blalock draws back into the technical problems of theory itself, from which position he seems to gain the confidence that sociology can advance in spite of the nastiness of this world. "I assume that it is safe to assume that most of us wish to develop theories and a body of knowledge that will help us understand a very complex reality" (1973:2). There is little doubt that those theories can be constructed.

It is not fair to picture Blalock's position as naive. When it comes to his theoretical method, he takes this complexity quite seriously. He objects to simpleminded empiricism. He pays careful attention to issues involved in the necessary differences between operational and theoretical languages. He acknowledges that in sociology measurement must always be indirect and, accordingly, that sociological theory must invest itself in a painstaking struggle with the effect of this indirectness upon the general theory presented. This is necessitated by the mysterious complexity of reality.

This amounts to the fact that Blalock is not a triumphant believer in the unqualified grandeur of man's reason. He believes mightily in rationality, but this faith does not cover its capacity to reach out over the whole of the complex social world. Blalock respects the gulf between theory constructed by sociology and the real world that theory ought to represent. In this respect his view of knowledge is marked by a grudging awareness of the finite limitations of human reason. At points he is downright humble before this world his theories can never fully represent. At one point he even likens the world to a trickster (1969:56), capable of playing hoaxes on the careless theorist. The way around this trickster world is to cede to it its own ground and to retreat into the lexical world which, since it was created in the first place by the sociologist, is his to control and manipulate. Only within the lexical reality of theory can the precision, formality, and simplicity of Blalock's type of sociology be gained.

2) The subjectivism in Blalock's approach is found in the definition of the theorist as an inventor. The simplest expression of the statement that governs Blalock's thought is *theory invents explanations*. This ideal is basic to the theory constructionist strategy. Verbal propositions, diagrams, mathematical statements are all created by the sociologist. While rules control their treatment, the crucial lexical elements are inventions. Once set up, the theoretical system must be checked and rechecked and reinvented. The sociologist is constantly placed in the position where his/her intellectual judgment is the sole resource for making the crucial determinations: Is this causal relationship reciprocal? Should variable X_1 be stated as exogenous or endogenous? Could not endogenous variable X_2 be lagged and restated as an exogenous variable? What is an indicator of *discrimination*? Can data be gotten on minority migration patterns between 1955 and 1965? Are the exogenous variables intercorrelated? What happens to this equation if it is transformed by a multivalent constant? And so forth. It has been shown above that these are the intellectual manipulations around which theories are constructed. None are conclusively settled by general rules nor by reference to data. They are the inventions of the theorist.

The power of the sociologist's presence is well illustrated in the following:

Not only *must one locate* . . . truly independent variables, but *he must make* certain *a priori* (*usually untestable*) assumptions about which of these independent variables cause specific dependent variables. He *must not allow* for the possibility that every independent variable affects every dependent variable directly, or he will be back in the same situation of having too many unknowns. He *must introduce* these additional independent variables *selectively in order to be in a position* to resolve the chicken-egg problem. For example, the economist assumes that rainfall affects agricultural yields and therefore the supply of these goods, but *he assumes* that it does not directly affect customers' tastes or preferences for these goods. If this assumption were unrealistic, *he would have to find* some other causal variable to do the job. [1970a:78; emphasis added]

This passage is a very general statement of some of the problems discussed above under model construction and the identification problem. Note the importance given to independent thought: the sociologist "introduces," "selects," "assumes," "finds," "locates," and "makes" the content of a theoretical system. The dominant verbs are all active. The personal pronoun here shifts into a strong personal sense; the "he" that repeats itself throughout is the personal presence of the sociologist who enervates the string of active verbs.

This is a position that is very close to that of Homans. The sociologist, aware of the finitude of his knowledge and technical skills, draws the theoretical process up into subjective consciousness, into his/her own intellectual judgments. The difference between Blalock and Homans is only that the former is more radical than the latter. With Homans abstract theory is both invented *and* borrowed. With Blalock it is mostly invented. Blalock has very little interest in the history of sociological theories (see Blalock 1969:1–2; 1970b:297–300) What Weber, Durkheim, or Parsons may have said on such and such a subject may occasionally be interesting, but it is not a primary source of theory—theoretical suggestions, perhaps, but not theory. This is apparent even with respect to those instances where Blalock self-consciously sets out to borrow, that is, in the examination of empirical theories existing in the literature. Blalock clearly sees the primary task of sociology to be that of refining its theories (1973). Here Blalock's view is seemingly identical with that of Homans. But it differs in the crucial respect that Blalock seldom builds directly on the theories of others. This stems, in part, from his conviction that most existing theory is improperly constructed and therefore not in shape for use. His usual stance is to take into account other theories in order to demonstrate their inadequacies and open the way for his own formulations which typically bear little similarity to the original. Blalock describes this approach in the conclusion to his major effort in substantive theory, *Toward a Theory of Minority Group Relations:*

My own interest in this [propositional] . . . approach was kindled by Robin Williams' *The Reduction of Intergroup Tensions,* in which 100 theoretical propositions were assembled and organized under a number of interrelated headings. At that time, I undertook a rather extensive survey of the literature in the field of race and ethnic relations in order to expand Williams' list of propositions. I discovered, however, that there were so many gaps in our knowledge that it was advisable to focus more narrowly on the kinds of specific topics covered in this set of essays. The result is an *additional* 97 propositions which, like those given by Williams, are rather loosely interconnected by semideductive arguments. [1967:190; emphasis added]

This is indeed a curious result for an approach that gives much weight to advancing the work of others.

On the other hand, it would be unfair to picture Blalock as a theoretical isolationist. Indeed, he does borrow heavily from people like James Coleman and Herbert Simon. But these borrowings are for technical and methodological guidelines. When it comes to theory itself, Blalock is an inventor. Theory is *constructed*—not borrowed, not modified, not even transformed. This is a point easily missed. Those sociologists who are not native speakers in the realm of theory constructionism will look at the texts and see charts that appear to take the same shape even as one shifts from author to author. But as soon as one begins to learn this language it becomes clear that the formal statements—the propositions, the diagrams, the equations—are similar only on their material surfaces. Their interpretation depends entirely upon a reading of the definitions individual theorists give to particular terms and these definitions are by no means standard among all constructionists, as certainly they could not be by virtue of the fact that they arose in the peculiar judgments of individual sociological inventors.

3) The historicism in Blalock's thinking is similar to that of Homans. It is most prominent in his view of the challenges facing sociology as a discipline. This challenge can be stated from two perspectives. Blalock is concerned that the work of sociologists is not understood and appreciated by the general public. With few exceptions, politicians are unlikely to find sociological theories useful in their analysis of contemporary social problems, such as racial conflict (1970a:3–11). In addition, Blalock observes that within the discipline there has been little progress toward the goal of developing general theories that guide the research of most sociologists (1973). One challenge is external, the other internal. But both have the same cause: there is far too much dispersion of effort in sociology. Theoretical and empirical work is not coordinated; without coordination there cannot be progress and without substantive scientific progress sociology cannot hope to improve its image as a feeble science unable to speak to social concerns.

The classical historicism in Blalock's thought is seen in his recommendation that large-scale scientific institutions coordinate sociological work. He proposes (1973), for example, that research institutes be formed to conduct large-scale research projects, that official sociological journals sponsor and legitimate replication studies and that periodic conferences be held for the purpose of standardizing sociology's lexicon.

In other words, Blalock's vision is that of using the influence and resources of important sociological institutions (major institutes, journals, prestigious departments, the American Sociological Association) to pull together the divergences within sociology. The ideal result would be a coordinated history for sociology itself. Sociological theories must be cumulative. The goal is progress in science. The substance of this progress is a coordinated lexicon forming the basis for agreed-upon general theories. If the coordination is achieved then the history of sociology's theoretical vocabulary can move forward.

This ideal is pure homocentrism. Faced with the complexity of the real social world, the sociologist, acknowledging his/her intellectual finitude, retreats into the subjectivism of his/her own intellectual prowess. Discovering there the threat of difference and confusion, the sociologist then moves back out into the historical realm of collegial cooperation. Differences are overcome by the hard work and technical skill necessary to bring divergent sociological concepts into a single history. The money, machines, and technology of modern society are applied to the central task of creating a consistent theoretical lexicon.

Precisely the same manner of thought appears within Blalock's substantive theoretical concerns. It has been shown that the key to adequate research is replication. This is the conclusive test of a theoretical system. Replication is, of course, the creation of a history for a given theory. In the same way, the historical ideal intrudes upon the solution to specific technical problems. For example, one of the possible solutions to the identification problem is to create new exogenous variables by time-lagging endogenous variables (Blalock 1969:78–87). This is a basic step in the creation of dynamic as opposed to static theories. "In a dynamic theory the time dimension enters into the formulation in an essential way" (Blalock 1970b:288). Blalock makes it quite clear that one cannot avoid dynamic formulations. Even when one is interested in the equilibrium state of a given theoretical system, adequate formal explanation demands dynamic models (1970b:289). Closely associated with this conviction is the use of the notion of "feedback" derived from systems and information theory (Blalock 1967:21–26). In theory constructionism in general this idea has become a device for representing both the complexity and dynamism of causal systems. The effect of feedback relationships is that theoretical systems must be stated historically. They must be able to picture causal processes working at no less than two time periods. If discrimination influences minority behavior and, then, minority behavior feeds-back to influence discrimination (as when the migration of a poor minority group into an urban area causes a change in zoning laws), then the theoretical system has taken on an historical character. It both represents the flow of empirical events, and *becomes* a step in the historicization of the theoretical model itself. This is especially clear in Stinchcombe (1968:57–129) who argues that the three basic types of sociological explanation (demographic, functionalist, historicist) all assume this historical quality. In other words, the content of any specific theory is the statement of the history of the relationships of different concepts, just as these specific theories are expected to give themselves up to the coordinated theories of the discipline as a whole. The two processes—one at the level of the individual sociologist, the other at the level of the sociological community—constitute, under ideal circumstances, the historical framework within which man the sociologist labors.

4) Man does not appear prominently in the pages of Blalock's texts. He is not spoken of in the manner of Homans. But man is still the central presence. Has not this entire discussion been an elaboration of the ways in which man the sociologist is the central force in theory construction? To believe as does theory constructionism that theory is the invention of explanation is to rely upon man as the definer of theoretical lexicons.

If Blalock is read closely it becomes evident that he possesses a very traditional liberal faith in the ability of rational man to solve the mysteries of the complex social world. Blalock does not entertain the notion that some social realities could be too complex for the sociologist. He believes that with sufficient technical skill explanations can be created. He believes that in spite of the confusions within sociology the tremendous divergences can be coordinated. He even believes in the New Deal-type doctrine that sociological government (for example, the American Sociological Association) can succeed in pulling together the embarrassing contradictions in the profession. His faith in man is no different from that of Homans. In discussing one of the elemental propositions in his theory of minority groups he confesses: "This proposition is based on the assumption that individuals will act more or less rationally so as to maximize their chances of attaining all important goals" (1967:204). Could there be a surer translation of nineteenth-century ethical theory?

In short, Blalock would have virtually nothing to say were he not already convinced that man the sociologist possesses the central place in the history of the sociological lexicon.

4

Analytic
Realism:

Talcott Parsons

Explanation Is Theoretical

The second major group within lexical sociology is
that which places far less emphasis on propositions, mathematics, and deduction. Its concern is the construction of
conceptual systems. It is not set against deductive reasoning (which it often uses) or propositional expression (also
used, though implicitly). It is not even actively hostile to
mathematical formalization. In fact, it is itself a highly formal (though verbal) theory. The difference is priorities.
Those who favor the development of abstract conceptual
systems do so because they believe that *neither* empirical
work *nor* formal, deductive theories can succeed unless
what Parsons calls the "frame of reference" for analysis is
systematically and self-consciously worked out in advance.

If the theoretical position of Homans is summarized by
the statement *theory is explanation*, and that of Blalock
(and the theory constructionists) by the statement *theory
invents explanation*, the type of lexical theory to which
attention is now being directed is governed by the statement
explanation is theoretical. The former two make explanation itself the essential criterion of effective theory; theory
that fails to explain is not sociologically useful. *Explanation is theoretical* retains explanation as a basic criterion of

science but does not admit that all theory must directly explain empirical phenomena in order to be useful. The difference is subtle but crucial. This position judges explanation by its theoretical merit. Homans and Blalock judge theory by its explanatory value.

This position is one of the few which can be adequately described by the name of its principal figure: "Parsonsianism." Not since Durkheim and his followers founded sociology in France has a single individual so exhaustively defined the substance and perimeters of a major sociological school as has Talcott Parsons. This is not to say that Parsons has been surrounded by a group of passive underlings. On the contrary, those with whom he has collaborated and those who have been his students are—in many, many instances—independent intellectual leaders in sociology. The list is imposing: Robert Merton, Edward Shils, Robert Bales, Robert Bellah, Bernard Barber, Renee Fox, Clifford Geertz, Neil Smelser, Kaspar Naegele, Morris Zelditch, Harold Garfinkel, Theodore Mills, and others (see Parsons 1970b). Some of these have done work that differs in important respects from that of Parsons. (Merton, Garfinkel, and Bellah are the most obvious examples.) Nevertheless, the total picture is one of a major figure influencing a large number of important thinkers and thereby establishing a distinctive theoretical approach. Therefore, there is no problem finding a representative corpus of texts. Those of Parsons are the obvious choice. Whatever differences within this school, those of Parsons remain the clearest statement of this type of lexical sociology.

Unfortunately, the ease with which the corpus of Parsons is selected for analysis is *not* matched by a comparable ease in interpreting that corpus. One problem stands above the others. Is there one Parsons? Or two (or more)? The question has led to considerable controversy. One point of view is that there are no fewer than two Parsons. John Finley Scott (1963; 1974) has put the strongest evidence in support of this interpretation, though others hold the same position (Turner and Beeghley 1974:47). In the simplest of terms this point of view holds that, prior to the Second World

War, Parsons' theory was a voluntaristic theory of action. It held that individuals act on the basis of ideal values and are not completely determined by natural factors. Man is viewed here as largely free and creative. The key texts for Scott's early-Parsons are *The Structure of Social Action* (1937) and, especially, the essay "The place of ultimate values in sociological theory" (1934–35). Scott then argues that after the war Parsons shifted to a position of "cautious naturalism." The latter is understood to deprive the actor of creative independence, locking him into a social system and largely determining behavior to a much larger degree by naturalistic, biological factors. In Scott's opinion this is not a behaviorism pure and simple, but it does result in a loss of the voluntaristic principle of the earlier writings. This interpretation is not without warrant. Parsons does, in later years, develop more fully the idea of a social system as the context of an individual's action. His thought does become considerably more formal. And, by his own admission (Parsons 1970b), the role of biologistic categories does become more prominent after the publication of *The Structure of Social Action*.

However, a second point of view has been taken (Turner and Beeghley 1974; Turner 1974). This happens to be the one shared by Parsons himself (1970b; 1974). Turner and Beeghley insist that the voluntaristic theory of action has remained the foundation of Parsons' thinking throughout the corpus. The changes have been elaborations only, not renunciations of the original framework (compare Turner and Beeghley 1974:51). Even Scott (1974:59) seems to agree that voluntarism remains in Parsons' general theory though he retains his earlier conviction that it is lost in the formal theory of social systems.

Fortunately, it is not, for present purposes, necessary to resolve this controversy. Its importance here is the extent to which the debate hinges upon an appreciation of Parsons' unique strategy for theorizing. In a published colloquy (*Sociological Inquiry*, Vol. 44) Parsons, Turner and Beeghley, and Scott all agree that one cannot successfully explain the place of voluntarism in Parsons' texts without examining his view of theory as *analytic realism*.

On this topic, there is no serious dispute. Parsons has—from *The Structure of Social Action* (1937) to the present—maintained a consistent theoretical *methodology*. Whatever substantive changes there may have been, analytic realism still guides his thinking. What can be demonstrated is that analytic realism is precisely the type of theorizing that permits debates such as the above to arise. By granting considerable autonomy to the general theoretical framework, it allows for the possibility that the framework itself may remain constant even though its applications and substantive details may change.

Analytic realism attempts to incorporate the two essential modes of scientific reasoning—theory and empirical reference. It rejects the view that theory is either secondary or irrelevant to empirical understanding. This is what Parsons labels "particularistic empiricism" (1937:72) which would be the type of sociology that claims only to be studying "what is going on in the real world" and looks upon theory as an excuse for avoiding research. At the same time, Parsons rejects any position that overvalues theory for its own sake. This is "positivistic empiricism" (1937:71) which starts from a completely abstract theoretical system and will only look at specific empirical phenomena from the point of view of that system. It is interesting to note that Parsons himself is often accused of making the latter error. Whatever one may say about his actual theoretical statements, it cannot be said that Parsons is unaware of the dangers of reifying theory itself. As a matter of fact, his own theoretical strategy is taken directly from Alfred North Whitehead's famous critique of the "fallacy of misplaced concreteness" (Parsons 1974:55), which is the fallacy of confusing an abstract theoretical statement with concrete reality (assuming that an analytic construct—such as "social system"—is a real object).

Analytic realism, in contrast to these extremes, assumes the existence of a real world of phenomena and believes that it is the duty of sociology to deal with that reality by developing an analytic theory which is taken as an adequate representation of that world. The theory itself is analytic, but it must also possess an empirical reference. The theorist must constantly refer to empirical studies to support the system developed.

In more technical terms, analytic realism attempts to retain the essentials of an epistemological realism while avoiding the extreme of antitheoretical empiricism. Theoretical systems are understood not as fictions but as analytic constructs that "adequately 'grasp' aspects of the objective external world" (1970c). However, there is a very important qualification of this type of realism which has to do with Parsons' use of the term "analytical."

These [theoretical] concepts correspond, not to concrete phenomena, but to elements in them which are analytically separable from other elements. There is no implication that the value of any one such element, or even of all those included in one logically coherent system, is completely descriptive of any particular concrete thing or event. Hence it is necessary to qualify the term realism with "analytical." [1937:730]

For example, the general theoretical problem to which Parsons has devoted his entire authorship is *action*. Action is a "characteristic" of many different types of living systems, including biological systems, personalities, social systems, and cultures (see Parsons 1970c). The sociologist, according to Parsons, attempts to understand the place of social action in relation to all other action systems. But what exactly is "action"? Clearly the theorist who uses the term is *not* referring directly to the actions of real individuals, that is to specific occurrences of wife beating or diaper changing or typewriting. This is especially clear when one attempts to explain what one would observe in order to see a society acting or, for that matter, a tree acting. If action is restricted to observations of political campaigns or photosynthesis one is, at best, observing very minor aspects of the more complex process of action. Therefore "action" is entirely an analytical construct, a concept. It is not in itself "real."

But neither is it fictitious. Studies of living systems have convinced Parsons that "action" possesses certain common elements whether it is biological, personal, social, or cultural. Originally (Parsons 1937) these were: ends, means, conditions, and norms.[1] In regard to action in human society this means that action is always directed toward goals which are sought by choices made amongst existing means ("resources") capable of achieving the goal. Furthermore, action always is bound to preexisting conditions (such as heredity and environment) and social norms, both of which influence the type of action taken. These concepts—ends, means, norms, conditions—constitute a *frame of reference*. For Parsons they are the conceptual features of all action systems (1937:733). However, frames of reference are not empirical and cannot be taken as "'components' of any concrete system of action" (1937:733).

The task of the frame of reference is to establish the relevance of facts appearing in any actual act.[2] Without a frame of reference the observer would be literally overwhelmed by data. To take the example Parsons himself gives, think of the facts available in a concrete case of suicide. *At least* the following information could be obtained: height of the bridge, cause of death, velocity of the body upon striking the water, effect of wind on the trajectory of the body, amount of water in the lungs at the time of death, and so forth. This list is virtually limitless. There could be no coherent sociological explanation of the act of suicide without a method for selecting the sociologically relevant facts. The action frame of reference begins to solve the problem by selecting out such facts as the following. The actor is assumed to have had an *end*: his expectation that jumping from the bridge will result in his death by drowning. Likewise, of the possible *means* (holding one's head in a full bathtub, exposing oneself to pneumonia, and so forth) he has chosen jumping from a bridge into San Francisco Bay. The *conditions* include: the height of the bridge, the depth of the water, the destructive force of impact with the water, the inevitability of his lungs filling with water, the virtual certainty of death. Finally the actor can be assumed to have been guided by such normative information as the awareness that jumping from a bridge might have a more dramatic effect than disappearing in the desert. Now, it should be noted that the ends, means, conditions, and norms here described are only part of the information that even the sociologist would use (for example, the sociologist would certainly be interested in norms governing suicide behavior and, perhaps, economic conditions of the individual). Thus, the sociologist would further clarify the frame of reference so that it could eventually isolate those facts relevant to the social causes of crime.

The frame of reference is itself purely analytical, that is, it breaks down such concepts as "action" into the concepts which form the theoretical frame. It is not itself empirical, but it does permit the sociologist to construct an empirical system which corresponds to the theoretical system:

An empirical system, then, is a body of presumptively interdependent phenomena to which a given abstract analytical scheme is presumptively relevant. It is impossible to study everything at once empirically. An empirical system is a theoretically defined field of relevant phenomena, with reference to which certain problem-statements have been abstracted. [Parsons 1961:32]

It is very important to note that an empirical system is not the phenomena themselves, but their theoretical definition. "A fact is not itself a phenomenon at all, but a proposition *about* one or more phenomena" (1937:41). Systematic theory assumes a systematic world of phenomena as its counterpart. The former "grasps" the latter but does not contain it. The grasping is within the theory itself.

For Parsons, empirical explanation requires what he calls general theory (for example, 1970c). His view that one must analyze social action as a particular instance of the action of all living systems is general theory. Parsons is convinced that: "*All* theories of empirical science are dependent on philosophical assumptions, by virtue of the fact that all human knowledge is at some level a single organon" (1959: 704). The corollary of this belief is that theories of any given range of phenomena are intercorrelated with ever more general levels of action. There can be, for example, no theory of suicide without a theory of the social system and no theory of the social system without a general theory of action systems. Thus, for Parsons, action is a frame of reference pertinent to all living systems, to social systems, and to unit acts within a social system (and thereby relevant to concrete acts of suicide). If one wishes to explain a given case of suicide, one has no choice but to devise an analytical scheme pertinent to suicide acts, which scheme will be taken from the frame of reference given by the theory of social action, which theory is taken from the general theory of action. Thus the rationality of a given suicide is an instance of the goal-oriented rationality of social action which, in turn, is an instance of the "purposiveness" of all action systems.

It is at this point that Parsons has received his strongest criticism. He is accused of being speculative and thus unscientific. Whatever may be the case with his substantive theory, it is definitely untrue that he is being speculative, if by speculation is meant ungrounded theorizing.

He is quite concerned that "a theoretical system should be capable of statement in logico-deductive form starting with axioms or postulates, and proceeding to definitions of variables, theorems, parametric constants, deductions from theorems, etc." (1959:702). This is how a science explains and at this point his view is no different from that of Homans and Blalock. Where he differs from these other two lexicalists is in an unwillingness to derive general axioms by borrowing or invention. General axioms must also be grounded. This is what is meant by the statement that explanation is theoretical. In this respect, Parsons' scientific *intentions* are considerably more rigorous and less "speculative" than those of Homans and Blalock. Parsons wants to work out the derivations of even the most general axioms, while the other two stop considerably short of this.

It could be argued (and often is) that this is well and good as intention, but it is practice that counts. However well-meaning Parsons has been, his actual theoretical practice could be speculative. On this score, something can be said in Parsons' defense. Parsons does work with empirical information, though it is seldom of the kind that appears in tables or equations. It should be remembered that analytical realism is a type of theory that seeks to "grasp" the empirical world. For Parsons this means that all theory (even the most general) is designed with an eye to the empirical world. This is what is suggested by the phrase "frames of reference." The reference is an empirical reference.

How does the empirical reference enter for Parsons? It cannot enter from the bottom, so to speak; that is, from direct empirical testing. This comes after the theory is formulated (as it does for Blalock and Homans). The empirical reference is a far more dialectical process than opponents usually concede. For Parsons all theoretical concepts must be justified by an important empirical study. In practice, these justifying studies are heterogenous, quite unlike the kinds of empirical literature Homans uses. For Parsons they have ranged over at least the following sources (see Parsons 1970b): Robert Bales' study of small group behavior, W. B. Cannon's studies of homeostasis in biological process, Durkheim's study on division of labor, Freud's clinical studies, Weber's work on religion, James Olds' brain research, J. J. Henderson's illustration of Pareto's ideas with reference to biochemistry, Gerald Platt's survey research on the American university, and—most frequently—Parsons' own impressive grasp of Western history. Even such general concepts as action, system, and structure are derived in this way. Action is justified, in large part, by the arguments of the insect biologist Alfred Emerson upon which Parsons based his belief in the purposiveness in all living systems. Function is said to be derived, in part, from W. B. Cannon's work on homeostatic balance in physiological systems and Claud Bernard's Experimental Medicine. And system comes from L. J. Henderson (a physiologist), Schumpeter (an economist), and Whitehead (a philosopher). (See Parsons 1970b: 826–32; 1959:619–27.)

Now some would argue that this type of derivation is merely one theorist quoting another theorist. There is some truth to this. It is much like Homans' borrowing from Skinner, except that Parsons is considerably more daring and comprehensive than Homans. On the other hand, there is a fundamental sense in which Parsons is constantly reading through the theories of others for empirical justification. For him this is perfectly consistent due to his conviction that there are no free facts; all facts are lodged within frames of reference and therefore must be seen through another's theoretical eyes, if one is not himself going to construct the frame for finding them. What emerges as Parsons' empirical source is an incredibly rich and diverse set of books and personal conversations by and with experts in a variety of academic fields. For example, he has explained the empirical use of Freud in his theory of the personality system in the following way:

To me, it is a central methodological point that a fact is . . . a *statement* or proposition which has been empirically verified. It is stated in terms of a conceptual scheme and may be couched at any level of generality; of course, the more general the statement the more difficult it may be to verify, though this is not always the case. Hence a statement of Freud that the superego "represents," i.e., internalizes, the parent function in the family of orientation I consider a statement of fact. The important point is that the "immediate data" level, and the appropriate "language" for describing such data, is *relative* to the scientific problem at hand. To the sociologist interest in certain psychological problems, a generalization of Freud's may be an immediate datum, though to Freud himself only materials derived from the observation of particular cases would constitute such data. [1959:692]

This is why Parsons repeatedly insists that *The Structure of Social Action* is not a "mere" theoretical study. It is empirical in two respects: one, it treats the ideas of Weber, Durkheim, Pareto, and Marshall as data; two, it reads in the theories of these writers empirical phenomena (for example, rationality) occurring in modern society and confirmed by Parsons' own direct and historical observations (see Parsons 1937:725–26).

No one would ever want to label Parsons a hard-nosed

empiricist. But, it must be admitted that this is something quite different from mere speculation. In this respect Parsons is surprisingly more "empirical" than someone like Blalock. Compare the abstract and methodological essays of these two (for example, Parsons 1970c and Blalock 1970b). One finds Blalock referring to virtually no empirical sources while Parsons' essays are constantly documented with empirical references. In this special sense Parsons' epistemology is a far more systematic type of empirical realism than that of a good many sociologists (including Homans and Blalock) who chuckle at his abstractness.

Parsons' Analytical Lexicality

In the texts of Homans, lexicality took the form of filling a borrowed theoretical structure with terms supplied by the sociological imagination. With Blalock it appeared in the invention of sociological terms (variables) which were then translated into increasingly more formal languages, their definitions being adjusted to meet the requirements of different languages. Clearly Parsons' lexicality possesses features in common with both of these positions. Like Homans, he borrows certain of his basic terms (system, action, function, and so forth); but like Blalock he invents his own definitions. The most general thing that can be said of Parsons is that he is, without a doubt, more creative and distinctive in the use of terms. But this alone does not make his writing lexical.

The first sure sign of Parsons' lexicality appears on the material surface of his texts. The reader is confronted and sometimes overcome by words. So much so that it has been argued that much of Parsons' writing is excess verbiage (Mills 1959:Ch. 2). It is true that even the technical reader finds himself put off by the sheer volume and density of words. How indeed shall the reader penetrate such sentences as:

The collectivity component is the normative culture which defines the values, norms, goal-orientations, and ordering of roles for concrete systems of interaction of specifiable persons; the component of norms is the set of universalistic rules or norms which define expectations for the performance of classes of differentiated units within the system—collectivites, or roles, as the case may be; and values are the normative patterns defining, in universalistic terms, the pattern of desirable orientation for the system as a whole, independent of the specification of situation or of differentiated function within the system. [Parsons 1961:44]

This is a sentence with both volume and density, yet neither of these attributes explain why the reader is left out. One can read texts which are voluminous at both the sentential and corporal levels from which he/she is not excluded (those of Faulkner and Dostoyevsky). One has certainly read with understanding texts wherein the vocabulary is far more dense (those of Norman Mailer or John Updike, for instance). This is all the more confusing due to the fact that Parsons' words are not themselves semantically overweight. In the passage quoted, not a single term (with the possible exception of "collectivity") is alien to the everyday discourse of a reasonably educated reader. One is not tempted to turn to a dictionary in order to discover what is meant. One already has a fair understanding of the words themselves. More profoundly, the dictionary will not help because one suspects (accurately) that the meanings in common usage are not exactly the meanings of Parsons. This precisely is the basis of Parsons' lexicality.

His sociological writings constitute a denotative system. There is a sense in which this is true of all scientific writing, and certainly true of all formal scientific writing. So the important descriptive term is not "denotative" but "system." Parsons' discourse necessarily reflects his theoretical intent. A systems theory must be systematically expressed. This fact is all the more radicalized in Parsons' case due to his distinctive discursive site. Were Parsons doing general systems theory amongst systems theorists, then the preestablished technical vocabulary of the scientific group would open the way to a degree of connotative practice. Terms such as "differentiation" and "function" would be freed from an obligation to state their specific denotations in order to connote such things as: the author's point of reference in the discourse or his familiarity with standard vocabulary. But Parsons' discursive task is unique. He is using systems theory to speak to an audience largely unfamiliar with systems theory discourse. More importantly, he is using systems theory in his own special manner, so that even systems theorists might not recognize it (a fact which is documented by the sparse attention given to Parsons by systems theorists).

Therefore, Parsons' discursive position compels him to speak/write denotatively. When this is understood, one can see that the problem lies not with some inner compulsive verbosity on Parsons' part but primarily with the discursive task he has undertaken. In this respect Parsons is not only *not* verbose, he is extremely parsimonious. If anything, Parsons' writing is exceedingly disciplined and controlled. One may prefer a different style (and certainly there are many, many flaws in Parsons' style) but it is entirely unreasonable to demand either connotative richness or lexical simplicity of texts that are bound, by the author's discursive circumstance, to systematic denotative comprehensiveness.

The importance of defined terms to Parsons' theoretical system appears in another material feature of his written texts. Like those of the theory constructionists, Parsons' technical writings are written around highly elaborate diagrams and charts. This is most striking in such writings as *Toward a General Theory of Action* (1951b). There is hardly a text which is not either a prolegomenon to or commentary upon at least one of those multiple fourfold tables that have become the visible sign of Parsons' writing. What is the content of these diagrams? Nothing less than lexical items for which Parsons supplies careful definitions.

When one examines the writing itself for what Parsons is saying, it is clear that definitions are central. Methodologically, the frame of reference (upon which everything in Parsons' system is based) is a definition. It defines the elemental terms that govern theory and research. And, from where does the action frame of reference come? It could be said to have come out of the utilitarian lexicon which was, in Parsons' view (1937:699), deficient. *The Structure of Social Action* (wherein the action frame of reference is first fully stated) was written, in part, to show the historic emergence of this new theoretical perspective from utilitarian thought of the nineteenth century. The utilitarian lexicon contained only the terms ends and means. The basic lexicon of the action frame—ends, means, norms, and conditions—defined a new theoretical perspective by providing additional terms and placing them definitionally within a new theoretical relationship. As already noted, these frame of reference definitions—while indispensable—are not sufficient to scientific explanation. Thus, one may establish the theoretical system only by enriching the basic lexicon through the definition of unit and analytic element terms (1937:39).

Parsons has vigorously protested the claim that his work is nothing more than a lexical inventory (Parsons 1974:57). This is a proper self-defense. The defined terms are never merely listed. They are systematized. The definitions are always specific in their own right, but their final semantic value depends on their reference to other terms in the denotative system. Thus, in the original statement of action theory such a term as *conditions* is defined (roughly as the material, substructural features of Marxian thought), but its lexical value rests upon its relationship to other terms in the system, particularly *means* and *ends*: "Action . . . is rational insofar as there is a scientifically demonstrable probability that the means employed will, within the conditions of the actual situation, bring about or maintain the future state of affairs that the actor anticipates as his end" (1937:699).

This type of lexicality is nicely illustrated by Parsons' more mature theory, such as his famous "A-G-I-L" paradigm.[3] The theory may be outlined as follows: All action systems are subject to four functional imperatives. An action system: 1) possesses normative patterns which function to maintain the coherence of the system (L, pattern-maintenance); 2) is integrated in the sense that the normative patterns actually function to coordinate all of the internal units of system so that they "contribute" to the fulfillment of the system's norms (I, integration); 3) is composed of units each of which have individual goals arising from the needs of a particular situation, which goals must be attained for them to make their respective contributions to the integrated system (G, goal-attainment); 4) uses the resources (means) available for the achievement of goals in such a way that the use does not "cost" so much that goal attainment disrupts the basic patterns of the total system (A, adaptation). These functional relationships are, for Parsons, universal to all action systems, at all levels.

Thus, in his most general social theory, Parsons argues that action itself may be described by the fact that it meets these functional requirements. Cultural systems (L) provide the normative patterns. Social systems (I) function to integrate the individuals and collectivites of which society is composed under the pattern meanings of a culture. The personality (G) in individuals is understood as an action system that "creates" the goal attainment problem which—in a dynamic system—is resolved when individual personality goals are achieved within an integrated system. And the "behavioral organism" (A)—roughly the biological component of action—is the system wherein action is adapted to the tension between the energy resources of the biological environment and the goals of the personality within the total scheme of action itself.[4]

It is perhaps easiest to visualize this conceptual structure by focusing on the social system.[5] For the social system, culture and the personality are the two immediate environments. Culture provides the patterned control for society by means of general values which are institutionalized in the actual structures of the social system, while personality provides the motivational energy for society by means of individuals acting within roles that are normatively organized in the integrated society.[6] Thus, the basic "external" functional task of social systems is integration. But how— in very general terms—does this work?

Within a social system the general values of culture are

institutionalized into structural features that function to maintain the social system. The institutions of primary socialization—family and church—are the usual agencies for this function *within* social systems. The integrative (I) function is fulfilled by those institutional sectors which serve to apply specific norms to the divergent actors (collectivites and individuals) in specific roles within the system. Here the entire legal system of complex societies is the structural site for integration. At the next lower level, the political system (including government and its various agencies, as well as political parties) is the institutional basis for the goal-attainment function. Government (at least in Parsons' theory) functions to allow particular individuals and groups to act with respect to particular goals within the system. The difference between the legal system (I) and the polity (G) is that the former has a universalistic reference (as symbolized in the American system by due process of law) and the latter is particular to specific actors in specific circumstances (as symbolized by the "responsiveness" of government and political parties to the demands of social movements and lobby pressures). Finally, the economy is the primary institutional basis for adaptation in that its function is to distribute the various resources (wealth) of the society.

With these illustrations in mind, one can readily see the lexical status of Parsons' theory. The social system, as described above, is not real. It is entirely an analytic construct (Ackerman and Parsons 1966). Everyone with his wits about him knows full well that distinctions such as these do not exist in the real world (however "dynamically" they are described). Where is the boundary between the economy and the polity for societies in which business interests and politics are intermingled? What becomes of the family as an institution for the maintenance of general values when the economy turns it into a unit of consumption? Where in American society is the legal system distinguished from the polity (outside the Constitution itself)? Under the best of conditions these functions and institutions, seen as empirical realities, are very much mixed up with each other. This precisely is the point of Parsons' analytic realism methodology. In reality one cannot sort out everything that acts. Therefore, the social system is real only to the extent that it is a topic of theoretical discourse. It is a system of definitions. And there is no way around this because "in order to think at all, we must abstract, ascribe differential importance, select and establish analytical boundaries" (Ackerman and Parsons 1966:27).

Thus the substance of Parsons' social system is entirely in his lexical system. Concepts such as *pattern maintenance, integration, goal-attainment,* and *adaptation* are the basis of everything, but they are not themselves realistically defined. This is crucial. Parsons' definition of lexical items always has two moments. First, they are defined in terms of an empirical reference. They are not arbitrary in the sense that they have no reference to what Parsons thinks goes on in the empirical world. This is why the terms are relatively nontechnical in the sense that most readers can get a reasonable idea of what they represent at first reading. One generally knows, for example, what integration is about. But, at the same time, the second definitional moment is necessary. The concepts must be given a specific place in the definitional system. Thus, the first definition usually appears initially in a clear form such as: "The function of pattern-maintenance refers to the imperative of maintaining the stability of the patterns of institutionalized culture defining the structure of the system" (1961:38). But this is insufficient for theoretical purposes. The second definitional detail is necessary:

We have compared pattern-maintenance with inertia as used in the theory of mechanics. Goal-attainment then becomes a "problem" in so far as there arises some discrepancy between the inertial tendencies of the systems and its "needs" resulting from interchange with the situation. Such needs necessarily arise because the internal system and the environing ones cannot be expected to follow immediately the changing patterns of process. A goal is therefore defined in terms of equilibrium. [1961:39]

Even in this very simple illustration, pattern maintenance takes up its theoretical value by its relationship to goal-

attainment. And this lexical relationship requires the
duction of other analytic terms: interchange, interna
tem, environment, equilibrium—each of which is d▓▓▓▓▓
elsewhere in the systematic discussion.

It is true therefore that with Parsons everything is lexical,
but this does not mean that he is mindlessly spilling forth
a peculiar sociological dictionary. The lexicon is a closed
system of specific and remarkably clean definitions developed by means of a self-conscious theoretical strategy.

Man, Serendipity, and Theoretical Systems

Whether or not Parsons' writings are homocentric is a
deceptively difficult question. On the surface it is all too
easy to label them the ideology of middle-class conserva-
tism and, thus, to conclude that they are a kind of establishment humanism. Thus one of the most widely read and
extensive criticisms of Parsons says: "The mountains of
categories to which Parsons' labors have given birth are the
product of an inward search for the world's oneness and a
projection of his vision of that oneness" (Gouldner 1970:
209). The trouble with such an appraisal is that it is not
grounded in Parsons' actual written texts. It refers entirely
to presumptions with respect to his intentions. Gouldner's
assessment is an explanation of theoretical discourse from
a point outside the discourse itself. It ignores Parsons' actual discourse whereupon one discovers such evidence of
homocentrism.

1) The fundamental deficiency in the usual criticism of
Parsons is that it ascribes far too much self-consciousness
and design to Parsons himself. It ignores the impact of the
finitude of discourse on Parsons' writings. His published
writing simply is not a corpus that possesses the "oneness"
and systematic integration of a "projection of his vision" of
"the world's oneness." In this respect his actual discourse is

at odds with his methodological intentions. It is quite true that methodologically and theoretically he does see a systematic unity in the world. But this is not even remotely evident in his actual writings. There is only one text in the entire corpus (Parsons 1961:30–79) that could be called a comprehensive outline of the social system. Other texts (1951a, 1951b) have this intent, but they are at best partial outlines. Virtually everything else is published in long essay form. Many of his essays were written either in response to specific invitations (for example, 1959, 1965) or to special (often accidental) occasions for collaboration (for example, 1951b, 1953). The total corpus is diffuse.

Parsons himself has described his intellectual career as serendipitous:

It is quite clear that neither in the occupational sense nor in the sense of intellectual content has mine been a meticulously planned career. The furor over the dismissal of Meiklejohn at Amherst was not foreseen when I went there, nor was the shift from biomedical to social science interests planned. Within a limited range the year at London was, but the German venture, including being assigned to Heidelberg, very definitely was not. Similarly, though going farther with economic theory was planned, involvement in sociology at Harvard was not, nor was the life-long career anchorage at Harvard. Just as, when I went to Heidelberg, I had never heard of Weber, when I decided to come to Harvard I had never heard of Gay or Henderson. I was early predisposed to treat Pareto as rather indifferent as I was conditioned to consider Durkheim unsound. I also had no special attraction to or knowledge of Freud until well into my thirties, and I had no special interest in the professions until nearly the same period. [Parsons 1970b:866]

Parsons' way of explaining this serendipity is convincing. The systematization in his theory is that of the judge, not the engineer. It comes from responding to particular cases and attempting to solve particular problems with reference to a general understanding of the order of things. It does not emerge from predefined blueprints and specifications.

I hope I have reacted somewhat in the manner of a competent common-law appelate judge: namely, that I have considered the submitted topics and problems in relation to a theoretical scheme, which—though its premises were not defined with complete precision and henceforth assumed as fully given in a logically complete sense—has had considerable clarity, consistency, and continuity. In a sufficient proportion of cases, it seems to me that this kind of procedure has yielded empirical insight and rounding out, extension, and revision and generalization of the theoretical scheme. At certain points this has meant intensive concern with formally defined theoretical problems, but at other points primary concern with much more empirical issues. In any case this is essentially what I have meant by the phrase "building system theory." [Parsons 1970b:868]

Instead of projecting his own image of unity onto the world, the judge stands back from a world he is obliged not to prejudge. The diffuse nature of Parsons' corpus is a sign of the effect of finitude upon his epistemology.

In spite of the confidence with which he defines his terms *within* the analytic system, Parsons' attitude toward the real world is cautious and receptive. Events stimulate him, often in surprising ways. This shows in the theory itself. Even when one follows the line of continuity in the development of action theory, one does not have reason to believe that many of the advances were particularly intentional. For example, the discovery of Freud (absolutely crucial to his four-function paradigm and later to the introduction of cybernetic theory) appears to have been almost accidental. It came from a chance meeting while doing research on medical practice (1970b:835) and was deepened by his own experience in psychoanalysis (1970b:840).

One could ask: are we to take Parsons at his word and believe that a scholar of such far-ranging interest would not have eventually come upon Freud? Almost certainly he would have, but the point is that he did *not* at the moment one would expect: during the preparation of *The Structure of Social Action*. Why—in a book over which he temporized for several years before publishing (1970b:829), and which was supposed to be a systematic empirical study of "recent European social thought"—would Parsons give Freud only two passing references (1937:336, 338)? It cannot be argued that he was concerned there only with "ideas about the modern socioeconomic order, capitalism, free enterprise" (1970b:829). This fails because Durkheim did not *primarily* discuss these topics. Even more significant is Parsons' own claim that the "main concern here [1937] has been with the definition of structural elements" (1937:727). In light of his appellate-judge model for theoretical work, this must be considered a mildly disingenuous statement. It is known for sure that he studied Pareto because of L. J. Henderson, Marshall because of his experience at the London School of Economics, and Weber because of his doctoral studies at Heidelberg. What are the odds that someone starting out to define a theory of action would devote a long chapter to Marshall, while excluding Freud (who certainly qualified as a recent European thinker pertinent to action theory)? Very slim. One must take Parsons at his later word (1970b). *The Structure of Social Action* arose as almost anyone's first book arises. One begins with the materials and background at hand, extends the research and thought where necessary, and draws it up as systematically as possible. Many people will be eternally grateful that after nearly eight hundred pages Parsons did not take up Freud. But the important fact is that it took him several years *after* the first statement of action theory to come to Freud. The serendipity theory is quite plausible.

Of course, the fullest justification for this evidence of finitude is in his theoretical strategy itself. Analytic realism is, perhaps, the most radically Kantian of any major contemporary sociological method. As shown above, its fundamental assumption is that facts in the real world are not immediately available. They are definitions grasped within the analytic theory itself and their only contact with the outer world is that of reference. While confident in its internal manipulation of terms, analytic realism is exceedingly bashful in its relations with the empirical world. We really do not know for sure why Parsons has done so little empirical work. The usual view is that he has no use for data; that he is compulsively theoretical due to his moral commitment to order. It seems just as likely that the lack of empirical work is due to his keen awareness of the finitude of human knowledge.

Whatever Parsons is or is not, he is hardly the picture of a brash overconfident scientific technician setting out to remake the world. He is far more the picture of a writer at home in a lexical world that takes on great theoretical proportions precisely because it no longer bears the pretense of containing what is really out there. The lexical world of Parsons—as with that of Homans and Blalock—is a world of writers who have learned and accepted the lesson of finitude.

2) Those who doubted that finitude was relevant to Parsons will be more perplexed by the proposition that his discourse is subjectivistic. The subjectivism of Parsons is first encountered in the fact that his writings must be read from the outside. The reader does not easily find a comfortable place in Parsons' discourse. One does not readily get the sense of "being spoken to," as some do upon reading more rhetorical authors such as Gouldner or C. Wright Mills. It must be noted that there is more than one type of subjectivist writing. One is rhetorical. The subjective dispositions and styles of the author are *thrust outward* onto the text. The reader is confronted in these texts by the stimulation of contact with another person materialized into writing. Thus, Mills' *The Sociological Imagination* begins with a confession of the author's personal experience: "Nowadays men often feel that their private lives are a series of personal traps" (1959:3). At the other extreme of subjectivist discourse lie the writings of Parsons wherein the author is withdrawn from the text. One does not meet Parsons directly in his writings. The author occupies some netherland that is both mysteriously behind the written text yet in touch with it. This is perhaps the most distinctive feature of Parsons' writing. The reader knows from the first sentence that he is dealing with an idiosyncratic text. This is why one does not turn to the dictionary for help. At the same time, the idiosyncracies of the author himself are not visible. One could read the entirety of his corpus and not gain a very clear mental image of Parsons himself.

This is the subjectivism of lexical homocentrism. It is the subjectivism of a theoretical style which depends on a system of terms defined by an absent author. The emphasis of lexical authority in the text is in a paradoxical relationship with the fact that the source of these terms is a human subject. The terms are set forth to assure the "objectivity" of scientific discourse, yet they cannot be explained without reference to their inventor or borrower. Thus, the author is essential to the lexicon and, thereby, cannot remain totally absent. He is a hidden, lurking presence of which one catches only occasional glimpses.

Parsons' writing is akin to that of Blalock and even Homans. It is subjectivistic in precisely the same way: the subjectivism of those who deal with the finitude of knowledge by retreating into a lexical system defined entirely in the mind of the sociologist. The author is no less the integrating presence than in more rhetorical styles. He remains the central force of the text in spite of his absence.

Parsons, in a remarkable passage, confesses his subjectivism: "Every system, including both its theoretical propositions and its main relevant empirical insights, may be visualized as an illuminated spot enveloped by darkness" (1937:17). The real, empirical world is darkness to the sociologist who is, himself, the "searchlight" which brightly illuminates a theoretical spot in that darkness (1937:16). This spot is where the lexicalist works.

One can now appreciate why Parsons (like Homans) is a methodological individualist: "the basic dynamic categories of social systems are 'psychological'" (1954:234; compare 1961:33, n. 4). Why would a systems theorist remain a methodological individualist? Why, in the general theory of action, is it the personality that provides the energic and motivational force to action itself? Of course, there are good theoretical arguments for such a view, but with Parsons one strongly suspects that it is the reasonable conclusion from his epistemological subjectivism. One would not expect a writer who claims that all theory is the work of the theorist himself to believe that, in the real world, action could come from another source than the individual.

This, in turn, helps to explain an aspect of Parsons' serendipitous intellectual development mentioned above. His primary resources for ideas and data have been those concrete persons who were his teachers, students, or companions at Harvard and elsewhere. People such as Henderson, Whitehead, and others either gave him his primary ideas or lead him to them. This does not in any way undercut Parsons' own personal genius. It simply reinforces what one sees in the texts themselves. Parsons' homocentrism depends heavily upon subjective judgments whereby the theoretical lexicon is invented or borrowed. "It is impossible even to conceive of 'knowledge' except as something *known by* a subject" (Parsons 1937:745).

3) Of all the features of homocentrism, it is historicism that offers the greatest resistence when it comes to Parsons. If the historicism of classical homocentrism is the world of continuity set up by man suddenly aware of his finitude over against nature, then it appears difficult to label Parsons an historicist in this sense. Action theory is based on the assumption of a continuity between the social and the natural. "The central thrust of the argument . . . is that the four-function scheme is grounded in the essential nature of living systems at all levels of organization and evolutionary development, from the unicellular organism to the highest human civilization" (1970c:35). This is confirmed by the centrality of organic and biologistic metaphors in his writing (1970b:850). Function, system, action, homeostasis, cybernetic control, environing systems are all central biologistic concepts expressing Parsons' sense of the interpenetrating closeness of the human and natural worlds. And yet, he is not a sociological naturalist! How is the contradiction explained?

One begins to see the answer by returning to his view of finitude:

[I]n addition to the limitations on complete realism necessitated by common human limitations, there are others which determine the fact that knowledge at any given time in any given field is less than this totality of humanly possible knowledge. These may be said to be of two orders: *those* inherent in the nature of the cognitive aspect of the human mind and those *owing to the fact that this cognitive aspect is never completely isolated from the other aspects: man is never exclusively Homo sapiens.* [Parsons 1937:754; emphasis added]

Man is cognitively finite both inherently and "situationally." The latter is relevant to Parsons' historicism. It is precisely because man is lodged in a highly complex system of living things—including those of the biological order—that human knowledge is severely limited.

[I]n so far as description . . . is applied *not* to a total concrete system, but to parts or units of it isolated from their context, a further element of abstraction enters in to the extent that the system is organic and has emergent properties. There is no a priori reason to limit the number of important emergent properties as such systems increase in complexity. . . . The empirical reference of a . . . concept is not necessarily a concrete phenomenon even in the above relative sense, but may be one aspect of it; the particulars corresponding to the general concept may constitute only a small part of the many facts ascertainable about the phenomenon in question. [Parsons 1937:755]

In other words, man in the theoretical world of the sociologist occupies a special place precisely because it is believed that man in the empirically real (though unknowable) world is intermingled with the organic. The very complexity of reality in which the human interpenetrates with the biological and the physical requires that knowledge (including knowledge of man) must be abstracted. It finds its clarity only within the finite realm of a theoretical system. This turns out to be a resolution exactly parallel to that of Homans and Blalock, in spite of the fact that Parsons has worked out the implications to a far greater extent. Lexical

historicism is founded in the "inner history" of the sociological community.

Parsons' special interpretation of lexical historicism is
seen in his definition of the place of sociology among the
sciences.[7] Sociology is an empirical analytic action science
"which attempts to develop an analytical theory of social
action systems insofar as these systems can be understood
in terms of the property of common-value integration"
(1937:768). In other words, the social sciences (including
sociology) are concerned with the integration function
among the general action sciences (as noted above). Because
it is analytic, it is to be distinguished from history (1937:
760). Because it is empirical, it is different from the humanities (1937:762; 1970a). Because a spatial frame of reference
is not involved in sociology and because it is concerned
with means/ends relationship and human subjectivity
(1937:764), it is an action science and not a physical science. And because it is not primarily concerned with rational action as such, or power relationships or the personality as such, it must be distinguished from economics,
political science, and psychology, respectively (1937:768–
70).

However, one cannot conclude that sociology is a residual
science. On the contrary, sociology is the most general of
the *social* sciences (1937:772, 3).[8]

The problems of social integration and pattern-maintenance stand
in a different relation to the motivation of the individual than do
adaptation and goal-attainment. The latter two are concerned
primarily with the mechanisms of "rational" orientation to the
conditions of action, a conception most highly developed in economic theory. The former two, on the other hand, to have to do
with "nonrational" factors, that is, those involved in the operation
of *internalized* values and norms. This process . . . is the essential basis of the phenomenon of *institutionalization* as seen from
the point of view of the relation of the individual to his society.
[1961:35]

In other words, economics (the social science concerned
with adaptation) and political science (that concerned with

goal-attainment) are action sciences that focus on specific situational *conditions*. Integration is the theoretical site of that science dealing with the crucial function problem of institutionalization which is a general (extrasituational) problem in the systems of social action. In other words, sociology treats those topics that give the culture a footing and economics and political science a frame of reference. Though he does not say it in so many words, Parsons seems to think that sociology is *the* crucial theoretical science in action theory.

Thus is recognizable the special importance of sociology's unique empirical topic, value integration. It must be remembered that the problem created for homocentrism by its acknowledgment of finitude is: How can difference be overcome? The consistent homocentric answer is: By setting the individual differences along the continuous axis of history. Value integration in the sciences of action does just this. It is precisely that function which unifies the particular differences which constitute the goal-attainment and adaptation functions by relating them to the ongoing patterns of culture. "In contrast to the constancy of institutionalized cultural patterns, we have emphasized the variability of a system's relation to its situation" (1961:39). Here, in another form, is the basic dichotomy of Parsons' general theory. Variability/constancy, specificity/universality, difference/repetition—these are the operating tensions within social action, within the social sciences, and within action itself. Sociology is that social science which stands at the crucial boundaries in these dichotomies. Its concern with integration is, fundamentally, a concern with that basic problem created by the intrusion of finitude into the homocentric world.

What then is the vital force in this process? With Parsons (as it was with other lexicalists) it is the sociologist. Now it is no surprise that Parsons himself occupies a crucial place in Parsons' history of sociology. It was Parsons who, in *The Structure of Social Action*, discovered the convergence among the great nineteenth-century thinkers: "What has happened in the minds of these men is not the appearance of an unorganized mass of arbitrary subjective judgments. It is part of a *great deep stream* of the movement of scientific thought. It is a movement of major proportions extending far beyond the works of the few men considered here" (1937:775). What better figure of speech than "*great deep stream*" to characterize the lexical elongation of sociology in time? Similarly Parsons understands his own sociological vocation to be that of developing a sufficient general lexical theory which will permit sociology to move forward from these "sound theoretical foundations" (1937:775).

It is, therefore, irrelevant to attribute Parsons' view of his own importance to characterological arrogance. Whatever else it is, it is at least the reasonable conclusion taken by a very systematic thinker from the implications of his own discursive practice. Sociology is the integrating of the lexicon of all the social sciences, which in turn are the integrators of the lexicon of the sciences of action. This integration function is served by the only means available: the establishment of a lexical history. Therefore, for Parsons, one simply cannot do sociology without placing oneself at a vital point in that ongoing stream in order to establish sociological theory on its own proper footing, the march of lexical history.

4) On the question of the place of man in Parsons' thought, there is now nothing to add. One can only repeat what was said of Homans and Blalock. Without man at the center, Parsons would not be able to speak sociologically. Parsons' discourse is entirely dependent upon the hidden postulate of the sociologist as the one who, in the face of an empirical world he cannot contain, defines sociological terms, situates them in the theory of action, then hollows out a vital place for sociology wherefrom it can explain the integration of that which is particular and differential. Man the sociologist speaks and thus gives discursive life to the terms he has created. "The components of a social system speak to each other: roles, collectivites, norms, and values speak, intend, mean, communicate, assess, decide, and refer" (Ackerman and Parsons 1966:36). But where do they do these wonderfully human things? Unable to know whether or not they speak to each other in reality, Parsons must play Edgar Bergen to their Charlie McCarthy and give them voice within his own theoretical discourse.

5

Symbolic Interactionism:

Herbert Blumer

Semanticality in Sociological Discourse

In linguistics, semantics is the study of meaning. In sociology, the label "semanticality" brings together those texts which consider meaning the most important sociological problem and, at the same time, consider language the principal source of social meaning.[1]

Without exception the texts discussed in the following three chapters are interpretations of social meaning as it appears in discursive interaction. "Semantical sociology" has two references: the primacy of meaning to the social; the importance of discourse to meaning. It will be shown that the discourse *of* these sociologists emphasizes the interpretation of meaning in natural discourse. Semantical sociologists share the intention of shaping sociological meanings to the meanings of the social world. Their sociological discourse is semantical because they view semantics as the basis of social life which, in turn, is basically discursive interaction.

The terms "naturalistic" and "interpretative" are most commonly used to classify this type of sociology. It is usually semanticalists themselves who use the label "naturalistic" to describe their view of the social world as a realm of activity with its own natural properties. These properties are not natural in the sense that they are built into the nature of things. A more romantic sense is understood. The social world is seen as free, spontaneous, and independent. To call it natural is to respect its own integrity. In this sense, the label "naturalistic" is as much a moral restraint upon the sociologist as a philosophical conclusion about the character of the social. The sociologist is obliged not to superimpose his own formal conventions on society. In short, the natural happenings of society are taken as the source of sociological discourse.

This is quite the opposite of lexical sociology wherein the sociologist defines the terms through which the social is understood. Therefore, the semantical sociologist is also an *interpreter* of these natural events. The social world speaks, the sociologist interprets. This too is different from lexicality wherein the sociologist speaks first, allowing the world to respond. What will be shown below is that, in spite of these differences, semantical and lexical sociology both share a traditional homocentrism. In fact, it may be said that semanticality is nearly a pure form of homocentrism. For only semantical sociology intentionally makes subjectivity the central topic. It alone explicitly imbues the finite, historical world with the power to speak. It alone is unembarrassed to assume for itself the proud title "humanistic sociology."

The three most important types of semantical sociology will be considered: symbolic interactionism, phenomenological sociology, and ethnomethodology.

Theory as Hearing Aid

With symbolic interaction speech has tended to take precedence over writing. For most of its history, symbolic interactionism has been reluctant to accept the responsibility writing requires. Writing is durable. It leaves a permanent trace. Once writing enters the public domain not even the author can suppress or deny it. Speech, on the other hand, leaves no trace (see, for example, Derrida 1976). Its utterances disappear into silence, leaving the audience with vague memories, usually attached to the presence of the original speaker. Symbolic interactionism's location on the speech side of the distinction is, perhaps, the most important of its discursive characteristics.

As seen in the previous section, with the lexicalists writing is dominant, producing the odd effect of hiding the author behind his texts. With symbolic interactionism the situation is reversed. In the absence of durable written texts, the speaker appears. It has been noted (M. Kuhn 1964) that, for nearly a generation, early symbolic interactionist theory existed largely in an oral tradition. There were many founders, including Charles Horton Cooley, William James, W. I. Thomas, John Dewey, and—the most important—George Herbert Mead. However, what is striking is that there are few published theoretical statements prior to the mid-1930s. Those of Cooley are a possible exception. However, though they contain the basic ideas of the position, they are not systematic theoretical works. Dewey's *Experience and Nature* (1925) was a systematic statement but it was not widely read by sociologists (M. Kuhn 1964:63). The most important single classical text was George Herbert Mead's *Mind, Self and Society*, which did not appear in print until 1934. Mead's relationship to the founding of symbolic interactionism is the clearest evidence of its oral tradition. *Mind, Self and Society* was not a book written by Mead, but an edited collection of class notes taken by students attending his lectures. For nearly forty years (1893–1931) Mead presented the classic formulation of symbolic interactionism in lectures at the University of Chicago. While his writings during this long career contained many of the central ideas, he reserved his most complete systematic consideration for his lectures—for speech!

It has been argued (M. Kuhn 1964) that beginning with the publication of *Mind, Self and Society* symbolic interactionism entered into an "age of inquiry," in which the theory was tested, divided into subtheories, and, most of all, written down. It was also the period which saw the emergence of two distinct schools (see Meltzer and Petras 1970), each with a leader. The Chicago School was dominated by Herbert Blumer who became the principal codifier of symbolic interactionism in sociology. The Iowa School was led by Manford Kuhn who developed the "Who Am I?" self-inventory test which became a widely used research instrument in self-theory studies.

The differences between the schools are discussed in detail elsewhere (Meltzer and Petras 1970). In rough terms they boil down to the fact that Blumer saw the self as a dynamic and spontaneous force and thus he designed research which resisted formalization, while Kuhn's self-theory was more deterministic and thus he saw symbolic interaction as more susceptible to formal, scientific research.

What is important for the present is the fact that even as these two distinct sub-traditions developed, symbolic interactionism retained many of the traces of an oral tradition. Blumer has published remarkably little. His theoretical studies have appeared as occasional essays, the crucial ones of which were gathered together as a book only as recently as 1969. Likewise, Kuhn's work was in essay form and no more expansive or systematic than Blumer's. Both Blumer and Kuhn, as Mead, served symbolic interactionism as teachers. While their students did much to make symbolic interactionism an important intellectual force in American sociology, the leaders felt no compulsion to write. When they did, their writing bore the marks of an oral tradition. These classical figures stand out bigger than life. For example, note the following portrayal of Blumer:

Several generations of students have found themselves and their careers while sitting in his classes. Some have been impressed by the elegance and vigor of his presentation; others have been shaken by the penetrating questions he raised. . . . Even those who disagree with him have found themselves forced to consider questions that cannot be avoided. [Shibutani 1970:viii]

There is little hiding behind written texts. Those writings that do appear are frequently reflections upon or systematizations of what people active in the theoretical tradition had known for some time (for example, M. Kuhn 1964; Blumer 1962; Rose 1962). The oral tradition takes precedence. And when symbolic interactionists actually write it is usually in a brazenly conversational style. The twelve articles brought together into Blumer's *Symbolic Interactionism* have a grand total of fourteen footnotes and only three bibliographic references! There is no index and no summary bibliography. Blumer simply will not let himself be forced into the stodgy, impersonal requirements of scholarly writing.

How does one explain this preference for speech over writing? Is it simply an accident that three of the most important figures in a major intellectual tradition were not primarily writers? No! These discursive facts are explained by something inherent to symbolic interactionism itself. It prefers the oral to the written because of its basic view that discourse itself is a dynamic, natural social activity. One is required to respect discourse, the source of meaning, and not to overformalize whatever interpretations one makes. Writing carries with it too much that is durable. So, speech is the natural discursive form, for speech alone retains the freedom and spontaneity of social interaction. The implications of this fact will be seen in the following discussion of Herbert Blumer.[2]

For Blumer, *theory is instrumental.* It is a tool. The scientific concept is a "tentative convenient conception" (1969: 170). Theory has no independent authority apart from the natural social world it seeks to describe. Here again is symbolic interactionism's preference for speech. If theoretical discourse is to be dependent upon the world for its content, then its utterances must avoid, where possible, the harsh restrictions of formal scientific writing.

Therefore, Blumer's sociology is explicitly critical of lexicality:

Its [lexicality's] divorcement from the empirical world is glaring. To a preponderant extent it is compartmentalized into a world of its own, inside of which it feeds on itself. . . . For the most part it has its own literature. Its lifeline is primarily exegesis—a critical examination of prior theoretical schemes, the compounding of portions of them into new arrangements, the translation of old ideas into a new vocabulary, and the occasional addition of a new notion as a result of reflection on other theories. . . . When applied to the empirical world [lexical] social theory is primarily an interpretation which orders the world into its mold, not a studious cultivation of empirical facts to see if the theory fits. [1969:141][3]

In other words, Blumer attacks lexical sociology at its presumed strength. While Homans and Blalock place great emphasis upon the simplicity and precision of theoretical propositions, Blumer would insist that these values keep them from discovering the reality of social process (1969: 138). This is not to say that Blumer is a scientific Luddite. His critique of lexicality is not that it is *too* scientific. Just the opposite. It is not scientific enough. In its adherence to formal scientific rules, in its operationalism, and in its devotion to the formalization required for replication research, it is unable to provide "the empirical validation that genuine empirical social science requires" (1969:32).

Blumer, therefore, must be seen as an empiricist. But one must use this label cautiously. Blumer's empiricism is not the naïve assumption that the social world offers its data freely. Quite to the contrary, Blumer's type of empiricism comes from his conclusion that the social world possesses its own secret meanings. The difficulty the scientist has in deciphering these meanings is the foundation for Blumer's respect for that world. In other words, Blumer's philosophy of science is based upon his philosophy of the social world as a world of interpreted meanings.

Here the difference between lexicality and semanticality becomes clear. For the former the world is dumb. It stands over against man the sociologist but does not speak without the assistance of the lexicon provided in theory. By contrast, semantical sociology envisions the world as a chatterbox. Every social thing speaks. Each has its meaning to communicate. Thus, in principle, every utterance of this world is potentially unique. The effect on science is to place theory in an awkward, secondary position. Theory cannot provide a lexicon to the world. It must humbly listen and, in the process, acknowledge that it cannot ever grasp all that is uttered. Thus, for the semanticalist, the scientific lexicon is a weak and blatantly artificial language that draws its power from social meaning.

In this natural world every object of our consideration—whether a person, group, institution, practice or what not—has a distinctive, particular or unique character and lies in a context of a similar distinctive character. I think that it is this distinctive character of the empirical instance and of its setting which explains why our concepts are sensitizing and not definitive. [Blumer 1969:148]

The over-all effect is the same for lexicalists and semanticalists. The theorist is cut off from the world, though for different reasons. For the one the world is too silent, for the other it is too noisy.

This leads to Blumer's famous notion of the sensitizing concept. Since the social world does all the defining (1969: 138), the sociologist must see this world through the "eyes and experiences" of people in everyday life (1969:139). "Whereas [formal] definitive concepts provide prescriptions of what to see, *sensitizing concepts* merely suggest directions along which to look" (1969:148). Blumer replaces formal definitions with sensitizing concepts which are the tools whereby the scientist listens to the world.

This understanding of science is the reason that Blumer and other semanticalists are often labelled humanistic sociologists. They want to place the human factor prior to the scientific. But it is entirely unfair to conclude that they have given up all scientific intent. Blumer is not a humanist in the sense that he would reduce sociology to an art, a kind of high poetry. Blumer is convinced that the use of sensitizing concepts is the only way to make sociology a science. They alone, in his view, overcome "difficulty of bringing social theory into a close and self-correcting relation with its empirical world so that its proposals about that world can be tested, refined and enriched by the data of the world" (1969: 151). In other words, the "concepts of social theory are *intrinsically* sensitizing" (1969:150; emphasis added).

The implications of this conviction are often missed by

the beginning sociologist. One is tempted to look at the tables, statistics, vocabulary, and formulae of the lexical sociologist and conclude that this is the difficult way to do sociology. Though seldom admitted in public, more than a few are attracted to humanistic sociology because it appears to be less imposing, more natural. For a semanticalist this distinction is ridiculous, for he/she views the task of research to be at times overwhelmingly difficult. For the semanticalist, research is the task of grasping a world of uniqueness without a given commonality, a world of meaning without a preestablished code (see Blumer 1969:148). For Blumer the world "*stands over against* the scientific observer, with a character that has to be dug out and established through observation, study and analysis" (1969:21–22). The metaphor is important. For Blumer theory must be "dug out." By contrast, it was shown that for a lexicalist such as Parsons the world is darkness and theory is a spot of light. This is an accurate summary of the differences. Both see the world as over against science, but for the semanticalist that world offers a greater resistance. Here theory is gained by the hard work of digging (1969:40). On the other hand, the lexicalist awaits illumination. Both involve work in a dark place, but it is the difference between work in the mines and work late at night by the desk. The latter can at least send out for pizza.

With Blumer the resistance of this obdurate world is active. Here the mine-digging analogy fails. For him, the fundamental mark of the reality of social life is:

that the empirical world can "talk back" to our pictures of it or assertions about it—talk back in the sense of challenging and resisting, or not bending to, our images and conceptions of it. . . . It is this obdurate character of the empirical world—its ability to resist and talk back—that both calls for and justifies empirical science. [1969:22]

Thus, another metaphor is necessary: "The metaphor I like is that of lifting the veils that obscure or hide what is going on. . . . The veils are lifted by getting close to the area [of study] and by digging deep into it through careful study"

(Blumer 1969:39). Though stylistically clumsy, this mixed metaphor conveys Blumer's praxis. Social life is an ongoing interpretative process. Its semantical nature hides its meaning from the scientist. He/she must lift the veils of these meanings. But this veil lifting cannot be like the voyeurism of a peep show. Since the scientist is also an interpretating creature, once the veils are lifted, he too is exposed. His digging into this world is, more accurately, a matter of the eavesdropper suddenly spoken to. He must enter into an ongoing discourse. The sensitizing concept is his way of speaking interpretatively from a place within a discursive world.

Thus, the semanticalist denies that there is an absolute discontinuity between scientific and everyday life discourse. Both sociology and everyday life are interpretative processes. However, this is not to say that there are no differences between the two, at least not for Blumer. Though he does not state it in so many words, what distinguishes the sociologist from the natural person is that the former is more aware of the interpretative nature of social discourse. The sociologist's job is to describe and explain the semantics of social life. This is obviously done with a great deal of caution and the caution pervades everything the symbolic interactionist does. This includes being quite explicit in acknowledging his/her own assumptions. As a result, much of Blumer's writing reads like a general philosophy of social life. This is a requirement of a sociology trying to speak another's language. Whoever attempts to speak a foreign language is required, by the uncertainty, constantly to explain what he is saying. Therefore Blumer's texts seldom lack a philosophical introduction. He wants everyone to know that he is not speaking native sociology, that he is speaking the language of the social world.

These philosophical introductions are stated in terms of "root images," a notion that is analogous to sensitizing concepts. While the latter are ways of speaking tentatively about the world, the former are ways of speaking tentatively about speaking tentatively about the world. Blumer grounds his semanticality in the following root images (see 1969:6–

20): 1) Society is composed of human groups which, in turn, are composed of individuals. All three exist only in *action*. 2) The nature of social interaction is that it is *indeterminate*. Individuals do not simply respond to stimuli. They creatively form human conduct itself. 3) Basic to this creative task is the predominance of symbols in social interaction. Acting human beings create by their ability to indicate what they think is going on. Persons can step out of the stream of action and think about themselves and others. These thoughts take the form of *indications*. The actor indicates to the other how he is expected to act and, conversely, interprets the other's indications in order to form his own individual conduct. These indications are symbolic. 4) There are three kinds of *objects* for human beings—physical, social, and abstract (such as moral principles). Thus, in order to "understand the action of people it is necessary to identify their world of objects" (1969:11). These objects change as people make different interpretations based upon different social situations. 5) Persons can act only because they can think of themselves as objects. That is, a person will act as a father only because he is able to think of himself in such a role. Action, therefore, is a symbolic process called *role taking*. 6) Human action is necessarily social because the individual can only interpret his own possible action by having first interpreted others performing that (or similar) actions. Conversely, "joint or collective action is an outcome of . . . a process of interpretative interaction" (1969:16). 7) Action, therefore, is not random. An individual's action is always tied to that of another. In order to act, the individual must fit his action to that of another. Thus, in society there emerges a fitting together of lines of action. This is the basis for the development of what is usually called *institutions*.

When one reads carefully the text in which Blumer describes these root images (1969:6–20), one sees immediately his distance from lexicality. The descriptive passages are sometimes painfully repetitive. Any one who wishes to categorize theoretical statements is frustrated. Even in the brief summary given here the numbers used to designate distinctions are arbitrary. It is not enough to say that he is talking about   1) action,   2) indeterminancy,   3) indication,   4) objects,   5) symbols,   6) role taking, and   7) institutions. Of course, Blumer is trying to talk about these subjects, but no single one of them stands out clearly. The descriptive language flows from one point to another. The repetitions are not logical circularity because his writing is not linear. Blumer's is not formally logical discourse, as one sees in his own summary of the root images:

This approach sees a human society as people engaged in living. Such living is a process of ongoing activity in which participants are developing lines of action in the multitudinous situations they encounter. They are caught up in a vast process of interaction in which they have to fit their developing actions to one another. This process of interaction consists in making indications to others of what to do and in interpreting the indications as made by others. They live in a world of objects and are guided in their orientation and action by the meaning of these objects. [And so on.] [Blumer 1969:20–21]

The discourse flows in a clear enough manner but one cannot break it up into pieces. No single piece stands by itself. Yet—and this is the most perplexing observation—it is possible to start reading at any particular point and not be confused. Try for example taking Blumer's text and reading it backward section by section beginning with the last section on lines of action fitting together. It makes just about as much sense. This is because the sense of Blumer's writing is the sense of conversation, not logic. In contrast to lexical writing, the reader is addressed and included by Blumer, which is exactly what one would expect from an author who believes that his theory is derived from people, like his readers, having first spoken it to him. Thus, Blumer's discourse is repetitive because it is the talk of someone who wishes to enter into an ongoing conversation. Blumer wants to speak sociologically, but not at the expense of changing the natural flow of social discourse.

These discursive qualities clearly reflect Blumer's understanding of the place of theory in sociological research. He outlines five basic steps:

a) The Possession and Use of a Prior Picture or Scheme of the Empirical World under Study. . . . b) The Asking of Questions of the Empirical World and the Conversion of Questions into Problems. . . . c) Determination of the Data to be Sought and the Means to be Employed in Getting the Data. . . . d) Determination of the Relations Between the Data. . . . e) Interpretation of the Findings. [Blumer 1969:24–25]

Theory is used cautiously. One begins with a picture. This is inevitable. Here Blumer agrees with Parsons. The world cannot be seen without some kind of theory. But with Blumer the frame of reference is replaced by an image, which is constantly reexamined: "The underlying picture of the empirical world is always capable of identification in the form of a set of premises. . . . The unavoidable task of genuine methodological treatment is to identify and assess these premises" (Blumer 1969:25).

It was seen that Parsons was highly sensitive to the premises underlying the action frame of reference. But once the frame was established, it became a working assumption. It was no longer open to fundamental doubt. Blumer's theoretical pictures are, in principle, open to constant doubt.[4] These pictures are used in the first stage of research, exploration (1969:40). Here the first three aspects of research are involved [see (a), (b), (c) above].

Exploration is by definition a flexible procedure in which the scholar shifts from one to another line of inquiry, adopts new points of observation as his study progresses, moves in new directions previously unthought of, and changes his recognition of what are relevant data as he acquires more information and better understanding. [Blumer 1969:40]

Exploration is then followed by inspection which is an examination of empirical contents corresponding to an analytic scheme thus developed (1969:43). Here is where sensitizing concepts come into play. While more definite than pictures, they are not definitions. Sensitizing concepts are used to guide theoretical explanation which is "exposition which yields a meaningful picture" (1969:120).

Thus, it may be seen that theoretical concepts are at work

in all research steps. They are indispensable. Furthermore, they are gradually clarified, if not formalized. Blumer is not antitheoretical, but he does intend to be cautious in the use of theory (compare 1969:154):

Throughout the act of scientific inquiry concepts play a central role. They are significant elements in the prior scheme that the scholar has of the empirical world; they are likely to be the terms in which his problem is cast; they are usually the categories for which data are sought and in which the data are grouped; they usually become the chief means for establishing relations between data; and they are usually the anchor points in interpretation of the findings. [1969:26]

Therefore, Blumer does not suggest that theory is a mere paraphrase of the natural world. Concepts are abstractions and they are the work of the sociologist. What distinguishes Blumer from the lexicalists is his view that the concept is "an incident or an episode of the scientific act" (1969:155). This is to say that the concept is the same order of phenomena as that which it studies, an element in a social act. Thus while even the semanticalist obeys the requirements of all science (1969:163–67), he treats the concept as a "gateway to the world" (1969:143), as an implement, not an archetype (1969:168). In other words, it is allowed no final authority. The concept remains a mere instrument, always subject to criticism and refinement by the world.

Sociology as Meaningful Interpretation

Semanticality has been described as a type of sociology which assumes that the creation of meaning is *the* essential social process and, accordingly, gives primary attention to the discourse by which that meaning is conveyed. Blumer's semanticality is most overt in his description of the three assumptions of symbolic interactionism (1969:2):[5] 1) The action of human beings is directed toward objects (physical, social, abstract) on the basis of the meanings those objects have for persons. 2) These meanings are created in social interaction. 3) This creative process is indeterminate in that the meanings are never given (or built in). They are always interpreted. In short, man is an interpreter of socially created meanings.

Sociologically, the most important of these is the third. To say that all meaning is interpreted is to deny easy sociological access to scientific measures of social meaning. This stems from the premise that "interpretation is a formative and creative process in its own right" (1969:135). Thus, variable analysis (and the whole of lexicality) is problematic (1969:132–39). One cannot simply state that black migration into white neighborhoods causes white out-migration. One cannot even say that black in-migration causes a certain type of meaningful response (such as a sense of threat to whites). For Blumer, what is at stake in sociological analysis is the interpretative process whereby black in-migrants and white potential out-migrants interpret the presence of each other as neighbors. These interpreted meanings are neither given in reality (as properties of racial groups in conflict) nor built in as a psychic attribute (such as racial prejudice). (See Blumer 1969:4.) Instead, they are built up in the interaction of the two groups. Neither possesses nor creates a meaning in isolation. Thus in the case of two neighbors (each representatives and members of a racial group), the black indicates his intention to buy and live in a home in a traditionally white neighborhood. The white neighbor, reading this intention, indicates his intention (to leave the neighborhood). A joint act is created when the two have interpreted the other's intentions and, accordingly, formed their own definitions of the situation (the black resolves to stay, the white resolves to leave). For Blumer, the sociologist is not interested merely in the fact that whites sometimes leave when blacks move into certain neighborhoods. He is more concerned with the precise ways in which the two interpret each other's intended meanings. Thus, for Blumer, meanings are not merely *aspects* of social situations, they are "central in their own right" (1969:3). Sociology is the study of the symbolic indications by which persons interpret each other's meanings. Literally every-thing important in sociology is included in this statement.

To illustrate Blumer's semanticality one of his substan-tive studies will be taken. Blumer has written influential essays on a number of topics including: social disorganiza-tion and deviance (Blumer and Hauser 1933; Blumer 1937), collective behavior (1959), industrialization and social change (1966, 1960), and race relations (1958). A survey of his writings reveals two facts which contradict the popular understanding of symbolic interactionism. Against the com-plaint that symbolic interactionism is exclusively interested in micro research, one must place the fact that with few exceptions Blumer's substantive writings are on macro problems. One commentator has accurately insisted that Blumer must be seen as a sociologist, not a psychologist or even a social psychologist (Killian, in Shibutani 1970:184). Against the criticism that symbolic interactionism tends to-ward purely descriptive studies with little explanatory strength, one must juxtapose the fact that there is little raw data in Blumer's writings, almost all of which are attempts at general explanation.

A prime example of both of these facts is the essay "Race Prejudice as a Sense of Group Position" (Blumer 1958). First, this study is an attack on "the rather vast literature on race prejudice [which] is dominated by the idea that . . . prejudice exists fundamentally as a feeling or set of feelings lodged in the individual" (1958:3). Blumer's counterar-gument is roughly this: Since, by definition, racial prej-udice presupposes persons belonging to two different racial groups, the feelings identified as prejudicial must be ex-plained with reference to those groups. In other words, prej-udice is a problem in collective behavior, not psychology. This leads to the second fact that Blumer's purpose here is general explanation: "There is need of showing how the feeling complex [prejudice] has come into being" (1958:3).

In the latter connection, one who begins reading Blumer

with his methodological statements (1969) will certainly be surprised by his substantive essays. All of the talk in the former of keeping close to the data leads one to expect a wealth of description in the latter. However, there is none. It is too easy to explain this anomaly away on the grounds that Blumer's career has been mostly that of a teacher and theoretical commentator on sociological problems. Obviously many, many studies in the symbolic interactionist tradition have been highly descriptive. But Blumer's essays show that semantical sociology can and ought to be general while remaining faithful to the symbolic indications of the social world. The more subtle explanation is that the form of his essays is influenced by his semanticality. Since he believes that everyday life is interpreted action, sociological discourse cannot be uninterpreted. Thus, his data cannot be pure description. They are found in the sensitive concepts by which reality is interpreted. Thus, in this essay (1958), the data are condensed into interpretative concepts.

This is seen in his understanding of the generic variable. He criticizes variable analysis for failing to employ truly generic variables which refer to "a dimension or property of abstract human group life" (1969:130). What he means is that in a great deal of empirical research such generic-type variables as "age" or "sex" are localized. They lose their generic quality by being tied exclusively to data taken from particular contexts, such as the age distribution in the rural counties of Illinois (1969:130). Another example is the use of such general variables as "social cohesion" and "social integration" which are specified only with reference to indicators pertinent to a particular problem (1969:129). The difficulty with these localized generic variables is not that sociology lacks the data to make them more general, but that they are improperly derived. They have been defined apart from the definitions real persons use and it is only in human interpretations that an authentic genus of meaning can be found. For Blumer, generic categories must be derived by tracing "the lines of defining experience through which ways of living, patterns of relations, and social forms are developed, rather than to relate these formations to a set of selected items" (1969:138–39). This is, of course, a rather vague statement, but its intent is clear in his understanding of race prejudice.

In Blumer's mind the trouble with psychological definitions of prejudice is that they refer only to particular feelings, such as hostility, intolerance, hatred. What is omitted is the fact that there can be no particular type of prejudicial feeling unless the prejudiced person belongs to a particular racial group. Why is this so? Blumer does not draw this conclusion from simple observations of racial groups in conflict. Instead, he refers himself to the general characteristics of interpreted action. For a person to be prejudiced he/she must, first, have a racial self-image. Secondly, one must have the ability to interpret an Other as being racially different. How are these indications formed? In the case of racial prejudice they are primarily formed by the fact of membership in racial groups. "To characterize another racial group is, by opposition, to define one's own group" (1958:4). Thus, the first element in prejudice is not the definition of a feeling of hatred or hostility toward another, but the definition of oneself as a member of a racial group:

To fail to see that racial prejudice is a matter (a) of the racial identification made of oneself and of others, and (b) of the way in which the identified groups are conceived in relation to each other, is to miss what is logically and actually basic. One should keep in mind that people necessarily come to identify themselves as belonging to a racial group; such identification is not spontaneous or inevitable but a result of experience. Further, one must realize that the kind of picture which a racial group forms of itself and the kind of picture which it may form of others are similarly products of experience. Hence, such pictures are variable, just as the lines of experience which produce them are variable. [Blumer 1969:3]

This is not a matter of biological self-definition. In the case of prejudice the crucial fact is not belonging to a race, but belonging to a racial *group* which defines itself as possessing a certain position relative to other groups. This crucial definition is experientially and socially determined. Groups create and interpret differing meanings associated with different group positions.

Thereby, Blumer isolates a generic concept: "the sense of group position." The operative word is "sense." He is not referring to given status arrangements, but to people's sense of orientation. A sense of group position "stands for 'what ought to be' rather than 'what is'" (1958:6). It is a "norm and imperative—indeed a very powerful one" (1958:5). It is generic in that it is not reducible to any specific feelings of hatred and hostility. It is a feature of meaning interpreted between racial groups.

Now, at this point, one may reintroduce the question asked above but not fully answered. Where is all the naturalism in this? How is Blumer staying close to and digging into the real world? And, is not this very much like what the lexicalists do? Taking the last question first, the difference between Blumer and, for example, Homans is that the latter would treat "sense of group position" as a formal term usable in a general axiom. For Blumer, even generic concepts are sensitizing in two respects. One, while general they must always be viewed as susceptible to unique definition in particular contexts. Two, they refer not to the scientific logic of deductive propositions but to everyday assumptions regarding the meaning of social interaction. The latter is decisive. Blumer's assumptions are different from Homans' axioms in that they are working assumptions rooted in his own ongoing sense of how people make meaning. The line between the two is fine, but decisive. It appears in Blumer's texts in his constant practice of embedding generic concepts in qualifying descriptions of their variability. A concept like *sense of group position* "may undergo quick growth and vigorous expansion, or it may dwindle away through slow-moving erosion. It may be firm or soft, acute or dull, continuous or intermittent. In short, viewed comparatively, the sense of group position is very variable" (Blumer 1958:5). Thus, naturalism is retained by a discursive practice. In a short essay, which could not possibly summarize or present descriptions of the generic concept,

Blumer attempts to retain a contact with the natural world by interspersing possible if not actual pictures of reality. This is quite different from the lexicalists with whom reality testing is always isolated in separate books, chapters, or— at least—sections. Furthermore, even when Blumer is making what lexicalists would recognize as a causal-type statement, he insists on using language that serves the purpose of bringing the experience of real people into the discourse. "The source of race prejudice lies in a *felt* challenge to this *sense* of group position" (1958:5; emphasis added). A lexicalist might read this as a verbal theory to be translated into formal propositions. Blumer, on the other hand, is not being merely sentimental in his refusal to do this. His semantical theory rests upon the assumption that reality is interpreted; therefore, one is required to speak of a *"felt* challenge."

Blumer is talking about definitions, but definitions that he wants to place in the natural world. The definition (sense) of group position is discovered by the sociologist in the actual discourse of persons in a racial group. "Through talk, tales, stories, gossip, anecdotes, messages, pronouncements, news accounts, orations, sermons, preachments and the like definitions are presented and feelings expressed" (1958:5). For Blumer the relevant sociological information is contained in discourse because social meaning is always symbolically interpreted and language is the surest carrier of symbols. It is in discourse that one discovers the definitions provided by people, which definitions are the source of the generic concept. This is seen clearly in his complete theory of the relation between sense of group position and racial prejudice.

Having established sense of group position as the generic concept, Blumer then turns to the feelings of prejudice:

There are four basic types of feeling that seem to be always present in race prejudice in the dominant group. They are (1) a feeling of superiority, (2) the feeling that the subordinate race is intrinsically different and alien, (3) a feeling of proprietary claim to certain areas of privilege and advantage, and (4) a fear and suspicion that the subordinate race harbors designs on the prerogatives of the dominant race. [1958:4]

Blumer makes no claim that these are logically exhaustive of all prejudicial feelings. In fact he does not really say where they come from. He does associate each one with an example, such as the fact that the feeling of superiority is expressed in the prejudicial downgrading of the qualities of the subordinate group. But this gives no real answer to the question, why these four? A partial answer is available. One finds that his generic concept quickly comes into play:

It should be clear that these four basic feelings of race prejudice definitely refer to a positional arrangement of the racial groups. The feeling of superiority places the subordinate people *below*; the feeling of alienation places them *beyond*; the feeling of propri-etary claim excludes them from the prerogatives of position; and the fear of encroachment is an emotional recoil from the endan-gering of group position. As these features suggest, the positional relation of the two racial groups is crucial in race prejudice. The dominant group is not concerned with its position vis-à-vis the subordinate group. This is epitomized in the key and universal expression that a given race is all right in "its place." [1958:4]

In other words, these four feelings fit meaningfully into the picture painted by the generic concept. They help to ex-plain how the dominant, prejudicial group interprets the world, and its place in it. "It supplies the dominant group with its framework of perception, its standard of judgment, its patterns of sensitivity, and its emotional proclivities" (1958:4). This is what makes a generic concept generic. Its central place in group life.

In this process we see clearly Blumer's semanticality. His theory remains an interpretation of the interpretation of others. Thus, even when he is presenting a general explana-tion he sees himself, as theorist, standing in the midst of some aspect of the world attempting to pull out its mean-ings. He is not seriously bothered by the possibility of logi-cal incompleteness. Nor does he feel compelled to offer all the data. This is the discourse of someone keenly aware of his audience who believes that those listening already un-derstand what he is referring to. This is particularly true in the case of the essay here analyzed. It was originally read at the dedication of the Robert E. Park Building at Fisk University. Robert E. Park is the first great American expert on race relations. Fisk is one of the country's foremost black universities. But the observation does not rest on this particular fact. It merely emphasizes a more general feature of his discourse. While the lexicalists are always speaking to fellow sociologists, one senses that Blumer is speaking to people who understand the meaning of the world. This observation is not the banality it may seem. It further illustrates the type of discourse Blumer uses. He is not speaking so as to define, but to interpret social definitions he believes people are using. This is why even his writing is conversational. While the lexicalists write in a tight denotative fashion, Blumer's language is suggestive and connotative. Take the sentence quoted above: "This is epitomized in the key and universal expression that a given race is all right in 'its place.'" Blumer is not troubled that there is no way of documenting the universality of the expression because his universality is not statistical in nature. It is the universality of people in natural social circumstances. ("Everyone knows that. . . . Everyone remembers bigots saying 'niggers ought to keep in their own place.'") The intent to remain faithful to natural meanings keeps him from speaking in the very way that lexicalists consider the only appropriate sociological discourse.

Man In a World of Meanings

There is not a great deal to say about homocentrism in Blumer's symbolic interactionism. Here it is nearly a pure type.

1)   The analytic of finitude is here so decisive that nature, as such, fades from view. Its absence creates a space, the space of man and his symbols. Even where Blumer talks of race, it is as though there is no biological foundation for racial differences. Not even a footnote or parenthetical clause acknowledges that racial conflict has something to do with biological conditions. It is only the *sense* of group position, and nowhere does the fact of group membership as a fact of nature enter in. It would be easy to conclude that this blindness to nature unleashes an arrogant liberal spirit. But the semanticalist—whatever he is—is not the dominator of a world of facts. Quite to the contrary, one finds a persistent awareness of the limitations of knowledge. The semanticalist does not even presume to initiate scientific discourse. He is a listener governed by the norm of attentiveness. He does not speak unless spoken to. Here the boundary created by nature's disappearance is seen. For Blumer does not listen to everything. For him the natural world is silent. He listens only to beings like himself, to other interpreters, and then he listens only to their interpretations. Their bodies are inert, lifeless—significant only as passive instruments for the conveyance of gestures. They are minds without brains, selves without viscera, and societies without territory. In short, it is a sociology of a people hunkered down into a small protected corner of reality. Their worlds are the worlds they have created by their discourse, worlds that totally lack reality or firmness outside the symbols by which they are perceived.

One might expect, on this basis, that within this retreat people would find for themselves a secure sense of reality. But not with Blumer. The limitation of sociology to discursive interaction serves only to establish barriers to certitude. Precisely because it is believed that reality is symbolically defined, even these defined realities are indeterminate. "Every object of our consideration—whether a person, group, institution, practice, or what not—has a distinctive, particular, or unique character" (1969:148). Thus, as seen above, the scientist interprets these distinctive features with caution. Concepts are tools for listening, definitions are experientially (and temporarily) created, universals are the consent of speakers listened to. The sociologist must dig into an obdurate world with the mere play tools of sensitive images. He is deprived of the steel of a strong scientific lexicon.

In summary, it can be said that the very possibility of semantical sociology derives from the assumption that nature and the social are utterly divorced. This divorce is what (beginning with Weber, Dilthey, and Mead) opened up the human world of meaning to sociological scrutiny. In this the semanticalists are not conclusively different from the lexicalists. They have simply retreated into different places —the lexicalist into the security of a scientific lexicon, the semanticalist into a partial world of friendly natural humans who do all the important speaking.

2) This contrast carries over to semanticality's subjectivism. While the lexicalists operate from the subjectivism of scientific intuitions defining a sociological lexicon, the semanticalists remain cautiously within a subjectivism of listening. In lexicality the sequence is intuition-speaking-listening. In semanticality it takes the form: listening-inter-preting-speaking back. In both, the crucial scientific act emerges from an inner dialogue. The lexicalist invents in response to what is completely inside himself. The semanticalist interprets by reflecting upon his self-understanding of what has been said by the world. It is simply two forms of self-communication: one with intuitions that come from no external place, the other from inner interpretations of another's interpretations.

Thus, the semanticalist Blumer permits no free-standing object. "The nature of an object—of any and every object—consists of the meaning that it has for the person for whom it is an object" (1969:11). All objects have meaning; all meanings are interpreted meanings; all interpretations are possible only because man has the capacity for self-indication. And the converse is equally true: we form ourselves because others interpret us to ourselves in terms of what we mean to them. We define ourselves by role taking, but we can only take roles because we can indicate to ourselves an image of ourselves taking the role. No matter how it is run— backward, forward, inside-out—the entire point of view hinges upon the inner self reflecting upon itself. And this differs from lexicality not as an entirely different image of scientific and social reality, but only as a more rigorously self-conscious reflection upon the role of the inner self in theoretical discourse. The lexicalist is far more bold. He ignores the niceties of subjective knowledge out of fear he will lose the security of formal definitions. The semantical-ist starts boldly by throwing aside this security but then finds himself surprised by a welter of possible meanings to which he must cautiously cede his scientific independence.

3) With respect to history, both lexicalists and Blumer face the problem of overcoming the differences invoked by an overwhelming subjectivism. Lexicalists do it by establish-ing a history of the lexicon. Surprisingly, Blumer does es-sentially the same thing though, as one would expect, with an additional complication. Obviously, Blumer could not be assured by a formal lexical history. Indeed, as seen above, his concepts are thrust into the differential world of common sense. In this respect, the scientific concept is no different from natural concepts:

> The concept involves an identifying mark or symbol; so it presents itself as a word or expression. . . . The word, then, is a symbol of a given process of conception. By reason of its verbal or symbolic character, the concept may become an item of social discourse and so permit the conception that it embodies to become common property. . . . In becoming social property it permits others to gain the same point of view and employ the same orientation. As such it enables collective action. [1969:159–60]

To this point in Blumer's description there is no fundamen-tal distinction between the commonsense and scientific concept, except perhaps that the former is based more on feeling than logic (1969:161). Both the scientist and the person in the natural world use concepts as vehicles for interpretation and the establishment of a social life. What then is the difference, if any? Blumer begins by rooting his idea of the scientific concept in circumstances common to all discourse. "It is by reason of the fact that the concept is an item of social discourse that concerted procedure is pos-sible as far as science is concerned, and that a structure of science may emerge in place of a mere assemblage of disconnected actions" (1969:160). Beyond this, the fundamental difference is that in science one reflects upon concepts, while in common sense they are taken for granted, "their character is just naturally sensed" (1969:161). Thus the difference: "Scientific concepts have a career, changing their meaning from time to time in accordance with the introduction of new experiences and replacing one content with another. Commonsense concepts are more static and more persistent with content unchanged" (1969:161). Therefore, commonsense concepts remain particular, "detached and disparate . . . [while] scientific concepts show 'a strain toward consistency'" (1969:162). The effect is quite similar to that in lexicality. Difference is overcome by establishing a "career"—a history—for the scientific concept. Blumer, however, is far less confident of the career of his concepts because he allows them to be exposed to the indeterminacy of common concepts.

The result is that in symbolic interactionism one has more of a tradition than a formal history. In American sociology there is no other group quite so tradition-bound. Symbolic interactionism continues to celebrate its founding fathers. The language of Mead still dominates its discourse. This is in part explained by the fact that symbolic interactionism allows natural concepts their own history. "Any instance of joint action, whether newly formed or long established, has necessarily arisen out of a background of previous actions of the participants" (1969:20). But precisely because this natural world is lively and ongoing, the semanticalist cannot (and will not) let himself move ahead of it. With lexicality, the history of the lexicon is divorced from the history of the world. With Blumer, the two are wedded. The history of the social world is the source and foundation of conceptual history. As a result, the semanticalist is less free to define his terms. His history is traditional because his scientific attitude is more cautious and passive. But it is a history similar to that of lexicality. Without it, symbolic interactionism would slide into a world made chaotic by the overabundance of meaning.

4) In conclusion, Blumer's semanticality is homocentric, though not a homocentrism of man the scientist. Here man literally bursts the narrow walls within which the lexicalists have bound him. Man is now the total subject and object of sociology. There is literally nothing that is not man. Man the indicator, interpreter, actor, role-taker, definer, and creator of the social world is merely a synonym for that mysterious presence which empowers all of these realities: meaning.

6

Phenomenological Sociology:

Schutz | Berger | Luckmann

Of all the theories examined in this book phenomenological sociology is the most difficult to define, for two reasons.

First, there is an astonishing number of theories that advertise themselves as phenomenology. Some (Bruyn 1966) have taken it as essentially equivalent to the technique of participant observation. Closely related is the view that phenomenology is the appropriate extension of symbolic interactionism's type of naturalistic sociology (Douglas 1970). Some have found in it a basis for combining themes from interpretative sociology with neo-Marxian critical theory (O'Neill 1972), while others (Tiryakian 1965) see it as a kind of existentialist social philosophy held by virtually every major classical theorist. Thus, Weber, Durkheim, and W. I. Thomas are all "phenomenological" (Tiryakian 1965: 678–86). Erving Goffman (1974) has incorporated it into his dramaturgical sociology. Finally, it has been employed as a *locus classicus* for American ethnomethodology (Garfinkel 1967). Though one cannot question the popularity of phenomenology, one must wonder what it is that finds so many different theoretical friends.

Secondly, this confusion is aggravated by the uncertainty

of *sociological* phenomenology's relationship to the classical philosophical phenomenology of Edmund Husserl. It has been convincingly argued (Heap and Roth 1973) that most who call themselves sociological phenomenologists have loosely and, often, inaccurately used Husserl's ideas. This uncertain use of Husserl has its origin in the fact that it is not at all clear that phenomenology can function as an empirical science. For one thing, it is known that Husserl himself denied that phenomenology could be used in direct conjunction with formal, deductive (that is, lexical) methods. But even its use as a semantical *sociology* is questionable. In this connection, it was Alfred Schutz, whom Husserl recognized as one of the outstanding students of his thinking (Walsh 1967:xviii), who sought to combine Husserl with Weber's *verstehen* method. Schutz thought he had proposed a workable empirical sociology based on phenomenology. But a problem arises with Husserl's most basic methodological idea—the *époché*, or phenomenological reduction—which requires the abandonment of what seems to be an essential premise of empirical work: "In the epoche . . . I abstain from belief in the being of this world, and I direct my view *exclusively* to my *consciousness* of the world" (Schutz 1962:123; emphasis added). How does even a semanticalist study that which one decides not to believe in?

The effect of this focus of attention on consciousness has been to make phenomenological sociology a method which intentionally ignores the apparent facts of the outer world in order to examine how that world appears in the experience of the sociologist. Its basic goal is similar to symbolic interactionism: It wants to get close to the natural world. But its difference is that it pays more attention to what the sociologist him- or herself experiences. Roughly put, the idea is that empirical truth is not objectively given. It is only a fact of the mind's reflection on experience. The result of this profound critique of the objective world has been that phenomenological sociology has written little in the way of what is ordinarily recognized as empirical research.

Yet one cannot omit phenomenology from any study of

recent sociology. The writings of Schutz are surely among the most widely influential with younger sociologists. When people think of sociological pluralism, they have in mind phenomenology, among other things (Friedrichs 1972a, Gouldner 1970, for example). Its influence has been exerted by two quite distinct bodies of writing: ethnomethodology, on the one hand, and, on the other, the writings of Peter Berger, Thomas Luckmann, and Alfred Schutz. In the former case there is reason to believe that ethnomethodology is not inextricably bound to phenomenology as is indicated by recent ethnomethodological interest in language theorists such as Chomsky and Wittgenstein (see Cicourel 1974a, Mehan and Wood 1975). The latter—Schutz/Berger/Luckmann—must be considered in its own right precisely because it is the most theoretically extensive attempt to bring sociology within the control of Husserl's writings.

Therefore, in this chapter Schutz/Berger/Luckmann will be read as an essentially independent, if not integrated, body of writings.[1] While it cannot be assumed that Berger and Luckmann are mere slaves to Schutz (for example, they include sources such as Marx, Sartre, and Durkheim of which Schutz made little mention), their basic ideas are phenomenological in a Schutzian fashion. In what follows, the work of Berger and Luckmann will be read as a supplement to that of Schutz. The latter's writings will be considered as a primary source for phenomenology's contribution to the methodology of the social sciences.[2] Berger and Luckmann, who more than Schutz have written on substantive topics such as religion (Berger 1969, Luckmann 1967) and knowledge (Berger and Luckmann 1967), will be the source for illustrations of applied phenomenology.

Theory as Typical Motives

In order to understand this strange proposal of a science based upon the suspension of belief in the empirical world, one best begins with a description of its special sociological use of Husserl's ideas.[3]

Phenomenology believes it is necessary for science to question its faith in the outer world, precisely because, in everyday life, persons accept reality naively. In the conduct of day-to-day life, one is able to act in the empirical world only by taking most of it for granted. The phenomenological assumption is that persons can only pay attention to specific projects one at a time. Thus we must become naïve about extraneous events, thoughts, and stimuli which could tempt us to act on some other project. When I am writing, I do not pay attention to the mechanics of my typewriter, its source of electricity, the reliability of my chair, and—under the best of circumstances—I even ignore completely such things as the weather, noise from the children, my fatigue.

Since naïveté is characteristic of everyday life, phenomenology argues that it must be gotten around in order for a true science to be founded. This then is the reason for the époché or "reduction" of the commonsense world by suspending belief in it. But it is very important to note that this suspension is methodological, not metaphysical. Phenomenology does not thereby conclude that this world does not exist or is not real. "For transcendental phenomenology . . . there is no doubt that the world exists and that it manifests itself in the continuity of harmonious experience as a universe" (Schutz 1962:122). The central conviction is that scientific thought cannot be based upon *belief* in that world. Science must be based on the world created in the *experience* of the world:

Phenomenological philosophy claims to be a philosophy of man in his life-world and to be able to explain the meaning of this life-world in a rigorously scientific manner. Its theme is concerned with the demonstration and explanation of the activities of consciousness . . . of the transcendental subjectivity within which this life-world is constituted. Since transcendental phenomenology accepts nothing as self-evident, but undertakes to bring everything to self-evidence, it escapes all naïve positivism and may expect to be the true science of the mind. [Schutz 1962:120]

But how is such a science possible? Clearly it is based upon one idea more central than the others: that an individual's consciousness is the only sure place that the world can be grasped. Thus phenomenology begins thought with the life-world (*Lebenswelt*), that is, with the world that one brings into view by reflecting upon conscious experience. It is held that both philosophy and the sciences (natural *and* social) must begin here because here "every reflection finds its evidence only in the process of recurring to its originally founding experience within this life-world" (Schutz 1962: 133).

This attempt to base science on the originating experiences of consciousness is the unique methodological feature of phenomenology. However, one immediately must ask if this does not make phenomenology irretrievably relativistic, a kind of intuitive science of the private mind. For Schutz it does not because consciousness is formed *intersubjectively* (Schutz 1962:123–27, 133). Knowledge, though based on consciousness, is social because consciousness itself is socially formed. While knowledge is grasped subjectively, it can only be *explained* intersubjectively.

The phenomenologist uses a series of reductions, first, to suspend belief in the world *and*, secondly, to suspend belief in the *individual* consciousness of that world because "in this way, I can return fundamentally to the originary experience of the life-world in which facts themselves can be grasped directly" (Schutz 1962:123). By going behind even consciousness one arrives at the original *intersubjective* elements of the experienced social world.

Phenomenologists are willing to take the risk of relativity in order to achieve a truly presuppositionless philosophy. In other words, they want to avoid the lexicalist error of formalistically and abstractly summarizing the social world by means of presuppositions or primal axioms. They reject, therefore, both axiomatic *and* empiricist methods in order to use what they consider to be a more certain scientific method, "in fact the only method which seriously claims to be a radical explanation of the world through the mind" (Schutz 1962:123).

This is a bold claim. Its effect on Schutz's view of sociology is important. He claims that phenomenological analysis is the *only* basis for an adequate social science (1962:133). Here one discovers what phenomenological semanticalists are doing when they are speaking theoretically.

The central idea is the distinction between the world of commonsense in everyday life and the world of scientific constructs.

> The thought objects constructed by the social scientists refer to and are founded upon the thought objects constructed by the common-sense thought of man living in the everyday life among his fellow-men. Thus, the constructs used by the social scientist are, so to speak, constructs of the second degree, namely constructs of the constructs made by the actors on the social scene, whose behavior the scientist observes and tries to explain in accordance with the procedural rules of his science. [Schutz 1962:6]

Obviously, the approach is similar to Blumer's in that scientific theory is based upon what is said and done in the social world. Schutz explicitly rejects the lexicalist view that allows the sociologist to define the relevant facts (Schutz 1962:5, 58). Moreover, like other semanticalists, Schutz holds that roughly the same rules of interpretation govern social science and everyday life. However, with Schutz there is an important difference. Man in the commonsense world does not speak freely to man the scientist. The sociologist cannot go to the world with the listening tools of sensitizing concepts because phenomenology suspends belief in that world. However, this does not completely silence the world. It is permitted to speak indirectly through the consciousness of the scientist. Thus, phenomenological listening is, so to speak, through the "inner ear."

This comes, in part, from a conclusion Schutz shares with Parsons. There are only interpreted facts (Schutz 1962:5). However, Schutz is far more radical than Parsons. Instead of freely constructing an analytic frame of reference to which facts are fitted, Schutz' approach seeks to remain empirical in the phenomenological sense. The interpreted facts of sociology are based upon commonsense interpretations. Thus, one has a paradox: an approach to theory that takes the world seriously by the curious tactic of refusing to believe in it. While the lexicalist, in effect, gives up on the world and withdraws into theory, the phenomenologist sets it aside in order to rediscover it in consciousness.

The difference between Schutz and others who acknowledge the interpreted nature of facts is that Schutz understands all reality to be interpreted. There is no knowable reality that is discoverable outside of consciousness. Thus, both the scientific and everyday life attitudes—though different—share this condition. Both are states of mind which develop constructs around what the subject considers relevant. The scientific attitude differs only in the extent to which it sets aside the naïveté of commonsense thinking in order to analyze the structures of consciousness themselves. Therefore, if one wishes to know what the phenomenologists mean by scientific theory it is necessary first to look at what they mean by commonsense thinking.

If phenomenological science proceeds by suspending belief in the outer world, then conversely, commonsense thinking proceeds by suspending *doubt* in its existence (Schutz 1962:229). The result is the natural attitude of naïveté. However, this naïve attitude is not passive dumbness. Quite to the contrary, it is a necessary condition for the practical interest which dominates everyday life. We experience this world as a life-world which, among other things, means that it is also a world of working (1962:225 f.). The fundamental work is those projects necessary for meaningful life in a given time and place and with other persons. It is for this reason that everyday life must be naïve. One cannot carry out meaningful projects if he pays attention to every aspect of the world.

Thus, life in the life-world is based on the *structures of relevance* persons create in order to permit the accomplishment of meaningful projects. The conscious individual, in everyday life, is a point of awareness around which, for him/her, the life-world is ordered. This state of "wide-awakeness" (1962:213) is one in which "the self traces out that segment of the world which is pragmatically relevant, and these relevances determine the form and content of our stream of thought" (1962:213).

The wide-awake self is further understood as a point which meaningfully integrates its own time, self, social relations and space:

[T]he wide-awake self integrates in its working and by its working its present, past, and future into a specific dimension of time; it realizes itself as a totality of working acts; it communicates with Others through working acts; it organizes the different spatial perspectives of the world of daily life through working acts. [1962:212]

These are integrated by the intentionality of consciousness (see Berger and Luckmann 1967:20; Schutz 1962:208–14). This is to say that man is an intentional creature who creates meaning as a condition for pragmatic action in the world. Thus, for Schutz, any moment in daily life is biographically determined: "I, the human being, born into the social world, and living my daily life in it, experience it as built around my place in it, and as open to my interpretation and action, but always referring to my actual biographically determined situation" (1962:15).

At any given biographical moment, the self organizes *time* around itself in such a way that it is able to imagine the completion, in the future, of a given project (Schutz 1962:214–15, 219–22). A future action, however, is relevant only to a present project. Likewise, with respect to *social relations*, the individual is bound in time and space (1962:15–19) primarily to those who share a "face-to-face relationship" (parents, children, lovers, friends, and so forth). Still others exist in varyingly more anonymous relationships to the self. Thus, "mere contemporaries" are those who are less directly relevant because they are not in a face-to-face "we-relationship" (1962:16) to the self. And, similarly, *space* is ordered with respect to the dominance of the "manipulatory area" or the "world within reach" (1962:122–29). The body is the pivot for the self's spatial world.

Those things closest to our body are the most relevant; those more distant are in a relationship of "restorable proximity" and are, at a given moment, less relevant.

In other words, everyday life is dominated by consciousness (1962:207–59) wherein everything—time, space, social reality—is organized according to its degree of relevance to the self. This outer world is one upon which the individual works intentionally in order to make it practically relevant. However, the world offers resistance to the self and must constantly be made meaningful. This relevance is, of course, produced by the interpretations which create the relevance of that world to the self's projects. This is the self's life-world.

Obviously the phenomenological view is semantical insofar as everything in everyday life is knowable only to the extent that it is interpreted in consciousness. In effect, Schutz' phenomenology is a social psychology of knowledge. The interpretations by which the life-world is created are meaningful knowledge for the individual. Phenomenology attempts to describe how this knowledge arises.

The most important idea in this theory of knowledge is *typification*. The individual knows (that is, interprets) on the basis of types constructed in consciousness. These types are the basis for ordering and explaining the events and actions we encounter in the world. Typification is possible for two primary reasons: man learns from his history; man is social. The two are interrelated: "Only a very small part of my knowledge of the world originates within my personal experience. The greater part is socially derived, handed down to me by my friends, my parents, my teachers and the teachers of my teachers" (Schutz 1962:13). Man is historical in the sense that "all interpretation of this world is based on a stock of previous experiences of it" (Schutz 1962:208). However, the individual has no purely individual experience. Our experience is basically a social experience. Therefore the knowledge handed down is unavoidably social. Here is the previously noted irony in the phenomenological view. Knowledge originates subjectively. Its primary reality is in the consciousness of the individual, however, consciousness cannot be created unless individuals act on their social world. I can know nothing of the socially defined manners for eating in a first-class restaurant unless I first act by visiting such a place. Yet, at the same time, I will not act in this way unless something in my previous social experience allows me to think of this as meaningful course of action. Thus, since my previous experience is social (for example, my parents often went to first-class restaurants), the subjective knowledge depends upon my social relations. Thus my subjective history is, inescapably, an intersubjective history. "I am born into a world which is inhabited by others who will confront me in face-to-face situations" (Schutz 1964:25).

From this intersubjective history individuals develop a repertoire of typical meanings. One learns that there are certain types of behaviors and assumes that underlying these behaviors are consistent subjective meanings, or motives. Generally speaking, there are two classes of relationships in which these typical motivations appear: the face-to-face and the anonymous. The former is crucial. Here there is reciprocal typification (Berger and Luckmann 1967: 31 f.; and Schutz 1962:11–13). In one sense even in the face-to-face relationships two persons are separated from each other. They occupy different spaces, possess different biographies, and have had different social circumstances. This is a barrier to social interaction. However, this barrier is overcome by two practical, naïve assumptions: 1) that each other's standpoints are interchangeable, and 2) that each other's systems of relevance are interchangeable (1962: 12). These are what Schutz calls the *reciprocity of perspectives* assumptions. Here is where naïveté functions to permit social action. Obviously it is not so that either standpoints or systems of relevance are precisely interchangeable. But persons must make this naïve assumption, for without it there would be no basis for interaction. Without it, one could not imagine himself communicating with another person. These assumptions are the beginning of types. The two persons assume roughly the same general motives for each other. "By the operation of these [typical] constructs of common-sense thinking it is assumed that the sector of the world taken for granted by me is also taken for granted by you, my individual fellowman, even more, that it is taken for granted by 'Us'" (Schutz 1962:12). From these very general typical assumptions, persons develop specific interpretative schemes. Thus, for example, a parent eventually learns that a certain type of crying from a new baby is a sign of its hunger, another type of crying signifies wetness, another fear. The cry is interpreted as a sign of a specific motivation. "He is crying because he is hungry; thus he is crying in order to get me to feed him."[4] The parent develops these types on the basis of a face-to-face relationship with the child. Previous experience indicates that this motive is intended. But it can only be learned when the relationship is reciprocal. Even a new infant reciprocates, participates in developing the shared type. At some point in the relation between parent and baby, parent responds to baby's crying by feeding him. The crying stops. Thus parent develops the cry as a type construct for baby's hunger and baby takes the same cry as a type for "getting parent to feed me."

Phenomenologists allow for the fact that these types also operate in relatively anonymous relationships (1962:17). For example, the parent undoubtedly knew—even prior to the birth of the baby—that crying is typical baby behavior associated with motives such as desire for food, comfort, cuddling, and so forth. This is learned through relatively anonymous relationships often with mere contemporaries, such as: movies, television, neighbors, child-care manuals, doctors, and so forth. In these cases the type is general and relatively inflexible. It may be nothing more than: "Babies typically cry when they are hungry." These anonymously formed types are important because without them the parent would not be able to recognize the cry of his/her baby as a sign of a motivation. But in the face-to-face relationship, both mother and baby modify the general type. Different babies have different cries, and different parents have different styles of response to crying. So one baby's hunger-cry may be close to another's "change-me" cry. The different meanings are interpreted as different types in the respective, particular face-to-face relationships.

Typifications constructed in this way are the substance of commonsense knowledge. Though they vary from subjective personal types to objective "course of action" types, the same basic social process of interpretation takes place (Schutz 1962:19). Typifications, furthermore, furnish the individual with constructs whereby reality is ordered in terms of its relevance to him. They constitute a social stock of knowledge: "The social stock of knowledge . . . supplies me with the typificatory schemes required for the major routines of everyday life, not only the typifications of others . . . but typifications of all sorts of events and experiences, both social and natural" (Berger and Luckmann 1967:43).

It is now possible to consider the place of social science in phenomenology. In short the position is this: The sociologist does the same thing as a person in everyday life, that is, he constructs types to explain the subjective motives of persons. The only difference, as noted above, is that the sociologist creates "second-degree" types, that is, types built upon the types of everyday life. Max Weber is, of course, the source of Schutz/Berger/Luckmann's term typification. The phenomenologists have simply clarified the way in which these types also operate in commonsense thought. Except for the second-degree quality of sociological thought, both are similarly constructed: "Thus, the postulate of the 'subjective interpretation of meaning,' . . . is not a particularity of Max Weber's sociology or of the methodology of the social sciences in general but a principle of constructing course-of-action types in common-sense experience" (Schutz 1962:24–25).

However, this is not to say that there are no differences between the sociological attitude and commonsense. If this were true there could be no science. The sociologist must put him/herself out of the naïve attitude and assume the reflective or critical attitude of science. This, of course, is where the phenomenological reduction comes in. The scientist reduces the life-world of commonsense to those particular types under investigation. The sociologist no longer assumes that his motives are reciprocally tied to those of others in the life-world. Thus, he has available for study "merely the manifest fragments of the actor's actions" (Schutz 1962:39). That is, those superficial layers of action that present themselves to the sociologist's consciousness. The sociologist gives up his "Here" in the life-world and accordingly does not organize the world in layers about himself (Schutz 1962:40).

The sociologist becomes a disinterested observer. But this does not mean that he is excused from the general conditions governing knowledge as such. Though he attempts to ignore his own particular place in the life-world, the sociologist still possesses a social stock of knowledge which now defines his scientific system of relevances and is the basis for the scientific types he produces:

His stock of knowledge at hand is the corpus of his science, and he has to take it for granted—which means, in this context, as scientifically ascertained—unless he makes explicit why he cannot do so. To this corpus of science belong also the rules of procedure which have stood the test, namely, the methods of his science, including the methods of forming constructs in a scientifically sound way. [Schutz 1962:39]

However, this poses a problem for the sociologist. On the one hand, he has removed himself from the life-world wherein one gains relatively direct access to the meanings of Other's motives. This is necessary to science. At the same time, the social scientist retains an obligation to understand precisely those subjective meanings from which he has cut himself off. How is this dilemma overcome? By the creation of the second-degree types of sociology. What this amounts to is that the sociologist creates a puppet or, as Schultz puts it, an *homunculus*. That is, an artificial man who "was not born, . . . does not grow up, . . . and will not die" (1962:41). The sociologist gives this puppet all of his motives, his relevances, his projects. In particular, he gives him those motives under investigation.

The homunculus is invested with a system of relevances originating in the scientific problem of his constructor and not in the
particular biographically determined situation of an actor within
the world. It is the scientist who defines what is to his puppet a
Here and a There, what is within his reach, what is to him a We
and a You and a They. The scientist determines the stock of
knowledge his model has supposedly at hand. . . . The relevance
system pertinent to the scientific problem under scrutiny alone
determines its intrinsic structure. [Schutz 1962:41–42]

A given homunculus can then be interacted with other
homunculi similarly created. In short, the social scientist
literally creates in his mind an entire social world pertinent
to his problem.

It may be asked: where does the sociologist get the material with which to create these homunculi? He gets it from
his own phenomenological reflection upon the life-world
which, as was noted above, the phenomenologist assumes
is an adequate basis for deriving the general structures of
human consciousness.

Schutz was well aware of the fact that this sounds like
pure subjectivism. Thus he provided what to him was a
plausible account for the objectivity of social science. Both
he and Berger and Luckmann insist that the same general
procedural rules of the natural sciences apply to social science (Schutz 1962:65; compare Berger and Luckmann
1967:189). The phenomenological method is merely a device applied within those rules to account for the special
quality of human subjects. Thus, Schutz holds that there are
at least four general procedural rules assuring the objectivity of the social sciences.[5] These are: 1) The postulate of
logical consistency whereby it is a requirement that all constructs follow the rules of formal logic. 2) The postulate
of *compatibility* whereby it is necessary that the ideal types
"must contain only scientifically verifiable assumptions,
which have to be fully compatible with the whole of our
scientific knowledge" (1964:19). These two are clearly
applicable to both the natural and social sciences. Schutz'
remaining two are unique to the study of human action,
but Schutz seems to understand them as subsumable under

the general rules of science insofar as they are intended to assure the objectivity of the ideal types. These are: 3) The postulate of *subjective interpretation* in which scientific interpretations are set forth with reference to the subjective meaning of actors. This rule (taken from Weber) allows for objectivity because it is assumed that man is defined in terms of subjective meaning and, thus, no science of man could possibly be objective if it omitted this unique quality. 4) The postulate of *adequacy* requires that:

Each term in a scientific model of human action must be constructed in such a way that a human act performed within the lifeworld by an individual actor in the way indicated by the typical construct would be understandable for the actor himself as well as for his fellow-men in terms of common-sense interpretation of everyday life. [Schutz 1962:44]

To many the fourth postulate is not very convincing. Presumably it involves taking an ideal type of, say, masochistic behavior to an actual masochist or someone who knows masochists for verification. More likely than not your average masochist will not be a reliable source of information on masochism, if for no other reason than that his masochism in everyday life is performed naïvely. Thus the phenomenologist still is left with the problem of verifying his models by his own understanding. What is most important, however, is that Schutz and the phenomenologists worry about objectivity and, given their approach, these are the available possible rules.

Semanticality and the Theoretical Consciousness

There are two discursive facts that, above all else, strike the reader of phenomenological sociology: 1) Though it claims to be sociology, phenomenological writing is not apparently empirical. There are no "data"; no descriptions; only a few historical references. Everything seems to return to a theoretical discourse. 2) The texts are repetitive. Each seems to begin anew. Schutz' essays (1962, 1964) repeat themselves; Berger and Luckmann (1967) repeat Schutz and Luckmann (1973 [publication date]); Berger (1969:1–51) repeats Berger and Luckmann (1967). The effect of these repetitions is that the writings convey a conversational style. Both of these superficial textual marks provide a basis for examining the special way that phenomenological theory becomes a form of semantical sociology.

In the first case they are not apparently "empirical" because here the distinction between theory and "data" is, in effect, irrelevant. There are no data from the outside world because phenomenologists are interested primarily in what appears in consciousness. But, as seen in the previous section, nothing appears consciously to consciousness unless it is typified. Thus, this discourse is so exclusively "theoretical" precisely because it has only theory (typifications) to speak about. What appears to the phenomenological mind (in everyday life and in science) are types, not pure data. This is quite different from Parsons' view that all facts are interpreted. With Parsons, and the other lexicalists, theory is always straining against the outer world, trying earnestly to fit it to a lexicon. Phenomenology makes no pretense of such a struggle because its "data" are already elementary theories. Thus, it can be said that phenomenology is regulated by the statement *theory is consciousness reflecting upon itself*. This rule is what requires phenomenology to write as it does.

Therefore, the fact of repetitiveness must be seen as more than a simple courtesy to readers unfamiliar with philosophical phenomenology (Wagner 1970:4). Repetitiveness is, instead, a result of the view of theory as consciousness reflecting upon itself. To the same extent that it cannot derive an automatic objectivity from data, neither can phenomenology capture an easy legitimacy from what sociologists call "the literature." It is unable to quote other writers as a means of locating what is being said. Of course, phe-

nomenologists do borrow ideas. To read Berger and Luckmann or Schutz is to be constantly flipping from text to
footnotes and back. But, for example, when they cite Durkheim as a source it is never in the lexicalist manner of taking
a term or proposition. Durkheim appears as a weak external
point of reference; his ideas are completely remade within
phenomenological discourse. Everything must be reworked
in the theorist's own consciousness. Deprived of the possibility of direct borrowing, phenomenological texts must
rely upon repetition. They must, so to speak, bring their
readers along with them, constantly informing the reader of
the general theoretical type in use. The writing moves forward, stops to reintroduce the general theory, moves on.

The effect is writing in the form of a conversation. But,
this is a very, very different conversational form than Blumer's. Blumer's writing is a dialogue with a reader to whom
he would, in principle, listen. Schutz/Berger/Luckmann's
conversational style is more distant. The reader does not
feel addressed. It is as though another hidden presence has
somehow, without being introduced, taken his place as the
Other in the conversation. Or, to put it figuratively, if Blumer's writing is that of the "heart-to-heart chat," then the phenomenologist's is that of a patient to his/her psychoanalyst.
It is talk in a highly private vocabulary about an idiosyncratic experience; the primary conversation is entirely internal; the reader, like the analyst, provides the occasion for
talk and is only included remotely by the repetitive form.

From these two surface features one can begin to understand the semanticality of phenomenology. If theory is consciousness reflecting upon itself then the task at hand is
interpretative, not definitional. Its goal is the deciphering of
the meanings consciousness has to itself, which deciphering, is assumed to lead to the meanings of consciousness
itself. Therefore, it is no surprise that the phenomenologists
(like symbolic interactionists) see language as the central
human activity upon which all that is social is built: "The
vernacular of everyday life is primarily a language of named
things and events, and any name includes a typification
and generalization referring to the relevance system prevail-

ing in the linguistic in-group" (Schutz 1962:14). Everyday life is itself a semantical activity, a naming process. Society, accordingly, subsists in the ability of fellowmen to recognize the meaning of typical names. Thus, sociological theory is the semantical process which names these common-sense names. To illustrate this semantical process, the following section will examine Berger and Luckmann's theory of language and its relation to the development of institutions.

The centrality of language rests on the following statement: "The central question for sociological theory can . . . be put as follows: How is it possible that subjective meanings *become* objective facticities?" (Berger and Luckmann 1967:18). The typifications of subject meaning, discussed above, are not constantly open to negotiation. One does not construct a new and different type each time he hears his baby cry or sees a friend offer a hand in greeting. In social reality, types have a constancy to them. The problem of the stability of types in consciousness is the problem of their objectivation. How do they come to be perceived as objective so much so that they are accepted naïvely?

For Berger and Luckmann objectivation is one of three crucial moments in the dynamic process underlying all social relations.[6] The first is externalization in which the wide-awake individual acting on a project "pours himself" out into the world (Berger 1969:4). The baby cries. The friend extends his hand. The lover produces a gesture of affection. That which is externalized in an ongoing social relationship becomes objectivated at that moment when persons in a we-relationship accept such gestures as these as though they are real in and by themselves. The parent and child forget that they created the cry as a sign. The parent, thereby, responds to it as an objective fact requiring him or her to feed or change or comfort the baby. The friends do not consider the handshake as their invention but as an objective form they use naïvely to greet each other. Thirdly, when persons treat these now-objective types in this way, the types literally act back upon the individuals using them such that they are formed by them. The mother becomes "one who responds to the cry." The friend defines himself, in part, as "one who greets another with a handshake." In short, identities are formed by the reflexive action of objective types upon those who participated in creating and sustaining them. This is the elemental form of internalization. The process is sometimes hard to imagine because it is not linear. These are not three serial steps. They are part of a constant, dynamic process in which, at a given moment in everyday life, all three are acting simultaneously. They have, in other words, a dialectical relationship. For Berger and Luckmann, these three ideas form the basis for their theory of society: "Society is a human product. Society is an objective reality. Man is a social product" (1967:61).

To say that society is composed of shared objectivations is to say that men who produce society are sign makers and users. Signification is the most important type of objectivation. The defining feature of a sign is "its explicit intention to serve as an index of subjective meanings" (Berger and Luckmann 1967:35).[7] Signs have two general characteristics. First, they are "detachable"; that is, when the baby's cry becomes a sign, it may be understood by both parent and infant apart from the particular situation in which it was first externalized and objectivated. Detachability is the mark of the sign's objectivity. Secondly, signs tend to form into sign systems. Usually the baby's hunger cry is systematically related to a slightly different change-me cry or another more general comfort-me cry. Furthermore, sign systems may be as simple as physical gestures operating in a we-relationship (cries, love-making gestures, handshake/hug/pat-on-the-back friendship gestures and so forth) or as complex as natural languages (Swahili, English, Russian and so forth). (See Berger and Luckmann 1967:36.)

Natural language, of course, is the most important sign system. Though in a minimal sense it is a "system of vocal signs," it is far more importantly the principal social device whereby the objectivations of everyday life are maintained (Berger and Luckmann 1967:37). When mother and father engage in conversation over their child's crying behavior they use language to organize and express the types observed. The simple linguistic act of naming a type of sound a "hunger-cry" puts it into a stable, socially shared sign-system whereby, among other things, the types they have observed and named can be related to others in the wider society such as those in Dr. Spock's baby manual. Without a natural language, parents and infant could depend only on what the three have agreed to as a sign of hunger. This would be a simple code of crying gestures. With this alone they could not even talk to their neighbors about the baby's crying without first exposing these "outsiders" to the gestures themselves. In other words, because of its range in society language permits a far greater degree of detachability. Accordingly, by permitting the meaning to be related to the meanings of many, many contemporaries, a language creates the possibility for making their interpretations much more legitimate (it appears as though they are "natural"), thus much more confidently held and maintained. Thus, the tremendous sociological importance of language. It literally allows the creation and maintenance of the meanings of which an individual's social world is constituted:

Because of its capacity to transcend the "here and now" language bridges different zones within the reality of everyday life and integrates them into a meaningful whole. . . . Through language I can transcend the gap between my manipulatory zone and that of the other; I can synchronize my biographical time sequence with his; and I can converse with him about individuals and collectivities with whom we are not at present in face-to-face interaction. . . . Put simply, through language an entire world can be actualized at any moment. [Berger and Luckmann 1967:39]

Language creates for persons in society "zones of meaning" within which they may individually understand themselves and collectively understand each other and their place in society as a whole. Language is both the principal means whereby individuals externalize themselves into the objectivations that make up society and the means whereby society talks back to these individuals shaping them to its intentions.

The centrality of language and sign systems in general is

seen in Berger and Luckmann's theory of institutionalization. Institutions, in their most elemental form, arise out of
the fact that actions are habitualized. Babies get into the
habit of crying when hungry. Lovers get into the habit of a
certain style of sexual intercourse. Friends get into the habit
of shaking hands. Obviously these are not inevitable actions, though the participants may view them as such. Some
babies use a soft gurgle as a sign of hunger. Some lovers use
exotic methods of love making. Some very close friends
never touch each other at all. What makes society work in
Berger and Luckmann's view is that we let particular styles
of action become habits in order that we may pay attention
to new, more important projects (1967:53). The baby habit-
ualizes crying as a sign of hunger, "so that" he may have
time to explore the colors or shapes he finds in the crib.
Without habitualization there would be no new projects,
hence no growth. However, having hunger needs met remains a necessity. This necessity is handled by the creation
of an elementary proto-institution: that of the "cry-parent
response-feeding-hunger satisfied" set of actions which, in
a given day, is repeated three, four, five times. "Institutionalization occurs whenever there is a reciprocal typification
of habitualized actions by types of actors" (Berger and Luckmann 1967:54). Thus, institutionalization appears in any
ongoing relationship between persons. And the process
taking place in these simple situations is taken by Berger
and Luckmann to be the same basic process that underlies
even very complex institutions in large-scale societies.

Institutions obviously take on the same features of any
other social products. They are externalized, objectivated,
and serve to control individuals. Thus, social institutions
(proto- or complex) have the following features. They are
objectivated and appeared to be "over-against" the individual. They are, nonetheless, socially produced and maintained. And, from the point of view of societies, institutions
tend to "hang together." That is, they possess a certain
"logic" (Berger and Luckmann 1967:63–64). This logic
need not be uniform. In complex, pluralistic societies institutions may appear to be at odds with each other. In some

societies the men are required to do all the economic work and the women all the child care. Yet, even under these conditions the segregation is explained by some kind of logic, such as: men are "natural" aggressors, women are "naturally" tender and better suited for child care. These logics are what Berger and Luckmann call legitimations which explain to the people involved the appropriateness of following such habitualized types of action.[8] Thus, the logic of an institutional arrangement becomes part of the stock of knowledge available to persons. People who are well socialized into an institutional arrangement are people who "know" that this is how things should be done. That, for example, men are the "breadwinners" and that "a woman's place is in the home."

How is this known in everyday life? Principally we learn it by and through language. It may be taught to us, in part, by the fact that a language uses the masculine "he/his/him" as a generic form. Or, by the fact that language is the medium whereby the society transmits this knowledge by means of stories, myths, adages, "scientistic" formulae, gossip, *Reader's Digest* articles, and so forth. "Language provides the fundamental superimposition of logic on the objectivated social world. The edifice of legitimations is built upon language and uses language as its principal instrumentality" (Berger and Luckmann 1967:64). Language does not merely "reflect" the facts of institutional forms to individuals. Language is fundamental to the creation and ongoing maintenance of these institutions (Berger and Luckmann 1967:65). Thus, it can be said that the most important social process is conversation (Berger and Luckmann 1967: 152).

In short, society rests on speech. It is only by talking to others that individuals discover themselves. It is only by talking to others that social relationships are formed. It is only by speech that types are developed and institutions formed. It is only by conversation that the basic social act is possible, that is, the interpretation of socially shared subjective meanings.

Sociological theory, therefore, is a peculiar sort of secondary conversation with constructed types of these conversations. Sociology is discourse on discourse, semantics on semantics, theory on theory. Its only distinguishing marks are that the language it uses is unnatural (not taken-for-granted), the institutions it forms are derivative, and the meanings it typifies are circumspect. In short, sociology simply takes up its place at a distance from the wonderful naïveté of everyday life in the world of consciousness reflecting upon consciousness. By throwing off the comforts of the naïve attitude, it deprives itself of a permanent "sense" of the logic of social institutional life, and confines itself to its own consciousness where it believes general truth can be uncovered.

Man Reflecting Upon Himself

The homocentrism of this type of sociology is found on both sides of the phenomenological paradox. Commonsense knowledge is held only in subjective consciousness, yet its necessary "source" is in social interaction. Theoretical knowledge is knowledge of the structures of consciousness, yet theory is a form of typification and the theoretician gets his types, as does everyone else, from social intercourse. Sociological phenomenologists mean by "data" the data of consciousness displayed in homunculi, yet these private constructs of the sociologist are taken from observations of social experience. The paradox takes the form: everything essential is subjective, yet the subjective requires the intersubjective for its content. Stated with reference to homocentrism: man is the central presence, the consciousness that empowers all meanings; at the same time, this man lives entirely in a manly world of social exchange.

Thus one discovers in phenomenological sociology the same man of the lexicalists. To be sure, he is spoken of in a slightly different fashion. With the lexicalists man is the hidden presence of the theoretician creating a lexicon. With the phenomenologist, man is brought more explicitly into theoretical discourse. With the lexicalists man is pure subject. With the phenomenologists man, likewise, is pure subject but now a subject who paradoxically is also pure object. Here is the distinguishing mark of semanticality and the mark of the phenomenologist's affinity with symbolic interactionism. Semanticality differs from lexicality in two basic respects: 1) it brings man the subject of theory into focus, and 2) it creates man as the sole object of sociology. Semanticality is, thereby, a sociology of manly discourse, of man the subject forming himself in conversation with man the object.

Schutz/Berger/Luckmann differ from Blumer only to the extent that they provide the theorist with an active consciousness and thereby endow him with the capacity for free speech. Blumer's sociologist is a listener above all else and a speaker only secondarily. Schutz/Berger/Luckmann's theorist speaks to others outside himself in order to speak to himself. Blumer's engages in man-to-man talks because he is less decisive in separating consciousness from perception. The phenomenologists have no effective idea of extraphenomenal perception, thus all that is finally meaningful is the conversation of consciousness to consciousness within consciousness, that is, the conversation of the patient to his psychoanalyst—consciousness speaking to another in order to speak more clearly to itself.

Yet, one finds no conclusive break with the homocentrism of lexicality. In all the cases examined to this point, there could be no sociological discourse without man in his subjectivity as the central presence of theoretical language. This is entirely evident in phenomenology's obedience to the basic rules of homocentrism.

1) The awareness of finitude is the point of departure for phenomenology. Husserl's eidetic science was founded upon a critique of positivism. There can be no positive science because the presupposition that the world presents itself positively to observation is considered unsupportable. Phenomenology as a science of consciousness stems from

the conviction that it is only in consciousness—not the perceptions of the outer world—that a true science can exist. Therefore, phenomenological sociology is, of all sociological styles, the most acutely aware of its own finitude. As a result, all knowledge of that which is outside consciousness is gained only by chance. There can never be certain, positive knowledge. This is as true of commonsense thought as of science.

[I]n common-sense thinking we have merely a *chance* to understand the Other's action sufficiently for our purpose at hand. [Schutz 1962:24]

There is a mere chance, although a chance sufficient for many practical purposes, that the [scientific] observer in daily life can grasp the subjective meaning of the actor's acts. [Schutz 1962:27]

Thus, both are risk-taking activities (Schutz 1962:33). Knowledge can only be built up after the finitude of man is accepted. Knowledge is knowledge of that which appears in consciousness, because man in his finitude is cut off from things that appear in themselves apart from consciousness.

However, phenomenological sociology differs from symbolic interactionism in that nature reappears as the visible boundary fixing man's limitations. Nature's most explicit presence is as man's body. The body, as seen above, is "the condition for all my experience of the spatial arrangement of the life-world" (Schutz and Luckmann 1973:102). It is the means whereby the individual's "Here" in the life-world takes on substance. It is the basis for the various manipulatory zones which spatialize meaning. The individual's sense of the objects within reach is, as noted above, one of the four axes by which man experiences himself as the meaningful center of the world. However, this physical world we encounter through our bodies is not a simple ally. Yes, it is one of the bases for coordinating our consciousness of reality, but it performs this function by offering resistance. Our natural body is the unyielding thing through which we encounter the physical world as that against which we must work (Schutz 1962:227). It is that which encounters the individual as an obstacle reminding him of his limitations within consciousness and setting before him the field of physical things that must be made meaningful, just as time, self, and others must be brought meaningfully into consciousness.

This theme is well developed in Berger and Luckmann's notion of world-openness. The basic distinction between man and animal is that the latter is born into a closed world of instinct (Berger 1969:3–6; Berger and Luckmann 1967: 47–48). For the animal, instinct closes his world by "building in" the "knowledge" necessary to survival. Man, on the other hand, is born into an open world. Deprived of instinct, he must create his own meaning world in which to live. This is a necessary precondition for man's creativity. Were his world closed by instinct, man would not be the maker of meanings. The effect of this principle is that nature is absorbed into man: "While it is possible to say that man has a nature, it is more significant to say that man constructs his own nature, or more simply, that man produces himself" (Berger and Luckmann 1967:49). With the phenomenologists, the natural is first of all experienced as a limit (Berger and Luckmann 1967:182) and secondarily as that which— within this limit—is taken into consciousness (Schutz 1962:127).

Man is biologically predestined to construct and to inhabit a world with others. This world becomes for him the dominant and definitive reality. Its limits are set by nature, but once constructed, this world acts back upon nature. In the dialectic between nature and the socially constructed world the human organism itself is transformed. In this same dialectic man produces reality and thereby produces himself. [Berger and Luckmann 1967:183]

This view of nature as limit thus determines the phenomenological view of the limits of sociology. The nature of the physical sciences is different from the nature of the social sciences. For the former, nature is an object world, for the latter it is "an element of the life-world . . . [and] thus has its place exclusively in the mental sphere" (Schutz 1962: 127). Thus, one returns to the basic fact that social science is a science of second-degree constructs, while natural science is that of first-degree constructs (Schutz 1962:6). Even though all the sciences are assumed to share the same general procedural rules (as noted above), they cannot approach the natural world in the same manner. Even natural things with which man cannot hold an intersubjective relationship are nonetheless brought under the requirement of second-degree concepts. The social scientist concerned with nature constructs types of people's types of natural things. Meaning remains the decisive feature of social science, whether treating people's relationship to people or people's relationship to nature. The social and natural sciences are distinct as a result of the recognition that nature is the limiting condition within which human finitude becomes the basis for a science of culture alone. Here one sees the classic semanticalist distinction by which sociology is lodged exclusively within the sphere of man's meaning and its productions. Thus, "sociology takes its place in the company of the sciences that deal with man *as* man; . . . it is, in that specific sense, a humanistic discipline" (Berger and Luckmann 1967:189).

2) In the final analysis, phenomenology leads to a sociology of loneliness, of finite man thrown back into his own subjectivity. "[W]e can never grasp the individual uniqueness of our fellow-man in his unique biographical situation" (Schutz 1962:18). Accordingly, man is the subjective point of origin for social reality. He experiences the world about him as having a lawlike stability which is, however, oriented around his personality as a "null point" (Schutz 1962:127). In the natural attitude, "I experience the world as organized around myself as a center, . . . the center 'O' of a system of coordinates which determines certain dimensions of orientation in the surrounding field" (1962:306, 307). Thus, in everyday life man in his subjectivity is the point of origin, coordination, and domination (Schutz 1962:208) through which the social world is constructed and maintained. Though this subjectivity draws its life from intersubjective experience it is in the subject alone in which the semantic reality of life is founded.

The social scientist is in no way outside of these conditions. Sociological theory simply originates in another subjective null point:

The person living naively in the life-world can become . . . motivated so as to raise the question concerning the structure of its meaning. But, although he reflects in this manner, he in no way loses his interest in it, and he still remains the center, the "null point' of this his world, which is oriented with regard to him. But to make up his mind to observe scientifically this life-world means to determine no longer to place himself and his own condition of interest as the center of the world, but to substitute another null-point for the orientation of the phenomena of the life-world. [Schutz 1962:137]

Whether it is the incipient "theories" of commonsense knowledge or the theories of social science, their origin is subjective. Here, once again, is the curious trick of phenomenological sociology—its subjectivism is not intended to imply solipsism; rather it is a working out of the ironic conviction that only by retreat into consciousness can one discover the objective conditions of the world.

3) Therefore, history emerges as the context of meaning. Nothing can be explained—either in science or everyday life—without referring it back to its origin in a meaning designated in consciousness. "I cannot understand a cultural object without referring it to the human activity in which it originates" (Schutz 1962:10). All knowledge is "biographically determined." It is founded entirely in the meanings the individual has defined, the world he has created. By uncovering these meanings, one thereby finds not simply the history of the individual but also the history of the social realities of which he is the vital force. Thus the history of the social world is recovered in the biography.

To say that this definition of the situation is biographically determined is to say that it has its history, it is the sedimentation of all man's previous experiences, organized in the habitual possessions of his stock of knowledge at hand, and as such his unique possession, given to him and to him alone. [Schutz 1962:9; compare Berger and Luckmann 1967:67–72.]

Furthermore, as noted above, the projects of everyday life depend on the individual's historical consciousness. One cannot project himself into the future, without reference to his previous experiences. "The reason for recollecting formerly experienced social realities . . . originates in my present situation and is conditioned by the problems and interests of the Here and Now" (Schutz 1962:57). The types upon which knowledge is founded derive entirely from the subjective and intersubjective history of the individual.

Phenomenological sociology, therefore, is an historical science, though in a sense different from that of the lexicalists. It is not a history of a free-standing lexicon. It does not hold as an explicit project the cumulation of theories. This cannot be a formal project in phenomenology because it is already incorporated as an assumption. There is no need of stating it is a project because history has already been given its primary place in the construction of types and the return to the origin of meaning in consciousness. Thus the difference between lexicality and semanticality is maintained. The former enunciates a theory founded in intuition, but the enunciation is displayed on an external linear space of propositions, charts, formulae, tables. The emphasis is on thrusting the lexicon out into a hard objective world of formal texts. By contrast, the latter utters theory to theory. The scientist speaks the theory of himself to his homunculi who speak it back to him. Here one has a free flow of discourse unpunctuated by charts and numbers, unmarred by translations from language to language. It is a discourse that flows forward, repeats itself, and regains its origins. But this movement forward is through a succession of spirals in which basic ideas are repeated so as not to deprive them of their relationship to the vital presence of their subjective origins. One reads Blalock chapter by chapter. One reads Berger and Luckmann chapter by chapter, but within each chapter one finds a recapitulation of what has previously been stated, which repetition drives the reader back—to previous chapters, to the footnotes, to corollary texts—in order that he may go forward with a vivid impression of *all* that is being said.

Yet, in spite of these differences, semanticalists and lexicalists achieve the same result. History serves to bind together the world of differences created by the subjectivation of knowledge and discourse. With lexical texts that subjectivity is deceptively hidden behind the texts in order that differences may be cloaked in the superficial similarity of linear form (similar charts, similar notations, similar procedures, and so forth). One must be attentive to discover the sea of differences behind these common forms. With the semanticalists, subjectivity is brought directly into the texts and the differences are reconciled by the literary tactic of repetition. In short, one must read back through lexicalist texts to discover their point of origin in intuition. In semantical texts, one has no need to "go back"; the point of origin is constantly presented to the reader. Though the discursive strategies differ, the essential presence of finite man in his subjective history remains the organizing presence of sociological writing.

4) Thus, once again, man is the presence without whom these texts could not exist. The man who in daily life "considers himself the center of the social world" (Schutz 1962: 37) is also the man who creates, vitalizes, and maintains a world of homunculi with whom the lonely sociological man talks out his theory.

7

Ethnomethodology:

Aaron Cicourel

Ethnomethodological Indifference

Not very many non-ethnomethodologists appreciate ethnomethodology. Typically, people want either to dismiss it
as a bizarre sect (for example, Coser 1975) or translate it
into a more familiar sociological language (for example,
Coleman 1968, Deutscher 1975). For some reason it so un-
nerves one's sense of sociological security that readers want
either to escape it or, at least, to remake it in line with
proper sociological talk. Common to both of these defensive
reactions has been a high degree of agitation over ethnomethodological discourse, which has been variously described as: an esoteric "language disease" (Coser 1975:696–
97); "inarticulate, obtuse, and utterly incomprehensible"
(Deutscher 1975:14); "tortuous" (Gidlow 1972). Coleman's
comment on Garfinkel is typical: "There is an extraordinary
high ratio of reading time to information transfer, so that
the banality is not directly apparent upon a casual reading"
(Coleman 1968:130).

Readers feel excluded, annoyed, victimized in a way that
goes beyond mere confusion. Persons confused by Parsons,
Blalock, or Stinchcombe are more often humbled than annoyed, sensing perhaps from the technical terms, tables,
diagrams, equations that these lexicalist authors know

something of which the reader is culpably ignorant. In this case the blame is assumed by the reader. But confused readers of ethnomethodology are inclined to pass the blame to the authors.

Yet, in spite of the disquietude it animates, ethnomethodology will not go away. It has taken a most unusual position in sociology's discursive formation. People think of it as marginal, yet cannot keep themselves from taking it seriously. Many (Turner 1974:321–31, Gouldner 1970, Ritzer 1975:137, Attewell 1974:207) are sufficiently intrigued to call it a new "paradigm," without ever being able to say why it should receive such respect. This fascination is presumably prompted by the fact that ethnomethodology does bear an important relationship to other semantical sociologies—interactionism and phenomenology (see Attewell 1974). However, it is not a completely legitimate offspring of these movements. Ethnomethodology clearly rejects the naïveté of interactionism (see Zimmerman and Wieder 1970:280–98) and is far more "empirical" than phenomenological sociology. In other words, it can be seen as, at once, familiar and strange, and as worthy of attention in spite of its marginality.

To begin to explain this peculiar discursive event, one must look at the relationship between its literary style and its most basic theoretical idea, ethnomethodological indifference. As a literary form, ethnomethodology is neither paradox, nor irony, nor comedy—though in some sense it is all three. The nearest rough equivalent is what Richard Coe has said of Ionesco's absurdist drama: it is an apotheosis of the platitude (Coe 1961). The mundane is taken with utter seriousness so that the reader is confronted by the fact that his/her own ordinariness is set forth and made a topic of scientific discourse. The platitude is apotheosized; the extraordinary is platitudinized. The former is typified in Zimmerman and Pollner's phrase "the strangeness of the familiar world" (1970:98) which is the strangeness appearing when the ordinary world is transformed into an object of sociological reasoning. The latter is even more crucial. To platitudinize the extraordinary involves what Garfinkel and

Sacks (Douglas 1970:346) call "ethnomethodological indif-ference," which requires that all social phenomena "wher-ever and by whomever they are done" be counted as equal. The special result of this conviction is that "persons doing ethnomethodological studies can 'care' no more or less about professional sociological reasoning than they can 'care' about the practices of legal reasoning, conversational reasoning, divinational reasoning, psychiatric reasoning, and the rest" (Garfinkel and Sacks 1970:346). Ethnometh-odology is indifferent to attempts to make of science some-thing extraordinary. Thus, Garfinkel's (1967) "practical so-ciological reasoning" is a way of saying that everyday life is sociological. Everyman is a sociologist. This is a far more radical view than that of Schutz, with whom sociological reasoning was of the same sort as commonsense reasoning but different in that the sociologist does second-degree thinking. With the ethnomethodologists everyone does at least second-degree thinking. Practical and scientific con-cepts are exactly alike.

But, it may be asked, if ethnomethodology is aiming to make sociology more mundane, why is its discourse so un-like normal conversation? The answer is that ethnomethod-ology is not simply "naturalizing" science. The platitudi-nizing movement is not divorceable from the apotheosizing movement. Ethnomethodology makes the extraordinary ordinary by making the ordinary extraordinary. It is not attempting to make sociology natural, but to see the natural as sociological. "[Ethnomethodological] studies seek to treat practical activities, practical circumstances, and prac-tical sociological reasoning as topics of empirical study, and by paying to the most commonplace activities of daily life the attention usually accorded extraordinary events, seek to learn about them as phenomena in their own right" (Garfinkel 1967:1). Thus, there are two senses in which the commonplace is made extraordinary: first, simply by paying attention to it, by bringing the common to light; second, by seeing commonsense reasoning as sociological.

Here is the uniqueness of ethnomethodologists relative to other semanticalists. The symbolic interactionists pay heed to the common by respecting it, "listening" to it. The phenomenologists treat the common as a source and model for sociological thinking, but keep scientific reasoning within the consciousness of the scientist. In both of these positions a distinction is maintained. In ethnomethodology that distinction is virtually eliminated. This is why ethnomethodological discourse appears bizarre. It is the discourse of professional sociologists speaking about (practical or lay) sociologists to ("professional") sociologists. All of the traditional distinctions—subject/object, participant/observer, science/common sense, theory/data, objectivity/engagement —are questioned.

Accordingly, the strangeness of its language comes from the fact that ethnomethodologists are working in an entirely new field of research. They are neither merely sociologists of sociology nor simply empirical field workers. They are studying neither science as such, nor the real world. Their domain of interest is "a member's knowledge of his ordinary affairs" (Garfinkel 1974:18). That is, ethnomethodology is the study of how people in social interaction create for themselves a sense of social structure or order. It is not concerned with social order itself but "only with how it is being made visible, hence 'created' for practical action" (Zimmerman and Wieder 1970:293). Ethnomethodology is the study ("ology") of people's ("ethno") "methods" for producing a sense of structure to social life.

For ethnomethodologists all language is indexical (that is, roughly, context-bound). By taking this as fact, ethnomethodology sees the common property of lay and professional reasoning to be the clarification of the inescapable indexicality of its own language:

The indexical properties of natural language assure to the technology of sociological inquiries, lay and professional, the following unavoidable and irremediable practice as their earmark: Wherever and by whomever practical sociological reasoning is done, it seeks to remedy the indexical properties of practical discourse; it does so in the interests of demonstrating the rational accountability of everyday activities; and it does so in order that its assessments be warranted by methodic observation and report of situated, socially organized particulars of everyday activities, which of course include particulars of natural language. [Garfinkel and Sacks 1970:339]

This becomes the basis for ethnomethodological indifference. Since professional sociologists use natural language they cannot avoid indexicality. Thus, to borrow an example (Garfinkel and Sacks 1970:338), when a professional sociologist employs Durkheim's statement "The objective reality of social facts is sociology's fundamental principle," such a statement is understood by professionals with reference to its context. It may be a way by which a sociologist indexes his theoretical bias, or it could be a type of bragging ("I've recently reread Durkheim"). Accordingly, all discourse must take the indexicality of language seriously and attempt, as far as possible, to make it objective. The practice of making objective (or making "accountable") what one means is the reflexive property of discourse, and it is precisely here that ethnomethodologists focus their attention for it is in this activity that social structures (orders) are constructed.

Thus, ethnomethodology is explicitly critical of lexical sociology for having ignored the indexical property of its language (see Garfinkel and Sacks 1970, and Cicourel 1964). An objective context-free lexicon is impossible. However, objective discourse is not ruled out. Both lay and professional sociologists attempt to construct it. Ethnomethodology is only (but powerfully) a critique of the naïve arrogance whereby lexicalists see sociology as an autonomous reason, defining reality without reference to reality.

At the same time, however, ethnomethodology is quite different than even semantical sociologies insofar as ethnomethodological discourse is so manifestly bizarre. While Blumer uses conversational discourse and Schutz uses the discourse of the analysand, the ethnomethodologists employ the discourse of speakers trying to converse in and understand second languages. Speakers using nonnative languages are always confronted by meanings that go so far beyond dictionary definitions that only native experience can grasp. Few Americans will ever be able fully to understand the semantical range covered by the French *gauchiste* and the French will seldom be able to appreciate the American meanings attached to *liberal*. Likewise, ethnomethodologists are not fully understood by speakers of standard American sociologese because the latter are not experienced in the nether world between the lexicon and reality itself, the world of ethnomethods.

Theory as the Theory of Methods

Aaron Cicourel has a distinctive place in the short history of ethnomethodology. He is, at the same time, a "founding father" and its prodigal son. His *Method and Measurement in Sociology* (1964) provided an outline to the movement's program three years prior to the *locus classicus* of ethnomethodology, Garfinkel's *Studies in Ethnomethodology*. Here (Cicourel 1964) are the basic themes: the primacy of language in social research, the reliance upon (but translation of) Schutz for the study of reflexive procedures, and the insistence upon the indexical nature of both lay and professional sociological language. Though these themes have been developed by ethnomethodologists in several different directions (see Attewell 1974), they were clearly evident in Cicourel's first major publication and elaborated in the crucial later works (1968, 1974a, 1974b). If not a father, Cicourel was, in this regard, at least a founding uncle.

However, he is also a prodigal son in as much as Cicourel, of all the major ethnomethodologists, has been least comfortable with the label ethnomethodology. Thus, the important collection of his most definitive essays, *Cognitive Sociology* (1974a), suggests in its title a departure from the remainder of the movement. Though written over the period between 1964 and 1972, the essays in this collection do in fact emerge as a departure (see Cicourel 1974a:7). *Cognitive Sociology* is an important event within ethnomethodology in the following respects. It is the most sophisticated ethnomethodological use of linguistics' literature and research methods. Accordingly, this collection places ethnomethodology in an explicit and positive relationship to major intellectual advances in the human sciences, especially Chomsky's transformational grammar and Schutz's phenomenology. As such it constitutes an independently significant intellectual event which, in many respects, is more important than the work of Garfinkel. The latter's writings have not been as theoretically explicit as Cicourel's on one crucial point: the cognitive processes of reflexivity. By a rereading of both Chomsky and Schutz, Cicourel sees in these processes the linkage between interpretation and social structure. It is precisely this point which remains unclear in the balance of the ethnomethodological literature preventing it from making a fundamental step beyond traditional semantical sociology. It is not at all assured that Cicourel has yet succeeded in this project, but the clarity with which he attends to this issue sets him off for special attention when only one ethnomethodologist can be studied in detail.

A general summary of Cicourel's view of sociological theory is the following: *Theory is the theory of measurement procedures.* At first this seems similar to Blalock's auxiliary theory. Actually there is no comparison. With Blalock, auxiliary theory is the attempt to reduce the theoretical variance caused by the context-boundness of measurement. It serves to manage the imprecision of empirical data by organizing methodological strategies in order to bring them into conformity with the formal lexicon to theory itself. Cicourel's position is just the opposite. He is openly critical of formal, context-free theory (see 1964, 1968). In general his view is that measurement is a normative process. It is the method whereby *both* lay and professional sociologists assign meanings to objects and events. Thus everyday life interpretations and behavior are based upon layman's "measurements" of their reality. As such, measurement is a universal human activity and normative in nature. "Research involves recovering both researcher's and actor's perspectives" (1974a:7). Sociological theory is a theory of these activities. Thus, rather than reducing the variation caused by contexts, ethnomethodology studies the ways in which measurement operates within contexts. The tactic is exactly the reverse of Blalock's. Cicourel wants to explain theoretical invariance with reference to contextual variation. As a result, Cicourel's criticism of lexical sociology is founded upon his assumption of the ethnomethodological equivalency between professional and lay sociology:

Traditional measurement seeks to assign numerals to objects and events according to some explicit set of rules or coding practices. In making such assignments researchers make use of interpretive procedures that remain an unwitting resource to them. Their coding practices are unavoidably embedded in a context-restricted setting having indexical properties. Thus, studying the researcher's coding practices becomes indistinguishable from studying speaker-hearer's use of interpretive procedures. [1974a:91]

Since sociologists assign meanings in the same way as ordinary people, sociological theory is the theory of professional methodologies *and* those of laymen.

This program is an attempt "to make explicit the role of cognition and context in ... social structure" (Cicourel 1974a:7). For Cicourel, this means two things: first, to draw attention to the cognitive processes which give rise to interpretive procedures (or methods); secondly, to require that these procedures be linked to social, ethnographic contexts. Together these constitute a basic goal of sociology: "the search for and measurement of invariant properties of social action within the context of changing social order" (Cicourel 1974a:197). *Invariant cognitive procedures/variable social context*: this dichotomy provides the structure to Cicourel's thought, and serves to locate his contribution. The former (cognitive procedures) relates him to Chomsky, while the latter (social context) is the basis for his critique of Chomsky's strong universalism. The former, furthermore, contains his implicit critique of prior semanticalist theories (Mead, Blumer, Goffmann and—to some extent—Garfinkel as well) which are seen as having insufficiently explained how actors develop and recognize shared meanings. The latter demonstrates his attempt to make clear the difference between the linguist and the sociologist. Without context there can be no sociology.

Together, cognition and context are concepts used to account for what professional sociologists call "social structure." However, with Cicourel, social structure is "a label for socially acceptable behavior" (1974a:11). He does not say in so many words whether or not he intends to collapse all social structures—including those usually called macrostructures—into this idea. One suspects that he does because this equation of structure with "sense of acceptable behavior" leads directly into his general interest in the classical sociological problem of order. "How members of a society or culture make sense of, or assign sense to, their environment over time is central to the persistent problem of how social order is possible" (1974a:42).[1] But ethnomethodologists are interested not in order itself as a theoretical axiom, but in the pragmatic consideration of how people come to believe in it. Thus, this view is inherently relativistic insofar as it calls into question the givenness of social order. While sharing this interest with other ethnomethodologists, Cicourel is unusual in his attempt to work out the procedural details of the interaction between cognition and context.

For Cicourel, "interaction is always a gamble for all concerned, [but] we have managed to exempt that abstract entity called 'society'" (1974a:29). In other words, how do we as professional sociologists account for the fact that lay sociologists give accounts of society as a seemingly invariant structure even though social interaction is unstable, variant, risky? In everyday life, persons interact with many others—merchants, parents, children, lovers, co-workers, and so forth—who are potentially (and sometimes actually) hostile, indifferent, jealous, competitive, rejecting, and so forth. We have no complete assurance that the others we encounter are more likely to be friendly than hostile. Yet, in a rough sense, we *assume* that they will be friendly (or at least not hostile), and this assumption is the basis for what the professional sociologist calls society or social structure, or just plain order. Obviously social order is not a given. It is not assumed to be built in to the nature of things. Rather, it is negotiated in the course of social action. But it is *not* negotiated into a thing, or a free-standing social fact. Social structure, it must be remembered, is entirely a cognitive reality, a "sense of acceptable behavior."

In this connection, one must understand Cicourel's two basic concepts: interpretive procedures and surface rules. The former are invariant, cognitive capacities that all social members possess. They provide the sense of social structure. The latter, surface rules, are what actors use in particular social contexts in order to explain what is going on. They are, therefore, variant norms. Thus, interpretive procedures are formal, cognitive devices; while surface rules are substantive norms. "The articulation of interpretive procedures and surface (normative) rules establish a basis for concerted interaction which we label the social structures" (1974a:40). Thus, persons overcome the gamble of interaction by applying interpretive procedures to surface rules in order to generate a sense of social structure. Accordingly, ethnomethodology is "the study of interpretive procedures and surface rules in everyday social practices and scientific activities" (Cicourel 1974a:51).

The above is only a partial introduction. More needs to be said. But one cannot hope to understand Cicourel's concepts without referring them to the sources from which they are quite explicitly drawn. Interpretive procedures/surface rules is Cicourel's way of modifying Chomsky's transformational grammar for use in sociology as a generative semantics. And interpretive procedures is a way of rephrasing the cognitive features of Chomsky's linguistics in terms of ideas taken from Schutz's phenomenological sociology. It is necessary therefore to provide a brief introduction to Chomsky's argument.

Noam Chomsky's transformational grammar is a description of the cognitive processes involved in linguistic competence. Its problem is to account for the fact that persons (children in particular) possess a high degree of linguistic competence even though they have had very little linguistic experience. This has led to the postulation of a universal grammar as a natural capacity of human beings such that transformational grammar eventually becomes "a study of the nature of human intellectual capacities" (Chomsky 1972:27). Specifically, the question is how do individuals generate and recognize normal sentences. Why, for example, is a five-year-old able to produce statements such as "This morning I *falled* and hurt my knee"? Though "falled" instead of "fell" is incorrect it is nonetheless a grammatically sophisticated understanding of the rules governing the modern American English past tense. Chomsky's general answer is that the mind possesses innate base and transformation rules which are the basis for linguistic competence.[2]

The themes in Chomsky's theory to which Cicourel pays attention are: 1) the rooting of linguistic competence in describable cognitive procedures, 2) the assignment of the semantic function to an action upon deep cognitive structures, 3) the subservience of the semantic component to the syntactic component, 4) the primacy of invariant universal rules over context. Of these four, Cicourel holds an unambiguously positive attitude toward only the first two. Ethnomethodology is the study of interactional competence with reference to cognitive procedures acting upon surface rules to generate acceptable behavioral displays. Similarily the semantics (meaning) of social interaction is located in the action of deep interpretive procedures. "The study of normative rules is no different from the study of linguistic competence" (Cicourel 1974a:80).

One understands Cicourel's positive theory by appreciating the points at which he *departs* from Chomsky. His objection to both is that they do not account for context. To subsume meaning under syntactic components which are ultimately understood in terms of universal, context-free rules is inadequate because this does not account for the way in which meaning is generated in precarious ongoing social interactions. Whatever its utility in linguistics (and Cicourel questions even this, 1974a:80–84), this proposal is clearly unworkable in a sociology:

The production of concrete social settings is an on-going accomplishment of their participants. The phrase "negotiated creativeness" is intended to underline the members' reliance on normative or syntactic general rules for finding and justifying the meaning of events as socially organized or as linguistically sensible. Despite the fact that the modern linguist's theory of deep structure is an elegant formulation, particularly in contrast with the sociologist's wastebasket usage of latent structure to disguise the inadequacies of his normative theory, both approaches to the idea of rules governing the production of grammatical utterances and social behavior . . . are deficient in their ability to account for the emergent, negotiated nature of meaning over the course of social interaction. [Cicourel 1974a:81]

This criticism is developed on two fronts. First, he presents data from both original and secondary sources to show that a syntactic theory cannot account for semantic processes among users of deaf sign language (Cicourel 1974a: 130–40) and in cross-modal communication situations (1974a:141–71). He shows, for example, that deaf-signers communicate by constantly referring to aspects of their ethnographic setting: body position, social environment, varieties of hand motions, and so forth. When nonnative users of deaf sign language attempt to translate a signing performance they are far less successful than native deaf signers in providing both quantity and quality of semantic detail (1974a:137 f.). "The conception of generative semantics proposed here assumes that the speaker-hearer selectively consults and intuitively presupposes features or particulars in a setting to invoke the tacit or explicit phonological, syntactic, lexical, social or legal rules to order and justify his speech" (1974a:101). Put differently, the evidence Cicourel provides demonstrates that there are numerous instances of semantically successful communication which do not rely upon the ideal oral grammar of Chomsky's linguistics.

This leads to the second, and for present purposes most

interesting, criticism of Chomsky. The background here is the general ethnomethodological insistence that all natural language is indexical. Obviously, a universal grammar that subsumes meaning under syntactics cannot explain indexicality. It is here that one discovers Cicourel's departure from Chomsky's linguistics. The linguist, like the lexical sociologists, does not provide accounts of the indexical nature of his own language. Thus, just as Garfinkel sees Blalock's use of formal theory as itself indexical, so Cicourel treats the idea of universal grammar as a gloss (1974a:114), that is, a reflexive process for correcting the indexicality of language (see Garfinkel and Sacks 1970). While both the transformational linguist and the lexical sociologist simply use these glosses, the ethnomethodologist considers the glosses themselves as interesting (1974a:109).

The above is central to Cicourel's thought. Repeatedly, he equates the following: the linguist (Chomsky), traditional measurement instruments in sociology, formal social science vocabulary (for example, Blalock), penal codes, and a judge (see 1968; 1974a:8, 13, 102). The common failure of all is that they prematurely code the data with which they deal (linguistic facts, crime statistics, even demographic data, and so forth). All ignore the indexicality of context-embedded facts.

The judge and linguist assign normative sense to sentences or their structure and thus detach utterances from their common sense and situated meanings, transforming them into context-free claims about social reality. [Cicourel 1974a:102]

Anyone engaged in field research will find that the shorthand vocabulary of social science is very similar to the general norms stated in some penal code: they do not correspond to explicit sequences of events and social meanings, but the fit is "managed" through negotiated socially organized activities of the police, prosecution, witnesses, the judge, and the suspect or defendant. [1974a:13; compare 1968]

Cicourel is not here using metaphors. The judge and the linguist, the social science lexicon and the penal code are not *like* each other. They are precisely the same. Here is an excellent illustration of the way in which ethnomethodology uses the ideas *indexicality* and *context* to equate all social practices as similarly sociological. This brings one back to ethnomethodology's problematic: Discourse is the primary data of sociology. Language is indexical and context-bound. Thus, meaning is embedded in social settings. ("The thinkable is expressible only through indexical expressions" [1974a:140]. Yet, actors must be able to generate and recognize general types (objectivations), otherwise social order (structure) is impossible. These conditions must be met by all actors (judges, linguists, laymen, sociologists, and ethnomethodologists alike) due to the requirement that all use language. What is at issue is how to prevent the premature coding which dismisses context in favor of reified ideal rules such as the ideal grammar of oral language which is clearly not operative for nonspeaking communicators. (See 1974a:161.) Cicourel provides the answer by means of his reworking of Chomsky's scheme and his understanding of interpretive procedures.

Cicourel replaces Chomsky's deep/surface structure pair with interpretive procedures/surface rules. The interpretive procedures are invariant but not natural capacities, they are learned developmentally (1974a:42–73). Interpretive procedures are intended as a way of capturing the function of Chomsky's idea of context-free rules operating on deep structures, while rejecting their overly strong syntactic control of meaning. "[A] concern with everyday practical reasoning becomes a study in how members employ interpretive procedures to recognize the relevance of surface rules and convert them into practised and enforced behavior" (1974a:51).

In a social setting, there are three active properties. One, the behavior itself which is understood as a *display* of meanings or intentions. Two, the surface structure rules whereby the actor makes sense of his social setting by cognizing and recognizing a connection between his and another's behavior and an appropriate norm which provides meaning to the behavioral display. Three, the interpretive procedures which "are invariant properties of everyday practical reasoning necessary for assigning sense to the substantive rules sociologists call norms" (1974a:52). As in Chomsky's linguistics, the latter two are entirely cognitive, while the behavioral displays are roughly equivalent to a phonetic signal.

As mentioned above, the interpretive procedures are invariant, formal capacities, while surface rules (norms) are substantive. Here Cicourel also retains the generative feature of Chomsky's scheme and, by this, seeks to overcome the static sociological notion of internalized norms. When it is assumed that norms are merely socialized into individuals, one is unable to explain how they operate in specific contexts (1974a:45). The generative action in Cicourel's theory is the cognitive action of interpretive procedures on surface norms in specific contexts.

The interpretive procedures provide for a common scheme of interpretation that enables members to assign context relevance; norms and values [surface rules] are invoked to justify a course of action, "find" the relevance of a course of action, enable the member to choose among particulars for constructing an interpretation others can agree to or an interpretation designed to satisfy the imputed interests or demands of others. [1974a:72]

Thus, for example, a transfer student arriving at the first meeting of a first class might discover a scene composed of the following: a single person seated at a desk at what must be the front of the room (there is a blackboard behind the person at the desk); also, a group of people seated in chairs facing the single individual. The stranger thereby encounters behavioral displays (two different "types" of sitting) which create for him the problem: which is appropriate behavior for me? Should I pull up another chair to sit with the single individual (who may be lonely) or join the larger group? The stranger (since he is a student) will cognitively process this scene and recognize that the relevant course of action is to sit with the larger group of people who are, accordingly, recognized to be fellow students. This recognition is the application to a specific context of a norm which an observer might describe thusly: "Students typically sit in groups facing an instructor who will at some point eventually speak to them."

But from where does the norm come? Obviously it is a part of the actor's acquired cognitive stock of knowledge (1974a:42–73).[3] Then, how is the acquired norm activated? The role of interpretive procedures is to allow the actor to recognize this norm and its applicability in the particular social setting. This is the absolutely basic idea of Cicourel's program. Cicourel builds his list of interpretive procedures upon Schutz' thinking (1974a:33). They are (1974a:52–57): 1) "the reciprocity of perspectives," 2) "the etcetera assumption," 3) "the existence of normal forms," 4) "the retrospective-prospective sense of occurrence," 5) "talk-itself as reflexive," and 6) "descriptive vocabularies as indexical expressions."

The et cetera assumption, for example, allows actors to overlook ambiguities in a situation so that the appropriateness of behavioral displays is taken for granted even though their meaning is not perfectly obvious. The new student may enter the classroom and observe that the person seated at the desk in front of the room appears to be very young and is dressed informally quite unlike your "normal" teacher. But the student can ignore this ambiguity by referring to other aspects of the scene. The et cetera assumption, therefore, instructs him in the following manner: wait and look for other information to confirm the normality of the situation. Accordingly, the student may use the rest of the scene (existence of a group, desk, chairs, blackboard, and so forth) as relevant data to conclude that the individual is the teacher and he ought to sit with the group. He would then seat himself in the group, expecting the single individual eventually to speak in a teacherly fashion.

Likewise, the normal form interpretive procedure is simply the assumption that there are normal types of behavior. The strange student could, in principle, behave in various ways: he could immediately proceed to wash the windows, or he could (particularly if he is a transfer student from Oral

Roberts University) offer to lead the group in prayer. But the ability to recognize normal forms considerably reduces the range of possible choices so that none of these will be actuated. The student will be able to select the appropriate substantive norm (sitting quietly with the group until the teacher speaks) because he knows that there are normal forms of behavior. The normal form procedure instructs him to look for a particular appropriate behavior and to ignore peculiar ones. The interpretive procedure is not the norm itself, but simply the ability to recognize normal forms.

In these examples one sees the emphasis placed on interaction as a gamble. Norms are not viewed as static, internalized things that automatically apply themselves. In any specific situation there will always be discrepancies because the order of any situation must be renegotiated. It should be noted, however, that this is *not* the same thing as reconstructing the norms on each occasion of application. The norms (surface rules) are learned and stored in memory. Likewise, interpretive procedures are learned developmentally (1974a:42–73). In the adult the latter are in effect "built-in" but only in the phenomenological sense of having become a part of one's stock of knowledge. They are not natural "instinctual" capacities for one can see in the development of the child a process of learning and rehearsing both interpretive procedures and surface rules (see 1974a: 58). Thus, the social scene plays an active role in the generation of meaning, a concept consistent with Cicourel's contextual semantics.

The interpretive procedures and their reflexive features provide continuous instructions to participants such that members can be said to be programming each other's action as the scene unfolds. Whatever is built into the members as part of normal socialization is activated by social scenes, but there is no automatic programming; the participant's interpretive procedures and reflexive features become instructions by processing the behavioural scene of appearances, physical movements, objects, gestures, sounds, into inferences that permit action. [1974a:58]

Thus, for Cicourel, social structure is made possible by the interpretive procedures. The latter's instructions to the actor directing him/her to activate surface rules provides the continual sense of order which is social structure (1974a: 33). Without them, norms can only be viewed as static. Without them, the professional sociologist lacks a way of explaining the basic sociological paradox: similarity/difference, invariance/variance, order/chaos, structure/context. "Social structure remains an accountable illusion of the sociologist's common sense knowledge unless we can reveal a connection between the cognitive processes that contribute to the emergence of contextual activities, and the normative accounting schemes we use for claiming knowledge as laymen and researchers" (1974a:7).

In conclusion, it may be seen through Cicourel, that ethnomethodology is a kind of boundary case within semantical sociology. The prominent relativism whereby attention is focused on methods for the construction of meaning and not meaning itself is undeniably a shift of some sort. But it is not possible to conclude that the semantical enterprise has been entirely abandoned. It must be remembered that ethnomethodology owes a debt both to interactionism and phenomenology. Interactionism, in spite of its ultimately empiricistic and behavioristic orientation, clearly provides an early critique of the lexicalist assumption that the sociologist may operate on a different plane from the real social world. Likewise, phenomenological sociology adds to this a clearer picture of the way in which sociological concepts are inextricably bound to the personal history of the sociologist as a commonsense man/woman. What ethnomethodology has done is to redefine these themes as methodological rather than substantive problems. The ethnomethodologist is no longer interested in describing the effective symbolic structures of the life-world. In the absence of a *prior* belief in the giveness of order, everything of interest is technique, and all social actors are equally caught in a world of radical freedom. Having lost the comfort of a preestablished meaning, they must make their own. But once meaning is made, all that remains of interest is not the meaning itself, but how it came into being. It is in this respect that one *might* see in

ethnomethodology a breaking down of traditional sociological thinking.

But even with ethnomethodology there is reason to hesi-
tate before announcing the birth of a new "paradigm." Indeed there is something new here, but there is also a great
deal that is very familiar. What is entirely familiar in ethnomethodology is the retention of the classical concern with
order as the central problem of sociology and of the semantical assumption that social life is fundamentally a process
of meaning construction. True, neither meaning nor order
are givens, but they are in some sense assumed. They are
assumed to be that which must be explained. It is here that
one can appreciate the earlier observation that ethnomethodological texts evoke the eerie feeling of speaking with
someone who only halfway uses the language. Ethnomethodology can be understood as discourse out of a nether
world because it has fundamentally changed the topic of
sociological discourse, while retaining most of its elemental
vocabulary. Thus Cicourel introduces an entirely new sociological concept—interpretive procedures—yet lodges it
within the traditional themes of semantical sociology—
meaning, order, social structure, the primacy of language,
the nativeness of knowledge. It is for this reason that one
is required to examine the place of homocentrism in ethnomethodology. The non-ethnomethodologist, confused
though he is, still hears familiar echoes and wants to know
whether they come from the mountain crossed or the mountain ahead.

Ethnomethodology's Necrophilia

Crude though it may be to say so, ethnomethodology still
admires the body of man whom it is helping to kill. Ethnomethodology remains ambivalently homocentric. It can be
said to be a participant in the slaying of man because, more

than any other sociological enterprise, it has brought language to the fore.[4] Language has been present in sociological discourse since Freud, Durkheim, Weber, and Mead. With ethnomethodology, however, it clearly becomes the primary focus of attention. This is particularly evident in Cicourel with whom one can never be absolutely certain whether ethnomethodology is anything other than a form of sociolinguistics.

The incompatibility of man and language is, from one point of view, a paradox. Humanistic sociology has founded itself on the claim that language is the distinguishing feature of the human. It is that which sets the human off from the natural and the animal. Yet, language as it has been treated in the twentieth century from Saussure through Chomsky has established linguistics as a science by the decisive step of describing rules peculiar to language alone. Thus, Saussure's linguistics depends upon the separation of *la langue* (language as a body of paradigmatic contents and rules) from *la parole* (speech itself). The speaking subject— man—is not the primal consideration in the study of language. Chomsky (whatever his differences from Saussure) shares this conviction. Transformational grammar is a grammar of natural universals independent of particular speakers. In these respects, language is not understood as the foremost symbol of the human presence in the world. In modern linguistics, man is rather a participant in language. One who is acted upon by language and its rules and, only remotely, a creator of language. These features of modern linguistics would be of little interest to sociologists were it not for the fact that sociology has been unable to resist their authority. As language has become the prominent topic in sociology, so has Chomsky been more widely read by sociologists.

Ethnomethodology was the first sociological activity to make language *the* problematic of sociology.

There is no way of getting at the social meanings from which one either implicitly or explicitly infers the larger patterns [of society] except through some form of communication with the members of that society or group: and, to be valid and reliable, any such communication with the members presupposes an understanding of their language. [Douglas 1970:9]

The notion of member is the heart of the matter. We do not use the term to refer to a person. It refers instead to mastery of natural language. [Garfinkel and Sacks 1970:342]

I assume first that methodological decisions in social research always have their theoretical and substantive counterparts; second, that the theoretical presuppositions of method and measurement in sociology cannot be viewed apart from the language that sociologists use in their theorizing and research. My basic assumption is that the clarification of sociological language is important because linguistic structure and use affects the way people interpret and describe the world. [Cicourel 1964:1]

The discovery of language is the source of ethnomethodology's relativism. It provided a substantive object the use of which is the method ethnomethodologists study. Thus all of the operative terms—glossing, indexicality, reflexivity, interpretive procedures, occasioned corpus, accounting—are discourse-specific. The extent to which this represents a shift is seen in the gloss given to reflexivity. It has been shown that for the phenomenological sociologists theory was a reflexive activity, an act of self-consciousness. However, there language was merely the medium of this reflexive action. The action itself was explained by the presence of an historic, conscious biography. Man there remained the visible dynamic of theory, thought, knowledge and reality.

With the ethnomethodologist, this program is considerably modified, even though man's presence is central. For Garfinkel and Cicourel, both indexicality and reflexivity are, first of all, properties of language and language use. Because all natural languages are indexical, language users are unavoidably involved in the reflexive act of accounting for and "correcting" the context-embeddedness of language. Thus, reflexivity is not primarily a property of man as man, but of the language man uses. Thus, man is no longer just a member of an historical continuity, he is a member of a language community. By studying methods for imputing meaning by language use, ethnomethodology takes a step in the direction of treating man as the medium of reflexivity, rather than its sole source. In Cicourel, the theoretical structure is eventually defined in terms of the problematics of language (Cicourel 1974a). Hence, it is understandable that Cicourel returns to Chomsky for the design of a cognitive sociology. Thus, standing behind ethnomethodology's surface problematic (how meaning is constructed) lies the depth interpretive procedure which instructs Cicourel: treat language as a normal form topic for sociological talk.

It is in this precise respect that ethnomethodology is a material witness to the death of man. However, its necrophilia is apparent. The lively ghost of man lurks seductively behind language. Chomsky is used to secure the centrality of language, yet Chomsky is also sternly criticized. The point of Cicourel's criticism is crucial. Chomsky's linguistics formalizes semantics too severely. Meaning is too divorced from context, too submissive to a universal syntax. In other words, Cicourel wants to use Chomsky to link language, social structure, and cognitive process, but equally to reject those aspects of Chomsky that erode the freedom of meaning's interplay with social context.

The result is the opening of a familiar space that requires explanation. With Chomsky meaning was explained by a universal grammar and thereby turned into a secondary element: that which is ruled by syntax. Cicourel's attempt to return meaning to a free state deprives meaning of this source. If semantics is not to be explained by syntactics, then from where does it come? Obviously, Cicourel's answer is the interpretive procedures which are curiously like and unlike Chomsky's deep structures. But from where do these invariant cognitive procedures come? Since they are not given by nature, they must be learned in history. And who is the learner? None other than man, who now lurks rather timidly behind discourse. But there can be no doubt that, even in Cicourel, man is still the guiding presence to sociology. However difficult it is to tell whether ethnomethology is something other than sociolinguistics, there is little doubt that, whatever else ethnomethodology is, it is primarily an attempt to explain how meaning is created in society. As seen above, that meaning is created by cognitive procedures which are, ambivalently, *both* invariant and learned. Since, strictly speaking, this cannot be, the invariance is merely a gloss in the following form: "virtually invariant, learned by everyone, thus part of the human condition." Since they are not natural, the cognitive procedures have no other safe place than the human. Thus, it is man who stands behind them as the one upon whom they act, yet by whom they are given life in any particular meaningful context.

Thus, as seen in other respects, the man behind ethnomethodology's methods is a man who speaks a broken language. His actual utterances, depending as they do on language and its rules, seem to announce the death of man, but when the ethnomethodologist tries to explain his own language (and, ultimately, this is exactly what ethnomethodology is all about), he can provide that explanation only by reinvoking man the speaker, the interpreter. Thus, from another perspective, one appreciates the confusion engendered by ethnomethodological discourse. Had they actually killed man and spoken unequivocally in the vernacular of modern linguistics, perhaps even nonethnomethodological reviewers could understand them. It is because ethnomethodology pronounces the death of man with words originating in man that it confuses. For even homocentrism can understand its own death. But instead of a death warrant one hears talk like that of the physician whose scientific side pronounces the patient terminally ill, but whose humane side tells the family to have hope. This, of course, is precisely the same type of discourse as that of speakers with two different native tongues. Their language hides what they want to reveal and reveals what they want to hide. With ethnomethodology the talk is: Man is dead to language, but there is hope because language lives only by man. The particulars of this ambivalence compose the homocentrism of Cicourel's thought.

1) The mark of finitude on Cicourel's texts is found primarily in the central but idiosyncratically glossed idea of sociological measurement. Earlier, it was noted that, for Cicourel, sociological *theory is the theory of measurement*. In this, one sees the completion of ethnomethodology's basic premise. To make of everyman a sociologist, to equate the theoretical with common sense, is to view common-sense thought as a form of measurement. In short, the distinction between theory and measurement (so prominent in lexical and most semantical sociology) is here obliterated. Theory is measurement. In other words, the statement can be put: *theory (that is, measurement) is the measurement of measurements*. The meaning of this seemingly elliptical phrase is perfectly consistent with ethnomethodology's program. On the one hand, it relates directly to the view that all cognitive processes are essentially normative. Both scientific and common thought generate meaning by assigning norms to contexts. There are no "obvious social facts," only "contingent productions" (1974a:166). On the other hand, it relates explicitly to the view that the scientist cannot escape the fact that he/she is first and ever a member before being a scientist. "The observer cannot avoid the use of interpretive procedures in research for he relies upon his member-acquired use of normal forms to recognize the relevance of behavioral displays for his theory" (1974a:36). Together, these assumptions form the view that all persons are sociologists because all use language and language is the means whereby everyone normatively evaluates "reality."

Thus, ethnomethodology shares in the finitude typical of semantical sociology. By unleashing the world of meaning, semanticalists deprive themselves of the gloss which holds that the world is given, its fact apparent. Knowledge, thereby, cannot extend confidently into the world as an autonomous force. It must be constantly mediated by meaning. At no other place is this more evident than in Cicourel's rejection of Chomsky's universal grammar. Finitude arises in the space created by the divorce of man and nature. Thus Chomsky's assignment of meaning to a universal nature-given capacity is intolerable because it contradicts the homocentric conviction that meaning's proper place is the human context isolated from the deadly force of nature.

Thus, within the substance of Cicourel's theory, man's body is subservient to his cognitive procedures. Speech is not a material, but a cognitive activity; phonetics is still a subdivision of phonology. Behavior is a display of meanings, not the action of the body upon the physical world. For example, in Cicourel's numerous analyses of deaf-signing (1974a), the body is clearly taken into account but only as the instrumentality of communication. Even deaf-signers are understood to be reading through the body to meanings processed by cognitive procedures. For Cicourel, meaning has no bodily weight because meaning is a property of the human alone.

From this one can see the progressive radicalization occurring within semantical sociology. With Blumer, theory is a tool. With Schutz, theory is self-consciousness. In both, theory is deprived of its autonomy, while in Schutz it is more starkly denuded of its cover as a representation of the world. In both, there is finitude, though in Schutz it is the more dramatic by virtue of the withdrawal of theory into consciousness. Yet, in Schutz there is retained the goal of finding the structures of reality within the secret places of consciousness. With Cicourel, even this modest hope is given up. Cicourel does not write about reality as such, only about its means of existence.

The conclusion that theory (measurement) is the measurement of people's measurement is attained by a definite line of thought. First is the idea that the meanings engendered in the flux of social action are measurements: "The interpretive procedures and the indexical properties of the particulars they process become a basis for measurement and a resource for the research in his studies of language behaviour" (Cicourel 1974a:97). Upon this basic concept Cicourel reflexively applies a second concept, the equation of researcher's and actor's measurements:

[S]tudying the researcher's coding practices becomes *indistinguishable* from studying speaker-hearer's use of interpretive procedures. By studying members' practices for assigning meaning during everyday interaction we simultaneously discover something about the problems all researchers encounter when they take for granted their own nativeness in trying to develop a system of measurement. The researcher's native or intuitive use of language while studying language behaviour in speaker-hearers, becomes an integral part of his research problem and theory. [1974a:91; emphasis added]

Thus, stated simply, speech is measurement (1974a:112, compare 62). All theory is spoken. Theory is measurement. With Cicourel, one does not find reality in the cognitive procedures because they are essentially empty, categorical tools. Interpretive procedures are the explanation for the creation of meaning (norms applied in contexts), but they have no substantive meaning themselves. They are the basis for social structure, without being a specific social structure themselves. In this respect ethnomethodology thrusts back deeper into consciousness than even Schutz, back beyond its structures, into its workings. But, instead of finding there the universal nature of reality, one finds finite man. The interpretive procedures are not, after all, given. They are made by this hidden presence, by man who performs the curious trick of creating that which is invariant. But what has he created? Not knowledge itself. Not specific norms. Not reality, nor statements about reality. He creates merely the empty tools with which he returns to social contexts to carry on the Sisyphean task of creating and recreating meanings that live but for a while then fall away. In short, this mysterious man is constantly working over against death. He is confined to a world in which no constructed meaning can last from context to context. His hope is found in the meager conviction that at least he possesses these empty procedures which are, in the end, all that there is to social structure.

2) Cicourel is also consistent with other semanticalists in that subjectivity is the response to finitude. Meaning is entirely a subjective creation. Even the interpretive procedures arise developmentally in the personal history of the individual. Here Cicourel's position is similar to that of Schutz. His cognitive procedures are not psychological attributes (1974a:85). He is writing a cognitive *sociology*

which means that these invariant procedures arise in social interaction and, once established, act on social norms in social contexts.

Where Cicourel differs from Schutz is that these subjective procedures, being contentless themselves, place those who are aware of them in an ambiguous situation. The ethnomethodologist who understands interpretive procedures threatens to wreck the ethnomethodological enterprise by assuming a privileged position, that of reestablishing the distinction between scientific and lay thought. Knowledge of interpretive procedures becomes the special knowledge of the professional sociologist. Thus, he too is susceptible to the problems most acute in lexical sociology—those of measurement by fiat (1964:33), which result in the observer treating the actor as a lifeless dummy (1974a:65). This points to the extreme methodological precariousness of ethnomethodology. Since language is indexical, all communication attempts to overcome context by measuring context reflexively with reference to social norms. Communication requires the overcoming of context, but because communication is by means of an indexical substance (language) context-freedom is an illusion. "In recognizing that we can generate only different glosses of our experiences, the ethnomethodologist tries to underline the pitfalls of viewing indexical expressions as if they could be repaired and thus transformed into context-free objective statements" (Cicourel 1974a:123).

What ethnomethodology cannot explain is precisely how the ethnomethodologist avoids the assumption of the normal form privileged position (belief in objective statements) by assuming still another privileged position (being the only lay or professional sociologist without a privileged position). This is left entirely up to the ethnomethodologist himself. It is an heroic act of the will. Presumably, it is achieved only by vigilance, by being that person who constantly remembers that his language is indexical and that there is nothing but measurement. Without a more explicit explanation we must assume that this accomplishment is made accountable only by reference to man, the subject aware of his finitude. Man, constantly seeking to submit himself to the rules of his discourse, becomes the isolated subject struggling to keep himself separate from the failings of all other sociologists. He is privileged to be the only one aware of the ridiculousness of privileged positions.

The extent of the ethnomethodologist's self-isolation is seen in Cicourel's distance at this point from Schutz. The latter permitted the sociologist to make homunculi, while the former insists that the observer cannot make of the actor a dummy (1974a:65). In other words, Schutz' tactic of creating types within the scientist's consciousness is a form of measurement that denies the authority of context. For Schutz the homunculus is the basis for types peculiar to sociologists, the basis for their communication with each other. With Schutz there was still some vague basis of difference between observer and actor, science and common sense. But with Cicourel, "in actual practice . . . the actor's everyday theorizing is probably not much different from the observer-researcher" (1974a:39). Thus, the ethnomethodologist, having made all equal on the plane of meaning, is cut loose in a world of meanings in which the only reliance is upon a single subjective possibility, the empty cognitive procedures which allow the *sense* of social structure, while withholding its substance.

3) Though considerably enfeebled, history remains for Cicourel, as for homocentrism generally, the only escape from the plentitude of differences created by a world of subjects. Thus, both interpretive procedures and surface rules are historical products. Both are learned in childhood and after. "The organization of cognition which served us on previous occasions is reconstituted in each new setting while we normatively reconstruct our speech, our social identity, and culture itself" (1974a:112). Man, in ethnomethodology, is one who moves through the variety of unfolding scenes (1974a:58) guided only by memory—procedures and norms. These memory features are what make speech, therefore identity, and therefore culture itself possible. By remembering interpretive procedures we can use them to activate remembered norms. It is from the past that the tools and standards of measurement are possible. Meaning cannot be generated without a man who lives in remembered history. Conversely, memory constitutes man's awareness of himself. "Past reflexive experience is central for humans" (1974a:118).

4) Accordingly, "the ethnomethodologist views meaning as situated, self-organizing and reflexive interaction *between* the organization of memory, practical reasoning, and talk" (1974a:100; emphasis added). It is precisely that which is between which explains ethnomethodology. Though he is never mentioned directly in ethnomethodological texts, it is clearly remembering man doing and talking practical reasoning who is the situated, self-organizing, reflexive interactor of whom the ethnomethodologists are reflexively talking.

8

Critical Theory:

Juergen Habermas

Syntacticality in Sociological Discourse

Syntax is the normative aspect of language. It is the set of rules by which normal sentences are constructed.[1] Syntactical sociology, therefore, is that type of sociological writing which derives from an interest in the norms governing both science and social life. In the United States this is more often known as "radical" sociology, by which label is commonly meant a sociology critical of the social and sociological status quo. One normally includes in radical sociology those texts that propose a fundamental change in the values of both sociology and society. Though often only implicitly, the vision of change normally derives from an ideal of human liberation and develops a sociology that presumes to contribute to the amelioration of human suffering. Even though the term *radical* is painfully overgeneral, it nonetheless suggests something of the nature of syntacticality: a sociology that concerns itself with the grammar of the good life.

There are in fact a number of different types of radical sociology. At least the following have been isolated (Colfax 1971): 1) *Participatory radicalism* seeks to fulfill radical goals in a direct way by producing research that could assist political action groups. A primary example is the use of sociological data in advocacy planning by representatives of urban neighborhoods who object to official, city-hall redevelopment programs. Other prominent outlets for this kind of research have been political campaigns, protest movements, social action groups, and underground newspapers. 2) Topical radicalism differs by taking the radical groups themselves as the topic of study. It also concerns the study of social problem areas, such as urban street corner culture. Here the implicit assumption·is that the publicity gained from published studies could have a radical effect. 3) *Cultural radicalism* is radical in the sense that it studies deviant or marginal groups that represent a challenge to normal culture. Studies of the occult, of new religions, of communes, and—in general—of "underdog" culture are the primary examples. The groups are not themselves radical in a political sense, but the strangeness of their culture is assumed to have a revolutionary potential. One thinks of work by Goffman, Truzzi, Tiryakian, and Becker. 4) Finally, *philosophical radicalism* seeks an explicit and scientific analysis of social conditions and sociology itself. It is usually associated, one way or the other, with the Marxian tradition, though this connection is often very indirect (for example, C. Wright Mills).[2]

One sees immediately that schemes such as this do not help to identify a particular type of theoretical (much less, discursive) practice. As Colfax (1971) points out, the first three types may (and often do) employ traditional sociological theories and models. A great deal of topic radicalism is lexical sociology and most cultural radicalism is semantical, for example. Used in this way, the term *radical* is virtually useless for comparative purposes. However, behind the term one can still see the common denominator of normativeness and, therein, an elemental hint of syntacticality.

For present purposes, however, one must examine that major radical sociology which is near to being a pure type of syntacticality. This is a prominent form of philosophical radicalism which historically has been known as *critical theory*, a name that owes to a 1937 essay by the German social theorist, Max Horkheimer (1972). Horkheimer was among those prominent in the Frankfurt School of Social Research.[3] From the beginning, this group has been engaged in critical empirical research, as well as critical theorizing. In the former instance, they have studied such questions as totalitarianism, mass communications, student rebellions, technologization—that is, topics concerning the oppressive features of modern, technocratic societies. The selection of these problems indicates their direct relationship to classical Marxism in which the principal problem was the alienating force of modern capitalism. In this work the Frankfurt School could be said to have followed the course of a topical radicalism which was prompted by their own personal experiences with totalitarianism in Nazi Germany. However, what keeps these empirical studies from being merely topical is that they have been supplemented by important theoretical texts in which Frankfurt authors have sought to work out a critical social philosophy. In this latter regard, their goal has been the reconstruction of social theory by means of the reformulation of the classical critical theories of Kant, Hegel and, above all, Karl Marx. The *critical* feature of this philosophy revolves around two basic convictions: the essential role of norms in theoretical work and the necessity of relating theory to a social practice, to action.

Perhaps because of its philosophical nature, American sociologists have not, until recently, been greatly influenced by or attracted to the Frankfurt School. In the past decade, however, this has begun to change due to the writings of a single author, Juergen Habermas. The successor to Adorno and Horkheimer as leader of the Frankfurt tradition, Habermas has recently been read widely and seriously by sociologists other than those who identify themselves as radical.

What Habermas has accomplished is to outline a critical social theory that is indisputably more than high ideology. As will be seen in this chapter, his theory of society is directly related to a comprehensive theory of science and knowledge. Due to his double competence in sociology and philosophy, Habermas' writings are evidently responsive to major intellectual sources known even to sociologists: Weber, Dilthey, Parsons, among others. In brief, he has rendered critical theory both intelligible and legitimate by writing with reference to familiar traditional texts. But, more profoundly, he attempts to set forth a critical theory that is normative without rejecting the value of other sociological practices.

To many sociological professionals who, especially during the troubled decade of the sixties, have borne the brunt of radical attacks on their alleged insensitivity to human suffering, Habermas offers a plausible alternative. His critical theory suggests a way of giving expression to human values without giving up science. To be sure, not all who read Habermas agree with (or even understand) him, but many agree that his work is important for having opened an alternative to the classical view that sociology must be *either* free of values *or* engaged. Habermas insists that both are possible and necessary for an adequate sociology. Whatever its deficiencies, his theory thereby opens a new discursive possibility in sociology and herein lies its importance and the reason for its popularity beyond the confines of a marginal antiestablishment sociology. Thus, there is now a growing list of texts influenced by Habermas (for example, Gouldner 1976; Wellmer 1974a; Schroyer 1972, 1973; McCarthy 1973; Mueller 1973) which are being read by a wide range of sociologists. Therefore, it can be said that if any aspect of radical or critical sociology can make the claim to being a "paradigmatic" departure then it must be the theories of Habermas. Moreover, Habermas is well chosen as the representative of syntacticality because his writing so clearly exhibits the marks of all syntactical discourse: material extension and moral tone.

Materially, Habermas' writings cannot be found in any one division of a library or any single set of professional journals. Reading Habermas is never a linear activity (page by page, book by book). Instead one must move in different directions over the spaces of his texts and their references, checking and rechecking meanings, terms, connections, sources. Such material extension is brought about by the sheer range and density of topics that cannot occupy a single shelf: epistemology, psychoanalysis, linguistics, mass communications, sociological theory, survey research, and others. Writers seeking to enumerate the basic grammar of science and society cannot confine themselves to a single discipline or a few topics. Syntacticality forces discourse to extend itself because when one is working out a code or grammar all of practiced language becomes a field of application. One encounters the same sort of extension in other syntactical writers—Marx, Mills, Adorno, Gouldner, Horkheimer.

What is conveyed, therefore, is a strong moral or homiletic tone. The reader has the sense of being preached to even when he/she does not fully understand the sermon. This is an unavoidable feature of syntactical discourse. As discourse, this moral tone appears in the fact that syntacticality is sentential. It is written neither around precise terms (lexicality), nor dialogues (semanticality) because its goal is neither to define nor explore the meanings of social life, but to speak of the rules of discourse and life themselves. Thus, the sentence governed by active first-person pronouns, imperatives, exclamations and declarations conveys normative talk about norms. The sentence is the unit of grammatical analysis just as the term is the unit of lexical writing and the dialogic-context that of semantics. Thus one can simply describe syntactical sociology as a sentential discourse that is written as an ongoing reflection upon the grammar governing its writing, its knowledge, its society.

Theory, Practice, and Reflexive Truth

What distinguishes Habermas from most sociological authors is the view that sociological theory must be written within a general theory of knowledge. Thus, for Habermas theory is *theory of the constitution and application of knowledge* (Habermas 1973b:7). Phenomenology and, in a derivative sense, ethnomethodology are also theories of the constitution of knowledge, but neither concern themselves with its application. With Habermas, the application problem is a principal mark of his syntacticality.

The application of knowledge concerns both the enlightenment of the theorist and strategic action—both of which are clearly understood as attempts to practice the ideal norms of humanity (1973b:2). This, in a general sense, is expressed in Habermas' recurring insistence that one must always speak of theory *and* practice (praxis).[4]

The mediation of theory and praxis can only be clarified if to begin with we distinguish three functions, which are measured in terms of different criteria: the formation and extension of critical theorems, which can stand up to scientific discourse; the organization of processes of enlightenment, in which such theorems are applied and can be tested in a unique manner by the initiation of processes of reflection carried on within certain groups toward which these processes have been directed; and the selection of appropriate strategies, the solution of tactical questions, and the conduct of political struggle. On the first level, the aim is *true statements*, on the second, *authentic insights*, and on the third *prudent decisions*. [Habermas 1973b:32; emphasis added]

Theory informs practice by generating *true* statements, *authentic* insights and *prudent* decisions. The adjectives are crucial indications of this theory's normativeness and reflexivity (its intent to think back on the origins of knowledge itself). For Habermas, truth, authenticity, and prudence are values ultimately explained by a metatheory of the constitution of knowledge. The normative standards for evaluating applications are tied to the theory of those natural human conditions from which theory derives. These conditions are called *human interests* (1973b:9).

The claim that knowledge is tied to natural human interests is, perhaps, Habermas' most distinctive idea because it is the key to his revision of the traditional Marxian doctrine of historical materialism (Habermas 1975c). For Habermas, historical materialism becomes much more than an economic explanation for social change. It becomes a description of the conditions within which members of the human species are able to reflect upon their humanity (1973b:1–2). Human interests are a theoretical frame of reference for the examination of knowledge and science: "I have let myself be guided by the problem posed by the system of primitive terms (or the 'transcendental framework') within which we organize our experience *a priori* and prior to all science, and do so in such a manner that, of course, the formation of the scientific object domains is also prejudiced by this" (1973b:7–8). These interests, though a priori, are *not* ontological (1971a:317). Here Habermas retains the general Marxian doctrine that interests are formed in the material conditions of social evolution (1975c:292). Their reference therefore is not to the *being* of the human, but to the historically real "socio-cultural life forms" of the human species (1973a:177; 1973b:9; 1970d:129).

Here one sees a conceptual relationship similar to that encountered in Cicourel's interpretive procedures. Interests (though not to be equated with Cicourel's cognitive procedures) are invariant without being purely historical (1973b: 8), *and* abstract and universal without being biologically innate (1973b:9). They are dependent neither on the whim of historical context, nor the conditions of biological being as such. Conversely, they are "historical" but not contextual since they remain universal. Cicourel solves this dilemma by rooting interpretive procedures in the history of the individual. Analogously, Habermas settles it with reference to a theory of social evolution. Interests are imperatives of a particular stage in sociocultural evolution (1973b:9; compare 1970a, 1970d, 1975a, 1975c). "The *universality* of cognitive interests implies that the constitution of object domains is determined by conditions governing the reproduction of the species, i.e. by the socio-cultural form of life *as such*" (1973a:177). Thus, Habermas attempts to integrate both transcendent categories and empirical reference, but in a way quite different from Parsons. While the latter used the transcendent frame of reference to define empirical facts, Habermas understands transcendent theory to be rooted in the empirical, just as the empirical is apprehensible only theoretically (Habermas 1973b:2, 21; 1970d: 129).[5]

From the empirical side of this dialectic, Habermas claims that there are two cognitive interests common to all knowledge, both commonsense and scientific: the *technical* and the *practical* (1973b:8). Roughly put, the former is the interest all persons have in gaining information that permits them to control their environment, while the latter is an interest in meaningful communication with other persons (1973b:3–10). The difference between the technical and the practical is that found in familiar dichotomies: instrumental/expressive, control/understanding, functional/personal, things/symbols. Both are deep-seated anthropological features of animals at the sociocultural stage of development, that is, the human (1975c).

For the present what is important about the technical/ practical distinction is that it underlines scientific knowledge (as well as mundane knowledge). From this, Habermas derives a crucial element in his philosophy of science, namely, the distinction between the *empirical-analytic* sciences and the *historic-hermeneutical* (1971a)—in other words, roughly the distinction that has been made here between the lexical and the semantical. Empirical-analytic sciences are those (natural and social) sciences that employ controlled observations. They are thus either experimental or quasi-experimental. That is, they manifest a technical interest insofar as they seek to produce knowledge by manipulation of what is taken for empirical reality in order to "control" for possible error and produce statements shaped to fit into technically formal propositions. By contrast, the historic-hermeneutical social sciences are governed by a practical interest. Thus they seek facts not by observation, but through understanding. Here the scientist places himself at the level of the persons studied and their communications with each other. The goal is to interpret, through intersubjective human understanding, the meaning of what is being and has been said. In other words, hermeneutical interpreters involve themselves in the historical tradition in order to know that of which they have some preunderstanding by virtue of their own status as intersubjective communicators. These two types of knowledge differ both with reference to the type of knowledge constituted and the manner of application of those knowledges.

Empirical analytic knowledge can assume the form of causal explanations or conditional predictions, which also refer to the observed phenomena; hermeneutic knowledge as a rule has the form of interpretations of traditional complexes of meanings. There is a systematic relationship between the logical structure of a science and the pragmatic structure of the possible applications of the information generated within its framework. [1973b:9]

To these two interests—technical and practical—a third is added: the interest in *emancipation*. As science, the third is the basis for the critical social sciences which are characterized, of course, by self-reflection. Stated syntactically, the first two are understood as those cognitive interests in respect to which one is unaware of the rules governing knowledge formation; the empirical-analytic sciences uncritically objectify facts, while the hermeneutical sciences hypostatize tradition. The critical-emancipatory sciences reflect on these rules as well as the grammar of self-reflection itself.

It is important to remember that Habermas identifies these interests *both* as empirical, anthropological facts of human knowledge *and* as quasi-transcendental frames of reference. This means that it is not a matter of good (emancipatory) versus bad (empirical, hermeneutical) sciences, since all three are founded upon natural human conditions. What is "good" or "bad" is the extent to which knowledge is aware of the relationship between knowledge and interests. The bold claim is that critical science is a necessary supplement to the empirical and the hermeneutical, but not a substitute. All three, therefore, are universal transcendent frames of reference. Thus, he attempts to maintain *both* a critique of traditional sciences from the point of view of the emancipatory interest *and* a viable theoretical pluralism that gives a place to technical and practical knowledge.

On the one hand, his critique is quite clear.[6] The empirical-analytic sciences suffer under the "illusion of pure theory" (1971a:315). Their objectivism—the assumption that facts are ontologically given, thus unrelated to values (1971a:303)—results only in technical manipulations and has nothing to contribute to enlightened practical action. By ignoring the questions of the constitution and application of knowledge, the empirical-analytical sciences are an illusion, particularly insofar as they assume that human history can be mastered by technical competence alone (1971a: 316). With respect to their own goal of nomological explanation they fail at the crucial point of being able to explain themselves. Everything is referred to a functional language of measurement and control (1973b:11) which itself has no explanation.

This criticism is not particularly unique to Habermas. It has been made—in a different form—by hermeneutical (semantical) sociology. What is distinctive in Habermas is the force of his criticism of the latter wherein he insists that the historical-hermeneutical sciences also suffer the illusion of pure theory. Here the failure is the inability to criticize tradition. The question is how can the hermeneutical sociologist reflect upon the very tradition from which he/she gains the preunderstanding which is the basis for his/her interpretations (see 1970d)? If hermeneutical science is based upon preunderstanding (the prior familiarity of the sociologist with the meanings of the activities studied), does not tradition become an objectivist criterion for truth? Or, put differently, if I claim to study middle-class suburban culture on the basis of my own prior experience as a middle-class suburbanite how will I know for sure that I am not being put-on? How does the hermeneuticist diagnose possible systematic distortions occurring within the tradition that equally effect both the scientist and the participant? What if it is true, for example, that *all* middle-class people (including the hermeneutical sociologist) are systematically unable to see that their relative affluence distorts their understanding of the world? Depending upon preunderstanding alone, the hermeneuticist cannot make this critical diagnosis. He cannot even know if it is untrue. This "may lead to the ontologizing of language and to the hypostatizing of the tradition-context" (1970d:125) with the effect that historicism becomes "the positivism of the cultural and social sciences" (1971a:303).

While Habermas insists that only knowledge aware of the emancipatory interest can be scientific, critical knowledge alone is not sufficient for science. It is in this respect that Habermas is a theoretical pluralist. Inasmuch as the technical and practical interests are anthropologically universal, sciences founded thereupon cannot be dismissed in spite of their inadequacies. "Orientation toward technical control, toward mutual understanding in the conduct of life, and toward emancipation from seemingly 'natural' constraint establish the specific viewpoints from which we can apprehend reality as such in any way whatsoever" (1971a:311). Therefore, Habermas is very careful to describe his view of critical science so as to demonstrate both its positive and negative relationship to alternative sciences (1973b:10–13, 19–24). Though the technical and practical are "lower interests" (1973b:21), they are, nonetheless, anthropologically universal interests constitutive of knowledge.

However, it must be remembered that Habermas is working out the ideal of knowledge. His critique of these objectivating sciences is of the way in which they are actually practiced in sociology. Conversely, his affirmation of their necessity is with reference to potential value were they to attain true reflexivity. Thus, he postulates an ideal science called depth hermeneutics (1970d) or explanatory understanding (1970c).

In order to examine Habermas' proposals for an ideal science it is necessary to return to his general view of critical theory and its obligatory relationship to praxis.

[T]heory thus encompasses a dual relationship between theory and praxis. On the one hand, it investigates the constitutive historical complex of the constellation of self-interests, to which the theory still belongs across and beyond its acts of insights. On the other hand, it studies the historical interconnections of action, in which the theory, as action-oriented, can intervene. In the one case, we have a social praxis which, as societal synthesis, makes insight possible; in the other case, a political praxis which consciously aims at overthrowing the existing system of institutions. Because of its reflection on its own origins, critique is to be distinguished from science as well as from philosophy. For the sciences focus away from their constitutive contexts and confront the domain of their subject matter with an objectivistic posture; while, obversely, philosophy has been only too conscious of its origins as something that had ontological primacy. Critique understands that its claims to validity can be verified only in the successful process of enlightenment and that means: in the practical discourse of those concerned. [1973b:2]

Theory is inseparable from action, but the two are not equated. The subtlety of Habermas' proposal is precisely in its attempt to make reflexivity undogmatic in order that it may be posed as an alternative to the dogmatism of traditional sciences. This is sought in his attempt to work out a theory of truth that retains an integral notion of practice. This is attained by hinging the truth of critical theory upon the *discourse* of scientists, which in turn requires a clear demarcation of the boundaries between scientific discourse, practical communication, and strategic action.[7] These three are, respectively, the domains that generate true theoretical statements, authentic insights, and prudent decisions. Roughly the proposal is that true statements have a direct effect on enlightenment (the production of authentic insight) but no direct effect on decisions involved in strategic action.

In general terms, the proposal is this. Action and experience are distinct from theoretic discourse and facts. We encounter objects in experiences, the validity of which observations is intersubjectively established (1973b:18). Experience produces opinions about objective reality. These become the "raw material" (1973b:20) which is submitted to argumentation in theoretic discourse (1974c:209–10). If substantiated, these opinions are transformed into assertable facts. Facts are necessarily returned to their appropriate fields of application. If they are statements about things and events, they are translated back into "orientations for goal-directed rational action" (1973b:20) as technologies or strategies. If they are statements about persons or utterances they are returned as "orientations for communicative action" (1973b:20) in practical knowledge. Throughout, theory and practice are distinct, though their unity is never lost. This unity is retained, as seen above, by the interested bases of knowledge. "The interests of knowledge can be conceived as generalized motives for systems of action, which are guided by means of the communication of statements which can be true" (1973b:21; compare 1973a:170).

Here is Habermas' proposed solution to the old problem of value-freedom in social science. He is, on the one hand, critical of the objectivistic sciences that eliminate value. On the other hand, he does not jump into "action research" (for example, participatory radicalism) wherein neither the objectivity nor the truth of scientific statements can be defended; thus, the necessity of divorcing experience and action from theory. Yet the divorce cannot be absolute because this would return science to the illusion of pure theory. The only way, then, to reunite theory and practice, discourse and experience, is a modified transcendental philosophy (1973a:181). That is, a general metatheory of knowledge which is able to refer both action and theory back to their constitutive foundations. However, for Habermas (as seen above) this is possible only in the form of a reflexive theory interested in emancipation. Thus, even the theory of truth is syntactical. "The truth of statements is based on anticipating the realization of the good life" (1971a:314).

Habermas' ideal notion of the critical sciences is not so abstract as the preceding might suggest. He has two quite explicit models which are, of course, Marx and Freud—both of whom are characterized as critical theorists aware of the limitations of technical and practical knowledge and, thus, conscious of an interest in emancipation (1973b:9; compare 1971a). However, of the two it is Freud who offers the most adequate source for a fully reflexive theory (1971a: part III; esp. 1971a:281). It is with reference to Freud that Habermas designs a critical science under the names ex-

planatory understanding (1970c) or *depth hermeneutics* (1971a:ch. 10; 1970d). As both of these interchangeable labels suggest, Habermas' critical science is worked out primarily on the boundary between hermeneutical and emancipatory interests with its application to technical strategies left in a somewhat secondary position.

The problem posed for traditional hermeneutics is, as noted, that of systematically distorted communication. How does the interpreter know that the unreflective practical communication which generates opinions (the raw material of discursively verified facts) is authentic communication? How can this approach avoid the objectivism inherent in taking the language used in practical communication for granted? This poses the problem of pseudocommunication for which the subject matter of psychoanalysis is a primary example (1970c:117). Obviously one cannot take the patient's reports literally. It is axiomatic that patient's reports are, in some sense, distorted communication. They are not analyzed for their literal meaning. Thus, psychoanalysis is unavoidably a theory and practice of language analysis (1970c:119). Psychoanalytic understanding involves three scenes: the original traumatic event in the patient's childhood, the symptomatic scene acted out by the patient outside the analyst's office, and the transference scene enacted during treatment sessions. The systematic distortion lies in the patient's suppression of the original scene and its deformed presentation as neurotic communicative behavior in symptomatic scenes. In the transference scene the patient forces the analyst into a role symbolic of the original conflict scene, such as the repressive father. The analyst, on his/her side, functions to reflect upon the correspondence between transference and symptomic scenes in order to reconstruct the original. "Scenic understanding bases therefore on the discovery that the patient behaves the same in his symptomatic scenes as he does in certain transference situations; such understanding aims at the reconstruction, confirmed by the patient *in an act of self-reflection*, of the original scene" (1970c:119; emphasis added).

Stated quite simply, what makes psychoanalysis an adequate model for critical science is the fact that the analyst cannot function in the treatment experience without a self-conscious theory. Specifically, this is a theory of communicative competence which includes a concept of nondistorted communication, a genetic theory of the systematic distortion of communication, and an explanation of the origin of deformed communication in childhood experience (1970c:121–29). The analyst's theory bases itself upon an emancipatory interest and serves as the guidance for his participation in communication with the patient and, thus, as a guide for the self-reflection of the patient. "For the depth-hermeneutical interpretation . . . there is no verification outside of an executed self-reflection which must be made by all the participants and which is successful only in dialogue" (1970d:128). What is crucial for Habermas is the prospect that psychoanalysis goes beyond the objectivism of traditional hermeneutics to provide explanation:

The analyst's understanding owes its explanatory power . . . to the fact that the clarification of a systematically inaccessible meaning succeeds only to the extent to which the origin of the faulty or misleading meaning is explained. The reconstruction of the original scene makes both possible at the same time: the reconstruction leads to an understanding of the meaning of a deformed language game and simultaneously explains the origin of the deformation itself. [1970c:129]

Thus, it is an explanation applied to experience while derived from a normative theory of the constitution of language and knowledge. Throughout, theory and practice inform each other.[8]

The Ideal Speech Situation and Syntacticality

It is clear now that Habermas' approach is strongly syntactical. Knowledge is ultimately the reconstruction of the rules of theory and practice with reference to the reconstruction of the meta-rules of knowledge itself. "[I]n the simultaneous process of the ongoing reconstruction of general rules and self-reflection we become masters of critique in an emphatic sense; that is, we become aware of the practically momentous distinction between norms of thinking and acting which are in principle revocable and those quasi-transcendental rules which first make cognition and action possible" (1970d:129). Behind this conviction lies the most general principle of Habermas' syntactics. The very possibility of competent communication contains within itself the ideal of perfect communication. Thus, necessarily, in science "we must presuppose an ideal situation of verbal communication, on both sides, whenever we wish to carry on discourse" (1973b:25).

With Habermas one sees the same radical shift that appeared in Cicourel (though worked out differently). Language appears as *the* primary topic of sociological theory. For Habermas, language is that universal in human nature which both contains and promises human emancipation. "Our first sentence expresses unequivocally the intention of universal and unconstrained consensus" (1971a:314). Emancipation is precisely the freedom of persons discursively to verify truth and to validate social norms. Accordingly, it is only by means of language that human action is possible (1970c:145). Language, therefore, is a "transformer" (1975a:10). It is the means whereby objective facts and norms are intersubjectively agreed upon; at the same time, it is that medium which contains within itself a metatheory of intersubjectivity (1975a:10; 1973a:170; compare 1976). Hence, Habermas' sociology has become a theory of communication and language. In particular, it is a sociological theory of communicative competence or what he calls *universal pragmatics*.

The central concept in this theory is the *ideal-speech situation*. "Truth is the peculiar compulsion toward unforced universal recognition; this is, however, bound to an ideal speaking-situation, and that means a way of life in which unforced universal agreement is possible" (1970d:126). The ideal speech situation always goes against the facts of actual communication. Empirically, speech is systematically distorted which, as seen, is precisely why neither technical nor practical reason are sufficient to themselves. Ordinary language always occurs, by definition, in the world of experience and action and, thus, is deformed. However, if this distortion is the final word, then it must be concluded that there is no communication taking place in the real world, which in turn involves the conclusion that language does not exist. Since this is absurd the problem becomes: how does one explain the apparently contradictory coexistence of deformed and yet—in some sense—effective communication. For Habermas, the solution lies in the claim that all speakers are communicatively competent because they are naturally able to recognize the difference between truth and falsity. "Reaching an understanding is a normative concept; everyone who speaks a natural language has intuitive knowledge of it and therefore is confident of being able, in principle, to distinguish a true consensus from a false one. In the educated language of philosophical culture . . . we call this knowledge *a priori* or innate" (1973b:17). Thus, "every speech, even that of intentional deception, is oriented towards the idea of truth" (1970c: 144). Therefore, even distorted communication is based upon the innate recognition of the ideal speech situation. "Communicative competence is defined by the ideal speaker's mastery of the dialogue constitutive universals irrespective of the actual restrictions under empirical conditions" (1970c:141). In other words, our knowledge of the metarules of speech, truth, and life makes it possible for us to use the rules of ordinary language which, in turn, is the precondition for truth and action.

The problem next encountered is how does this ideal operate within the facts of actual language use? It is here that Habermas presents his theory of universal pragmatics. Like Cicourel, Habermas takes his departure from Chomsky with whom he shares certain affinities. Habermas' criticism of transformational grammar is also that it does not allow for context. It is "monologic"—explaining linguistic competence from extra-contextual innate rules—and, thus, does

not account either for dialogue or for man as a social creature. Habermas seeks to overcome Chomsky's biologism by
arguing that there is evidence to support the existence of
semantic universals which are a posteriori and intersubjective. He wishes to expand Chomsky's monologic scheme
(1970c:133–36) by pointing to the existence of culturally
universal kinship terms and organically universal color
words as significant semantic universals. Both are a posteriori; the former is intersubjective, the latter monologic. Both
go beyond Chomsky. However, for present purposes, the
most important category is the a priori, intersubjective universal—of which dialogue-constitutive universals are representative. As will be seen, these are crucial because it is
Habermas' view that linguistic competence cannot be explained apart from a theory of intersubjectivity which is,
of course, a theory of communicative competence. "The
situation . . . in which speech, i.e., the application of linguistic competence principally becomes possible, depends
on a structure of intersubjectivity which in turn is linguistic" (1970c:138).

Habermas' alternative to Chomsky is constructed with
reference to the writings of J. L. Austin (for example, 1970),
and J. R. Searle (1969), and D. Wünderlich (1971, compare
1972) of which the last-mentioned will serve here as an
illustration. Habermas believes that the universality of utterances in language expresses the universal pragmatic power
of language. These are the dialogue-constitutive universals,
of which (following Wünderlich) there are five (Habermas
1970c:139–44, 1971c; McCarthy 1973). Only two—pronouns and performative verbs—will be considered here.
Without pronouns speakers could not indicate their respective places in intersubjective dialogue. One must be able to
say "I" in order to distinguish oneself from "You" without
which distinction neither could utter "We."

The system of personal pronouns enables every participant to
assume incompatible roles simultaneously, namely that of the I
and that of the Other as absolutely different. And yet at the same
time he recognizes himself in the latter as another I and is con-

scious of the reciprocity of this relationship; every being is potentially his own Other. These dialogue roles of I and You are reproduced on the level of We and You, while He, She, and They describe roles of a virtual or potential participation in the dialogue. [1970c:141]

In other words, the fact that speakers use pronouns properly indicates their innate comprehension of the social nature of language. Likewise, performative verbs are the means whereby speakers make assertions, promises, and commands and, thus, are means whereby the intersubjective basis of truth and norms is secured. For example, one class of performative verbs are those expressing normative expectations (order, obey, allow, demand, refuse, recommend, advise, warn, and so forth). Expressions containing these verbs (in either deep or surface structures) are essential for social norms. People cannot understand an "ought" without the communicative competence to use and understand verbs in this class. Similarly verbs such as to deny, to confirm, to certify, to doubt, and so forth, are the basis for discourse with respect to truth. Without them people would be left in entirely private worlds and have no possibility to ascertain public, objective facts.

Habermas argues that these dialogue-constitutive universals—discovered in the empirical facts of speech and language—are themselves only explained by the proposition that all speakers innately assume an ideal speaking situation. Specifically, therefore, the ideal speaking situation includes the assumption that I am as free as my partner in speech to: a) assert statements containing facts and to criticize such statements, b) to represent freely myself and my own sense of authentic experience to the Other, c) to share with the Other the duties and rights contained in norms under discussion and pertinent to our respective roles. In other words, the ideal speech situation is marked by equality of opportunity with respect to truth, experience, and norms, and, accordingly, by the absence of intimidation and other constraints. As a consequence, communicative competence rests upon the ideal of the good life, of emancipation:

The ideal speaking-situation is anticipated with the help of our linguistic means of construction. Through the symmetrical distribution of chance by the choice of and practice of acts of speaking which relate to a) statements as statements, b) the relationship of the speaker to his remarks, and c) the observance of rules, are *linguistic-theoretical designations for what we customarily comprehend under the notions of truth, freedom, and justice.* [1970d: 132; emphasis added]

Though he has often been so accused, Habermas does not intend that his investigations remain fixated at the stage of a new general epistemology. His aim is a substantive theory of social evolution that provides a critique of late-capitalism. As noted above, it is here that his critical relationship to classical Marxian thought is most prominent. He is offering a reformulation of historical materialism in which interaction (communication) is given a primary place alongside work. Thus, for Habermas, the question of communication replaces the traditional Marxian concept of the forces and relationships of production (work) as the point of departure for substantive critical theory. One sees the connection between his general and substantive theory in the fact that the syntactical rules derivable from the ideal speech situation are generalizable under substantive empirical conditions into the general rules of a given stage in man's social evolution. Thus, the theory of universal pragmatics permits an analysis of the deep structures of society (1975a:26–27) which are specified in terms of the idea of an organizational principle appropriate to a stage in social evolution (1975a:7).

One begins to see the effect of this general theory of ideal communication on the more purely sociological aspects of Habermas' work by noting the connection between distorted communication and the particular evolutionary stage with which critical theory is most immediately concerned: late-capitalism.[9] Late-capitalism is, roughly defined, that period in human social history when technical reason dominates the practical reason of everyday life (1970a:113). Here Habermas makes a specific substantive application of the knowledge-constitutive interests. In overly simple terms, late-capitalism is a stage in which the technical interest in control essentially overwhelms and suppresses (1970a:113) the ethical norms created in intersubjective communication. Roughly put, it is when the social system compels people to legitimate their behavior in terms of technological ends rather than human value. An important consequence is that the members of a society become depoliticized insofar as they prefer the success that comes from a smoothly running social system to the criticism and dispute normal to an open society. Thus, for example, the system leads them to accept the benefits of a welfare state which they might well lose were they rigorously to exercise their critical powers. Mass loyalty (1970a:102)—for example, "America: love it or leave it"—replaces public debate and controversy as the norm for good citizenship. Similarly, achievement replaces independence as a private virtue.

It is very important to note that this is a structural analysis. It is not a question of bad individuals doing evil to others. What happens in late-capitalism is a systematic consequence of that type of social order. The depoliticization of public discussion, the loss of practical norms, the suppression of criticism derive from the organizational principle of technocratic societies which *requires* a systematic distortion of communication.

The critique of distorted communication is, therefore, an analysis aimed at both the private and public levels. Here one sees that the function of psychoanalysis as a model for the critique of distorted communication in private/psychic life is both a source and an analogy for the critique of the technocratic ideology distorting public communication. Just as it is assumed that the private and the public are part of the same social system, so it is assumed that critical theory is unified. There can be no purely psychological nor purely sociological analysis. Furthermore, systematic criticism of distorted communication (private or public) depends entirely on the theorist's awareness of the ideal of emancipation, that is, ideal communication. Thus "the 'critical' sciences such as psychoanalysis and social theory . . . depend on being able to reconstruct successfully general rules of competence" (1973a:184). In other words, the ideal-speaking situation is more fundamental than the analyzed structures of distorted communication (1973b:17). The critique of present society is made possible by the theorist's understanding that the ideal society is one of free discourse (1970a:119). In this ideal situation, the emancipatory interest refers to the syntax of the good life in which there is undistorted communication in both private and public life.

Man Resurrected Beyond the Tomb of Language

If ethnomethodology is ambiguously necrophilic toward man, then syntacticality is ambivalently necrophobic. Habermas seeks both to destroy man and to revive the dead body. Like ethnomethodology, syntactical sociology has moved in the direction of inserting language into the center of sociology's discursive space, thereby displacing man. "Today the problem of language has replaced the traditional problem of consciousness; the transcendental critique of language supersedes that of consciousness" (Habermas, cited in McCarthy 1973; compare Wellmer 1974b). By this, Habermas claims to have displaced nineteenth-century homocentrism founded upon a critical philosophy of the subject (see 1971a), a move which is paralleled in his attempt to redefine the nineteenth-century historical materialist concept of value. Against the transcendental subject, Habermas poses a quasi-transcendent *inter*subjectivity. Against the reliance of norms upon labor, he poses communicative interaction as an anthropologically primary fact of human nature. Both developments, as seen, are founded upon the primacy of language in the interests constitutive of knowledge. Language is both the mark of man's freedom and that which is equally the subject and object of reflection. In short, language is the resource and topic of emancipation.

There can be no argument with the proposition that Habermas attempts to drive a wooden stake through the heart of nineteenth-century man. At the same time, it must be said that if he has succeeded in killing man, he is just as earnestly attempting to revive him beyond language. Here the similarity to ethnomethodology breaks down. Cicourel permitted language to remain the hard, irrevocable measure of social reality; man remains only as a ghostly presence necessary to explain language. With Cicourel, language and man are engaged in a struggle; a love-hate relationship which is primarily indicated in the ambiguous place of the sociologist who is like other men in his subjugation to language, but unlike other men in recognizing his subjugation. The latter theme is, of course, present in Habermas wherein the sociologist is the man reflexively able to think language. The result is homocentric ambiguity. But, with Habermas, the ambiguity is missing. The calling to reflexivity is, implicitly, set forth as the ideal calling of all men. Ethnomethodology apotheosizes professional sociology by reducing it to practical sociology; Habermas calls all men to the high vocation of the former. In other words, Habermas' sociologist will not submit to the ethnomethodological principle of indifference; he will not give himself up to language.

Thus, the difference between the two discursive styles. Ethnomethodological discourse *confuses* for having dislocated man without giving up on him entirely. Syntactical discourse *overwhelms* because, being normative, it cannot escape the very assertive monologism it hates. Syntacticality, therefore, becomes a normative theory of man in spite of the presumably fatal blow delivered to consciousness by language. The difference in discursive effect is due to a difference in discursive practice. Ethnomethodology speaks up from the grave of man, offering an affirmation of language that veils a lament for man. Habermas' critical theory speaks down from a throne of ascension, offering a homily in praise of the man beyond language. In the former case, the reader is bewildered by a duplicitous discursive practice; in the latter case, one is intimidated by an unattainable discursive ideal.

Within theory itself, one discovers this triumphalism in the fact that with Habermas the primacy of language always points beyond itself to the good life. The contents of the ideal speaking situation are not the sheer facts of language. They are linguistic features capable of redefinition as the signs of human emancipation: truth, freedom, and justice (1970d:132, 144). Language is not here the final fact. Language itself has become a signifier. Therefore, it comes as no surprise that one easily discovers man, finitude, subjectivity, and history collected under the very first of Habermas' five theses on human interests: "The achievements of the transcendental *subject* have their basis in the natural *history* of the *human species*" (1971a:312; emphasis added).

1) The first apparent sign of finitude in Habermas' writings is the consensus theory of truth wherein truth is deprived of a footing in being or nature. Since truth can only be gained discursively, it cannot be thought as that which is built-in or readily apprehensible. Even when Habermas speaks of communication being based upon a necessary compulsion toward truth (1970c:144; 1970d:126; 1973b:17; 1976:158), it is the *desire* for truth that is natural and not any presumptively true statement. Since truth can be gained only from the position of an emancipated reflection upon the constitutive grounds of knowledge, it is evident that there can be no necessarily true proposition. Radical reflexivity is obliged to hold all propositions in doubt. Indeed, for Habermas, reflexivity derives from a universal compulsion toward truth which, by its own inner logic, can never take a permanent form outside of intersubjective communication. Were discourse to cease or become virtually impossible, there would be no truth.

Having distanced himself from both lexical and semantical sociologies, Habermas has shifted to a new discursive space. By denying the validity of lexicality's technical language, he has undercut the role of man as the intuitive source of the lexicon. By demonstrating the effect of distorted communication upon semanticality's strong sense of history, he has thrown man out of his comfortable role as the integrating subject of meanings. In the space left void by the exorcism of these manly epiphanies, Habermas utters up a syntactical creature who, at first, seems to be something other than the man of homocentrism. It is a creature whose distinguishing mark is speech. As speaker, it would seem to be devoid of consciousness, of subjectivity. But, on closer study, it is evident that though this is neither a lexical nor a semantical consciousness, there is consciousness nonetheless. Syntactical man emerges as that creature able to speak by virtue of an innate consciousness of the ideal rules of speech, which consciousness is gained intersubjectively and which reacts back to secure the validity of speech itself.

Though it is worked out in a somewhat different manner it is clear that Habermas still writes from within a homocentric finitude, as one sees from his view of nature. One should remember that those interests constitutive of knowledge are both in and beyond nature (1971a:312). This crucial conviction surely gives nature a more secure place than it holds either in lexicality or semanticality. Habermas treats this nature/culture dichotomy in a very delicate and intentional manner in order to establish the concept of *quasi*-transcendental interests. The prefix *quasi* now assumes all the purposeful ambiguity with which Habermas has endowed it. As noted above, he has need of both the "quasi" and the "transcendental" in order to mediate between the requirements of universalism on the one hand and context on the other. To speak of quasi-transcendent interests is to provide them with a definite location in relation to history and nature. Thus nature/culture is situated by a theory of social evolution. Human interests are not merely natural because in this formulation work dominates the others and man is indistinguishable from the animals (1975c). At the same time, nature/culture cannot be explained by culture alone because then one lapses into historicism and has no way to account for the transcendental quality of interests which, should such an account be unavailable, would destroy the place provided for emancipation and the origin of knowledge.

Therefore, in a remarkably undialectical fashion, Habermas places nature/culture at a precise stage in human development. That stage, curiously, begins with the original moment in man's history when he transcended the social labor of the animals by establishing communicative interaction in kin groups (1975c:289). Thus, man appears when language is reflected upon (1975c; 1971a) but in this moment labor is not deconstituted. Emancipation and language combine with labor to make knowledge possible. Thus, knowledge originates with man. "The human interest in autonomy and responsibility is not mere fancy, for it can be apprehended a priori. *What raises us out of nature is the only thing whose nature we can know: language.* Through its structure, autonomy and responsibility are posited for us. Our first sentence expressed unequivocally the intention of universal and unconstrained consensus" (1971a:314). Both phylogenetically and ontogenically, knowledge appears only with the birth of man.

Therefore, while nature is not pictured as death to knowledge, it is that which must be overcome in order for knowledge to exist. "By becoming aware of the impossibility of getting beyond these transcendental interests, a part of nature acquires through us autonomy in nature" (1971a:311). Man, through labor, is tied to nature. He cannot know without a technical reason rooted in labor. But nature is not sufficient to emancipated knowledge. To be sure, nature is not starkly over against man as it is in classical homocentrism; but, at the same time, it is perfectly obvious that reflexivity is not given in birth. It must be learned in specific contexts. Our language may be an invariant and universal urge toward reflexive truth, but in historical fact communication can be distorted and, thus, even this anthropological endowment can be put in jeopardy.

One can more fully appreciate this uncertain relationship to nature by noting Habermas' description of social life trapped between inner and outer nature. Outer nature is the "resources of the non-human environment" (1975a:9) which are assimilated by means of production. Inner nature is defined as "the organic substratum of the members of society" (1975a:9), that is, the biological needs of individuals. Social man is that creature who lives *between* nature which imposes itself in two directions—from outside as natural resources, from inside as needs.

Outer nature is appropriated in production processes, inner nature in socialization processes. . . . Control over outer nature and integration of inner nature increase with the "power" of the system. Production processes extract natural resources and transform the energies set free into use values. Socialization processes shape the members of the system into subjects capable of speaking and acting. *The embryo enters this formative process, and the individual is not released from it until his death.* [1975a:9; emphasis added]

The last sentence in this passage exposes the finitude of syntactical man. He is confined to a world between natures.

Man becomes man only when he is technically able to control outer nature (resources) and practically able to shape inner nature (biological needs) to social purposes. Neither accomplishment is a given in human nature. Both are gained by cultural, historical man. And both ultimately require a competent grasp of the ideal emancipated life. Thus nature is con-text but not text for the writing of the syntactical rules governing human knowledge and life. True, syntactical man does not exactly cower before nature, but it is equally true that he lives only to the extent that nature is overcome.

2) To the same measure, Habermas holds an eccentric place relative to subjectivism. On the one hand, he is quite intentionally at odds with the pure subjectivity of critical philosophy (1973b:14). On the other hand it is clear that self-reflection is central to his theoretical program. Thus, while *pure* phenomenological subjectivity is rejected, subjectivity remains central in the form of intersubjectivity.

Just as we can understand "thinking" as the process of discourse-dependent argumentation internalized by a single individual—so self-reflection too can be conceived as the internalization of a "therapeutic discourse." In both cases the withdrawing of communication into the inwardness of a solitary subject by no means revokes the virtually retained intersubjective structure of the dialogue; the thinking subject just as well as the reflecting subject must play at least two roles of the dialogue, if argumentation is not to become merely analytic (and thus in principle reproducible by machines). [1973b:28]

One finds here a subjectivity interdependent with intersubjectivity, that is, a subjectivity analyzed from the point of view of social context. This intersubjective context ranges from the direct cooperative communication of investigators through their respective social subsystems to and including the sociocultural stage of evolution pertinent thereto (1973b:14). In short, the subject is bound up in an intersubjective nexus encompassing the totality of social and anthropological organization. This is clearly another sort of subjectivity than that of lexicality and of semanticality in which the theoretic subject (of intuitions and ideal meanings) is set apart from the reality of social context. In these cases, theory as theory is formed without immediate references to the social contexts of action and experience.

But does the displacement of the subject into community destroy the homocentric principle of subjectivity? One must conclude that it does not when the steps formulating the place of self-reflection are retraced. The line of thought is roughly this: Self-reflection is, in the first instance, reflection upon one's language. Language is necessarily interpersonal communication. This fact is discovered in communicative competence, the ability to employ the universally pragmatic rules of the ideal-speech situation. These are the universal rules of undistorted communication which permit all speakers to enter into language. When they are actuated the speaker simultaneously brings to life the desire for truth, which desire includes the potential to overcome empirical instances of distorted communication by means of reflection.

Thus, to embed subjectivity in intersubjectivity is not to destroy it but to bring it to life. At no point is this more evident than in the psychoanalytical model. The cooperative communications between doctor and patient are carried forth under the guidance of a positive theory of undistorted communication. Discourse between analyst and analysand validates statements and norms pertinent to the patient's experience (both within and outside of the relationship). These interpersonal discourses form the basis for the analyst's reflections which in turn become the basis for the patient's self-reflection. However, this self-reflection takes shape as an inner dialogue between the part of self which remembers the original scene and the newly emancipated self. In this sense self-reflection is both occasioned by and practiced as intersubjective communication.

Of particular importance is the interpretation Habermas places on this critical model of scientific thought. As noted above, it is seen as the ideal science of explanatory understanding, the chief merit of which is its ability to explain the *origins* of neurosis. Here precisely is the evidence that subjectivity is retained in a strong sense. It must be remembered that the characteristic function of homocentric subjectivity is to act as the central presence of thought. The principle of the origin is, thereby, another name for subjectivity. With respect to psychoanalysis the originary experience is that primal subjective event the discovery of which explains the constitution of the patient's knowledge. It is clear that this same subjective principle is also projected on the total context of human social life. For, as it has been seen many times over, human knowledge is ultimately explained by that collective originary experience in which man first discovered his own language by speaking.

There is no question that this is quite another subject than that found in phenomenological sociology. There all intersubjectivity, while crucial to self-understanding, was relegated to context. There subjectivity dominated insofar as the intersubjective was retained only by memory after the brackets had closed off the intersubjective world. With Habermas, the brackets are dropped. The original experience of the subject is constituted in communication with others. Therefore, to explain subjectivity by means of intersubjectivity is not at all the same as expelling the subject from thought. On the contrary, with Habermas it has served only to enlarge its authority. Here the subject, having been freed of confinement in consciousness alone, becomes the means for explaining the syntactical rules governing the constitution of knowledge itself.

The syntactical sociologist, therefore—try as he might—cannot escape the onus of a privileged position. He is, in Habermas' scheme, the one who can both explain and understand the original rules of human life. To be sure, he is able to attain this privileged knowledge by means of communication with others. But, once attained, the knowledge sets him apart from all others whose communication is empirically disformed. Therefore, regardless of the substantial value he places on dialogue, the syntacticalist cannot refrain from speaking monologically. Since truth is not given, dialogue can only produce controversy. And because there is only speech and no listening for the syntacticalist there is no permanent quieting of the critical discourse and, thus, no final truth. Yet for Habermas it is clear that the controversy is for the sake of the good life. The dilemma cannot be overcome within language. It must be overcome beyond language. The good life is never attainable but one can speak about it. However, one cannot speak so as to let this ideal be submitted to controversy, for without the ideal speech-situation discourse is impossible. Therefore, the syntacticalist must speak monologically from the other side of language. Even a consensus theory of truth is ultimately explained from an ideal place outside of science.

3) Syntactical man is frustrated at the crucial moment. He cannot explain that which explains everything else. As a result he has no choice but to return to history. Faced with a situation in which everyone must speak monologically about dialogue, the syntacticalist is no less alone than the lexicalist or the semanticalist. This is why Habermas' theory of history is his least daring and most unreflected writing. Syntactical history is the story of man's evolutionary progress between the arché and the telos. "[T]he certainty of self-reflection is based on the remembered process of self-formation, which in precisely that act of remembering, is relegated to the past" (1973b:40). "[I]n every speech act the telos of reaching an understanding is already inherent" (1973b:17).

As seen above, man lives in that communicative world between the moment when he arose from nature through the discovery of language until the death of his species. Within this history, his life depends upon an unattainable ideal of communicative freedom. This alone permits him to speak, to be man. But since that telos is not attainable in this world, it can only be gained on the other side on language, in the posthuman realm. Like all eschatological theories, that of Habermas bears the burden of explaining what one should do before the end. In particular, his problem is how to account for the contradictory confinement to monologism wherein there can be no dispute over the telos.

Thus, at this point, Habermas, no less than the lexicalists and semanticalists, is caught in a world of differences. "Monologic dialogue" is the pseudocommunication of people who have no positive theory of listening. Those who do not listen cannot question that which is their only resource for universal community: the telos beyond their distorted communication. Since the telos of free communication is not given in being or in nature, man is threatened by difference and thus chaos. Difference, in turn, threatens language, intersubjectivity, truth and, finally, man himself. The whole threatens to collapse. Such a situation can only be redeemed in exactly the manner of classical homocentrism: by means of a strong sense of history.

All eschatological theories wishing to escape this-worldly nihilism must be strongly historical. Thus, Habermas formulates the crucial relationship between knowledge and human interests with respect to a variant form of historical materialism. Likewise, he accounts for that discursive capacity with which truth is possible by means of a theory of communicative development (1976:162–65). Since the discursive recognition of truth is not biologically innate, its universality can only be accounted in the biographical history of the individual. But in both one is returned to those ominously volatile doublets—nature/culture, universal/contextual. If the universal strain toward truth in discourse is not natural, then it can only be cultural and contextual. But if it is contextual, how can it be universal? There is only one answer available within homocentrism: analogy. All nonbiological theories of universal developmental stages must rest on analogy since they are deprived of the security of ontogenic identity. In Habermas' case monologic difference is overcome by the illusory assumption that the compulsion to speak is, in fact, the desire for communication. This desire finds its plausibility as a universal trait only by the prior assumption that the desire for communication is the origin of man's collective and individual histories. However, analogic histories are redeemable only with reference to a central presence that is the representative source of the analogies. In this one sees that Habermas also uses man as the originating presence for a history of those who would otherwise be trapped in a hell of speaking without listening. Thus, the other-worldliness of the telos of freedom is embodied in a history of the species.

4) It is undoubtedly true that in specific features mentioned, Habermas is attempting to speak his way out of the homocentric discursive formation. That he has failed in this is evident in the fact that the telos of freedom is simply another name for man. At the eschaton even language bows to signify that which is truly transcendent. Everything necessarily rests upon the belief that: "The achievements of the transcendent subject have their basis in the natural history of the human species."

9

Homocentric Sociology in the Twilight

A discursive analysis has not hidden real differences within sociological theory. It has been shown that in each major group there is a different relationship between the theoretician and his(!) text with the result that the positive surfaces of theoretical statements are different. Lexicalists hide themselves behind their lexicons in order that the formality and precision of terms can overcome the complexity of social facts. Semanticalists thrust themselves into a more visible place in the theoretical text in order that they can give an account of the sociologicality of human reality and, conversely, of the humanity of sociological reality. Syntacticalists, even more so, insert themselves without embarrassment in the surface structure of normative sentences in order to make apparent the ultimate bond between rules, language and the ideal human life.

However, what makes one doubt that these differences are fundamental or "paradigmatic" is the fact that none of these texts could have been written without finite, historical man as their subject. Without man, lexicality would have no source for its terms. Without man, semanticality would have no consciousness from which to generate meanings.

Without man, syntacticality would have no telos of freedom from which to derive rules and norms.

Because man is the source and topic of each of these theoretical types one must doubt that modern, American sociology is as pluralistic as many think. Because man is so demonstrably a nineteenth-century theoretical center, one must doubt that sociology has truly escaped its classical age. Because one knows that both man and the principle of the center are in the twilight of their useful lives, one must question what sociology is to do in the future.

Outside sociology there is considerable conviction that homocentrism and all other centers are in their twilight if not yet their graves. In place of centrism, one finds relativity; in place of originating principles one finds a world of infinite differences. Gerald Holton has described the change to posttraditional thinking in the following way:

The reigning themata until about the mid-nineteenth century have been expressed most characteristically by the mandala of a static, homocentric, hierarchically ordered, harmoniously arranged cosmos, rendered in sharply delineated lines as in those of Copernicus' own handwriting. . . . This representation was slowly supplanted by another, increasingly so in the last half of the 19th century. The universe became unbounded, "restless" (to use a fortuante description of Max Born), a weakly coupled ensemble of infinitely many separate, individually sovereign parts and events. . . . The clear lines of the earlier mandala have been replaced by undelineated, fuzzy smear. . . . And now, a significant number of our most thoughtful scholars seem to fear that a third mandala is rising to take precedence over both of these—the *laby-rinth with the empty center,* where the investigator meets only his own shadow. [Holton 1965:xxviii–xxix; emphasis added]

In science, the empty center is the result of general relativity and indeterminacy in modern physics. In modern art, drama, and literature, it is the *void* (Coe 1961) left by the decline of representationalism and realism. In psychology it is the partial decentering effected as a result of Freud's critique of the rationality of human consciousness. In modern linguistics it is the *absence* (Eco 1972) created by the redefinition of the sign as a negative, differential value (Saussure 1959) which does not name or represent the real world. In music it is the *silence* (Cage 1939) created by the death of the composer as the single source of musical texts.[1]

Very few people would deny that the intellectual movements most characteristic of "modern," post-nineteenth-century thought are: relativity theory, cubism, atonalism, absurdism, dada, expressionism, structuralist linguistics, psychoanalysis, among others. What is common to each of these is that in place of a center, one finds *relationships* that cannot be explained, organized, or defined by a single perspective, principle, or origin. While it cannot be argued that either *man* or the *center* have completely disappeared, it must be assumed that anything put forth as a new "paradigm" must at least be relational, not centered.

More precisely, it is also evident that "modernity" thus defined is neither humanistic nor homocentric. The great dilemma of the humanities today is not simply that scientism has made people inhuman, but that the humanistic disciplines themselves have lost their consensus on the self-evidentness of man as the source of art and thought. Derrida (1970) and Foucault (1973:373–86) for example, have shown how the two distinctively twentieth-century human sciences—psychoanalysis and ethnology—were possible only with the critique of homocentrism in the forms of the primacy of consciousness and ethnocentrism, respectively.

Perhaps the most substantial evidence for the approaching death of man in the human sciences is the case of modern linguistics. As Culler (1976) and others have shown, modern linguistics was made possible largely by Saussure's discovery that language and its signs are not motivated by human speakers. The arbitrariness of the linguistic sign was, with Saussure, tied to the corresponding idea that language (*la langue*) is a series of complex, changing, differential relationships from which speakers borrow their terms and rules.

Though the historical connections have yet to be drawn one has very good reason to suspect that the power of Saussure's theory came as much from its relativity, as from its ability to formalize linguistic facts. It is in fact the compelling feature of modern linguistics that it is *modern* in the sense of accounting for relativity yet *science* in its ability to generate formal explanations. As some have speculated (Culler 1976:114), for this reason modern linguistics may well turn out to have effected a Galilean revolution in the human sciences.

Certainly the importance of linguistics and language to modern thought is readily documentable. There is hardly a major discipline within the human sciences which is not now being challenged by language-specific philosophy. The names of Chomsky, Wittgenstein, Searle, Austin, Saussure, Lacan, Lévi-Strauss, Jakobson are increasingly prominent in academic publications in literary theory, art theory, psychoanalysis, social theory, philosophy, and theology. With few exceptions in the last ten years, the function of language in these texts has been to criticize traditional practices while promoting a more relativistic perspective.

Thus, it is no surprise that a sociology living and working in the twilight of man has begun cautiously to turn to language. In each of the three theoretical groups studied above, there has been at least one movement of recent origin. And, in each case, that movement has been either explicitly or implicitly a language-specific theory. I have in mind, of course, theory constructionism in lexical sociology, ethnomethodology in semantical sociology, and Habermas' theory of communications in syntacticality. While all three remain homocentric, one finds in each the marks of a post-homocentric, relativistic theme. Theory constructionists are willing to relativize empirical accuracy for the sake of the purity of theoretical language. Ethnomethodologists relativize both the sociologist and his classical idea (order) for the purpose of opening up *talk* as the topic and resource of sociological discourse. Habermas uses language as the source for redefining the ideal of the good life. While none have successfully rid themselves of *man*, all have begun severely to question the more traditional nonrelativistic

notions of their immediate predecessors. The theory constructionists have attacked the absolutism of empiricism
and operationalism. The ethnomethodologists have profoundly questioned even symbolic interactionism's naïve
assumption that the sociologist can effectively listen to the
social world without questioning his/her language. And
Habermas has been among those who have tried to overcome the absolutism inherent in classical Marxian social
theory's devotion to an absolutistic and often deterministic
doctrine of historical materialism.

One is tempted to read these changes as mere technical
advances within separate sociological traditions. But this
does not account for the fact that all three have been developed as a theory of sociological language. Of course,
the ethnomethodologists and the critical theorists are the
strongest illustrations because in these cases language has
led to a more explicitly relativistic theory of sociological
truth. But when even Blalock is not embarrassed to sacrifice
empirical realism for the sake of a simpler theoretical language (Blalock 1970b:296), one must seriously ponder the
effect of language on discourse in the human sciences.

Everywhere else in the human sciences, language has
arisen at the expense of homocentrism:

> From within language experienced and traversed as language, in
> the play of its possibilities extended to their furthest point, what
> emerges is that man has "come to an end," and that, by reaching
> the summit of all possible speech, he arrives not at the very heart
> of himself but at the brink of that which limits him; in that region
> where death prowls, where thought is extinguished, where the
> promise of the origin interminably recedes. [Foucault 1973:383]

Though one cannot yet be sure, it is likely that this is the
twilight region where a surprisingly nonpluralistic sociology now finds itself. If one were to guess what sociology
might look like on the other side, it would be reasonable to
imagine a relativistic, decentered manless world of talkers
talking about talk and texts written about texts.[2]

To those who find this a morbidly cold place, one can ask
two speculative questions. What evidence is there that

when *man* makes himself the moral center that life is more human? What reason is there to believe that when sociology is done *homocentrically* that it is able to account reliably for the increasingly marginal position of human creatures in a technologically and biologically precarious world?

Notes / References / Index

Notes

1. Homocentrism and Sociological Discourse

1. This view derives, in part, from Saussurian semiotics in which it is held that there are no positive values whatsoever, only differences (Saussure 1959:117; cf. Eco 1976).

2. The most complete methodological statement in English for this kind of discursive analysis is Michel Foucault's *The Archaeology of Knowledge* (1972a).

3. See Saussure's (1959) distinction between diachronic and synchronic studies.

4. For critiques of the idea of the center see Derrida 1967, 1968, 1970, 1973, 1976; Foucault 1972a, 1972b, 1973:part II; Eco 1972; Lévi-Strauss 1966:ch. 1. Derrida (1970) relates the beginnings of the critique of the center to Nietzsche, Heidegger, Freud, and (later) Lévi-Strauss (cf. Foucault 1973). In this connection, note that the critique of the center is also a critique of *metaphysiques*, including what Heidegger called ontotheology.

5. There is considerable agreement that a fundamental characteristic of post-nineteenth-century "modern" thought is relational, not centered. See, e.g., Derrida 1970; Culler 1976; Lemert 1974, 1978; Eco 1972; Foucault 1973; Lemert and Gillan 1977.

6. The unfelicitous term *homocentrism* is used in order to avoid confusion. French discussions of the same phenomenon use *anthropologism*. The problem is with the adjectival forms (*homocentric* vs. *anthropological*) which, in American texts, permits a confusion with alternative and more general meanings of *anthropological*.

7. The following discussion is based on Foucault 1973:part II.

2. Axiomatic Explanation: George Homans

1. Three of his best known texts are devoted to this task: *Social Behavior: Its Elementary Forms* (1961), "Bringing men back in" (1964b), and *The Nature of Social Science* (1967). His other popular text, *The Human Group* (1951), was primarily a study of small group behavior but,

as Homans admits (1951:6), its secondary purpose was to demonstrate how sociology could synthesize its theoretical ideas.

2. See Turner (1974) for a discussion of Homans' change of mind.

3. For Homans, reduction and deduction are the same (1967:80–87).

4. Homans admits that he uses an idiosyncratic meaning for the term *induction* (1961:10).

5. He has changed his mind on a fourth. In *English Villagers* (1941) it was function; later (1951, 1961) it was norms.

6. The exact derivations need not be considered here. See *Social Behavior* (1961), chs. 2, 3, 4.

3. *Theory Constructionism:* Hubert Blalock

1. The following is based upon a diagram appearing in Blalock 1970b: 276.

2. Exogenous variables are defined by Zs; endogenous by Xs. The terms b and c represent coefficients for strength of influence by endogenous and exogenous variables, respectively. The Us represent unknowns. The equations are entirely fictional.

3. It should be noted that this is a very simpleminded illustration. There are rules governing the exact kind of exogenous variables that must be found (Blalock 1969:75). Furthermore, what is suggested here refers only to the simplest type of relation. Nonrecursive systems create another set of difficulties; see Namboodiri, Carter, and Blalock 1975: 492–535.

4. *Analytic Realism:* Talcott Parsons

1. The example which follows refers only to the earliest description of action systems. There has been considerable development. In fact the pattern variables scheme (1951a, 1951b) and, later, the four function paradigm (1953, 1961) are highly developed advancements on this scheme. For a later description of his general theory of action see Parsons 1970c. For an outline of his intellectual development see Parsons 1970b and Turner and Beeghley 1974.

2. The following discussion of frame of reference is based on Parsons 1937:727–53 and 1959. It should be said that *frame of reference* is only the most general feature of his theoretical method. The *unit act* and *analytic elements* (or, variables)—not discussed here—provide the particular working tools. See also Parsons 1937:727–53 and 1959.

3. The "A-G-I-L" or "four function paradigm" was an advance on his earlier pattern variable scheme (1951a, 1951b). It first appeared in con-

junction with his work with Robert Bales (Parsons 1953). Eventually it was fully developed with reference to Freud's thinking as well as the notions of hierarchy and control from cybernetic theory. It should be noted that it is clearly not an abandonment of action theory. The following discussion is of course quite simplified. The reader should consult Parsons' writings themselves (1961; 1967:192–219; 1970c, for example).

4. See Parsons 1961:36 and 1970c:43–48. The description of these general relationships helps one see two of the most important features of Parsons' theory: 1) each of the action systems constitutes an "environment" for another and 2) each "interpenetrates" with another. It should be noted that what is described here is entirely the functional side of Parsons' scheme. There are also structural relationships, such as: institutionalization, which is the structuring of patterned values (from culture) into the social system; and roles, which are the normatively directed structural relationship between the personality and its place in collectivities within society. The beginning reader will surely be confused if he/she attempts to think of the functional relationships, described above, as though they were structures.

5. Here Parsons has in mind complex societies in which integration is an obvious problem and adaptation involves choices among several and many resources.

6. The difference between values and norms is that the former are universalistic through the culture and the latter are particularistically relevant to specific roles in specific situations (Ackerman and Parsons 1966:35).

7. The following is drawn from Parsons' most specific discussion of the topic (1937:753–75). Though formed early in his career the general position has not changed significantly (cf. 1954:212–37; 1961:34; 1967:166–91; 1970a).

8. In this paragraph reference is to the place of sociology among the social sciences (cultural anthropology, sociology, economics, and political science). This should not be confused with the place of the social sciences among the other sciences of action (cultural studies in general, psychology, and biology). The latter, discussed above, is the next "higher" level of classification in Parsons' philosophy of science.

5. Symbolic Interactionism: Herbert Blumer

1. Of course, semantics in linguistics does not necessarily entail the assumption of man as a producer of meaning.

2. Blumer is selected as the representative of symbolic interactionism for several reasons. He could be considered as a classical figure insofar as he has been the tradition's principal codifier. At the same time he exerts a broad contemporary influence. He and the Chicago School are

purer types when compared to the Iowa tradition of formalization. The latter has essentially sought to locate symbolic interactionism within lexicalism.

3. The terms *lexicality* and *lexical* inserted in this passage are the present author's. Blumer is, of course, referring to strict, formalistic sociology.

4. The theoretical images or pictures are different from root images which refer to the premises behind a total theoretical position. The pictures are, roughly, the precursors of the sensitizing concept. The latter emerge after one has used a preliminary picture in exploratory research. It should be noted that Blumer's root images have not changed and, apparently, have not been subjected to continuous doubt.

5. The difference between these three assumptions and the root images described above is that the former are general and abstract while the latter are specific applications to topics considered in sociology. Blumer's resistance to formalization is noted in the fact that he makes no attempt explicitly to link the two. One can readily imagine any lexicalist immediately defining these assumptions as the primal axioms from which sociological propositions are deduced. Blumer's refusal to do this is not due to his ignorance of deductive reasoning (see 1969:140–70) but to his unwillingness to speak in a formal manner.

6. *Phenomenological Sociology:*
Schutz | Berger | Luckmann

1. Both Berger and Luckmann were heavily influenced by Schutz. Their important and popular book, *The Social Construction of Reality*, drew its basic initial chapter and its overall scheme from Schutz' *Die Strukturen der Lebenswelt* (see Berger and Luckmann 1967:194). The latter volume (Schutz and Luckmann 1973) was actually written by Luckmann using the outline and preliminary notes prepared by Schutz immediately prior to his death in 1959. Luckmann has admitted that the book is neither Schutz' nor his. It does stand roughly as a systematic summary of Schutz' earlier thought (1962, 1964, 1967). What this text lacks, however, is Schutz' ideas on the methodology of the social sciences. These appear—in their most mature, if not most systematic form—in the first volume of his *Collected Papers* (1962).

2. Neither Schutz' earliest work (1967) nor his latest (Schutz and Luckmann 1973) will be primary sources. The former says little that is not also said in a more mature manner in the first volume of *Collected Papers* (1962). The latter, as noted, omits the crucial methodological discussions and, more importantly, is better grasped for present purposes in Berger and Luckmann's *The Social Construction of Reality* where the

ideas are explicitly applied in a sociological as opposed to philosophical manner. However, those with a serious interest in Schutz are encouraged to study both of these volumes, especially the latter.

3. The following is based upon Schutz' summary of Husserl's basic ideas (see Schutz 1962:118–39).

4. See Schutz' discussion of "because of" and "in order to" motives; Schutz 1962:19–22.

5. In his different writings this list varies and sometimes includes as many as five. See Schutz 1964:18–19, 84 f.; 1962:43; 1967:241 f.

6. See Schutz and Luckmann 1973; Berger and Luckmann 1967; Berger 1969:1–52.

7. Actually, there is some question whether Berger and Luckmann allow for any objectivation that is not a sign. Though this is implied (1967:35), it is not clear how, according to their definition of sign, one could have an insignificant objectivation inasmuch as objectivation is the "proclamation of subjective intentions." Also they say: "all objectivations are susceptible of utilization as signs" (1967:35). This theoretical ambiguity demonstrates the extent of their semanticality. In effect, everything is signification.

8. Legitimation is a major feature of their theory. (See Berger and Luckmann 1967:92–128.) The use of the term *logic* here should not be taken as "formal logic." It refers to the "meaningfulness" of the institutions. It is a kind of naïve logic normally, but in the scientific attitude it could, of course, involve the use of formal logic. (See 1967:65.)

7. *Ethnomethodology:* Aaron Cicourel

1. Moreover, Cicourel is explicitly critical of the view that societies require a set of common, core values. See 1974a:ch. 1 and especially 1974a:72.

2. For a summary of Chomsky's basic scheme see Chomsky 1965:128–47 and 1972:24–64.

3. This concept is used in the same way by phenomenological sociologists. However, with the ethnomethodologists the *emphasis* is on the fact that the norm is renegotiated in the particular setting.

4. For detailed discussions of the way in which language is the death of man see Foucault 1973:part II; Derrida 1970; Lemert 1978.

8. *Critical Theory:* Juergen Habermas

1. Syntax combines with phonology (rules governing the proper formation of language sounds) to constitute grammar. In the following,

syntax and grammar will sometimes be used interchangeably with the understanding that phonology is not primarily at issue.

2. One could add a fifth residual category to identify those texts which are primarily an attack on bourgeois sociology without being particularly clear on either their philosophical position or their substantive research programs (e.g., Ehrlich 1971, Smith 1971). These could be called *radical socio-logism*.

3. There is now an extensive secondary literature on various aspects of the Frankfurt School and its recent developments. See Jay 1973, 1974; McCarthy 1973, 1975; Dallmayr 1972a, 1972b; Wellmer 1974a, 1974b; Shapiro 1970; Therborn 1970; Habermas 1973a; Schroyer 1972, 1973; Slater 1977.

4. *Practice* and *praxis* are interchangeable. However, with Habermas it must be noted that several distinctions are working at once to affect the term *practical*. Generally speaking practice/praxis is used in relation to the theory/practice dichotomy, while practical involves the technical/practical/emancipation trichotomy. However, as will be noted in the following, the two sets of concepts interpenetrate each other such that the action of practical communication is a primary domain for the practice of theory.

5. Habermas himself has rejected his own earlier use of the expression "quasi-transcendent" (1973b:14) because it implies too strong an affinity for a transcendental subjectivity. It is retained here in several places as a general term with the understanding that it functions to convey a qualified, empirical transcendentality.

6. The primary sources for his critique of science are 1971a, 1973b, 1974c, 1973c, 1970e.

7. Habermas' use of the term *discourse* is different from that used throughout this book. His reference is strictly to argumentation free of experience that serves to verify facts and validate norms. I have roughly followed Foucault and others who understand discourse more generally as the practice of language.

8. It should be noted that psychoanalysis is not a perfect model. Self-reflection in psychoanalysis is both more and less than scientific discourse (Habermas 1973b:23). It is less in that the patient and the analyst are not dialogically equal partners. The analyst retains greater authority. But it is more in that with psychoanalysis theory is more closely related to experience (1973b:23). The latter difference is generalized by Habermas to include applications to social action (1973b:38–39). Theory is not as directly applicable to action as it is to enlightenment as one realizes in the case of political struggle, which necessarily involves a rupture in dialogue.

9. The following is necessarily a superficial exposition of the many issues surrounding modernization and capitalism. The reader should consult Habermas' own texts, 1970a, 1975a.

9. Homocentric Sociology in the Twilight

1. For a more complete discussion see Lemert 1974.

2. This possibility is discussed in somewhat greater detail in Lemert and Gillan 1977 and Lemert 1978.

References

Ackerman, Charles and Talcott Parsons
1966 The concept of social system as a theoretical device. Pp. 24–40 in Concepts, Theory and Explanation in the Behavioral Sciences, edited by Gordon J. Di Renzo. New York: Random House.
Attewell, Paul
1974 Ethnomethodology since Garfinkel. Theory and Society 1:179–210.
Austin, J. L.
1970 Philosophical Papers. London: Oxford University Press.
Berger, Peter
1969 The Sacred Canopy. Garden City, N.Y.: Doubleday.
Berger, Peter and Thomas Luckmann
1967 [1966] The Social Construction of Reality. Garden City, N.Y.: Doubleday.
Bierstedt, Robert
1959 Nominal and real definitions. Pp. 121–44 in Symposium on Sociological Theory, edited by Llewellyn Gross. New York: Harper & Row.
Blalock, Hubert M.
1960 Social Statistics. New York: McGraw-Hill.
1964 Causal Inferences in Nonexperimental Research. Chapel Hill: University of North Carolina Press.
1967 Toward a Theory of Minority Group Relations. New York: Wiley.
1968a The measurement problem: A gap between the languages of theory and research. Pp. 5–27 in Methodology in Social Research, edited by Hubert M. Blalock and Ann B. Blalock. New York: McGraw-Hill.
1968b Theory building and causal inferences. Pp. 155–98 in Methodology in Social Research, edited by Hubert M. Blalock and Ann B. Blalock. New York: McGraw-Hill.
1969 Theory Construction: From Verbal to Mathematical Formulations. Englewood Cliffs, N.J.: Prentice-Hall.
1970a An Introduction to Social Research. Englewood Cliffs, N.J.: Prentice-Hall.
1970b The formalization of sociological theory. Pp. 271–300 in Theoret-

ical Sociology, edited by John C. McKinney and Edward A. Tiryakian. New York: Appleton-Century-Crofts.

1971a A dual-measurement problem: Indirect measurement and deviations about imprecise standards. The Australian and New Zealand Journal of Sociology 7, no. 2 (Oct.):19–22.

1971b Aggregation and measurement error. Social Forces 50, no. 2 (Dec.):151–213.

1973 Thoughts on the development of sociology. ASA Footnotes 1, no. 2 (Mar.):2.

Blumer, Herbert

1937 Social disorganization and personal disorganization. American Journal of Sociology 17:871–77.

1958 Race Prejudice as a sense of group position. Pacific Sociological Review 1, no. 1:3–7.

1959 Collective behavior. Pp. 127–58 in Review of Sociology, edited by Joseph B. Gittler. New York: John Wiley.

1960 Early industrialization and the laboring class. Sociological Quarterly 1:5–14.

1962 Society as symbolic interaction. Pp. 179–92 in Human Behavior and Social Process, edited by Arnold Rose. Boston: Houghton Mifflin.

1966 The idea of social development. Pp. 3–11 in Studies in Comparative International Development, Vol. 2. St. Louis: Social Science Institute, Washington University.

1969 Symbolic Interactionism: Perspective and Method. Englewood Cliffs, N.J.: Prentice-Hall.

Blumer, Herbert and Phil Hauser

1933 Movies, Delinquency, and Crime. New York: Macmillan.

Brown, Robert

1973 Rules and Laws in Sociology. Chicago: Aldine.

Bruyn, Severyn

1966 The Human Perspective in Sociology. Englewood Cliffs, N.J.: Prentice-Hall.

Buckley, Walter

1967 Sociology and Modern Systems Theory. Englewood Cliffs, N.J.: Prentice-Hall.

Cage, John

1939 Silence. Middletown, Conn.: Wesleyan University Press.

Chomsky, Noam

1965 Aspects of a Theory of Syntax. Cambridge: MIT Press.

1972 Language and Mind. Enlarged edition. New York: Harcourt Brace Jovanovich.

Cicourel, Aaron V.

1964 Method and Measurement in Sociology. New York: Free Press.

1968 The Social Organization of Juvenile Justice. New York: Wiley.

1974a Cognitive Sociology. New York: Macmillan.
1974b Theory and Method in a Study of Argentine Fertility. New York: Wiley.

Coe, Richard
1961 Eugene Ionesco. New York: Grove Press.

Coleman, James
1964 Introduction to Mathematical Sociology. Glencoe: Free Press.
1968 Review essay [on Harold Garfinkel's Studies in Ethnomethodology]. American Sociological Review 33, no. 1:126–29.

Colfax, J. David
1971 Varieties and prospects of "radical scholarship" in sociology. Pp. 81–92 in Colfax and Roach 1971.

Colfax, J. David and Jack L. Roach (eds.)
1971 Radical Sociology. New York: Basic Books.

Cooley, Charles Horton
1964 Human Nature and the Social Order. New York: Schocken Books.

Coser, Lewis
1975 Presidential address: Two methods in search of a substance. American Sociological Review 40, no. 6 (Dec.):691–700.

Culler, Jonathan
1975 Structuralist Poetics. Ithaca: Cornell University Press.
1976 Saussure. Glasgow: Fontana/Collins.

Curtis, James E.
1972 The sociology of sociology: Some lines of inquiry in the study of the discipline. The Sociological Quarterly 13 (Spring):197–209.

Dallmayr, Fred
1972a Reason and emancipation: Notes on Habermas. Man and World 5, no. 1 (Feb.):79–109.
1972b Critical theory criticized: Habermas' Knowledge and Human Interests and its aftermath. Philosophy of the Social Sciences 2:211–29.

Davis, Kingsley
1959 The myth of functional analysis as a special method in sociology and anthropology. American Sociological Review 24 (Dec.): 757–72.

Davis, M.
1971 That's interesting: Towards a phenomenology of sociology and a sociology of phenomenology. Philosophy of the Social Sciences 1:309–44.

Denzin, Norman
1969 Symbolic interactionism and ethnomethodology: A proposed synthesis. American Sociological Review 34 (Dec.):922–34.

Derrida, Jacques
1967 L'écriture et la différence. Paris: Seuil.
1968 La différence. Pp. 41–66 in Theorie d'ensemble, edited by M. Foucault, R. Barthes, and J. Derrida. Paris: Seuil/Tel Quel.

1970   Structure, sign and play in the discourse of the human sciences. Pp. 246–64 in The Structuralist Controversy, edited by Richard Macksey and Eugenio Donato. Baltimore: Johns Hopkins University Press.

1973   Speech and Phenomena. Evanston: Northwestern University Press.

1976   [1967] Of Grammatology. Baltimore: Johns Hopkins University Press.

Deutscher, Irwin

1975   Review essay [on Aaron Cicourel's Cognitive Sociology]. American Journal of Sociology 81, no. 1:174–79.

Dewey, John

1925   Experience and Nature. Chicago: Open Court.

Douglas, Jack (ed.)

1970   Understanding Everyday Life. Chicago: Aldine.

1971   American Social Order: Social Rules in a Pluralistic Society. New York: Free Press.

Dubin, Robert

1969   Theory Building. New York: Free Press.

Durkheim, Emile

1938   [1894] The Rules of Sociological Method. New York: Free Press.

1965   [1912] The Elementary Forms of the Religious Life. New York: Free Press.

Eco, Umberto

1972   La structure absente. Paris: Mercure de France.

1976   A Theory of Semiotics. Bloomington: Indiana University Press.

Effrat, Andre

1972   Power to the paradigms. Sociological Inquiry 42, nos. 1–4:3–33.

Ehrlich, Howard J.

1971   Notes from a radical social scientist: February 1970. Pp. 194–221 in Colfax and Roach 1971.

Emmet, Dorothy and A. MacIntyre

1970   Sociological Theory and Philosophical Analysis. New York: Macmillan.

Filmer, Paul, et al.

1972   New Directions in Sociological Theory. Cambridge, Mass.: MIT Press.

Foucault, Michel

1972a   The Archaeology of Knowledge. New York: Random House.

1972b   Discourse on language. In Foucault 1972a.

1973   The Order of Things. New York: Vintage Books.

Friedrichs, Robert

1972a   A Sociology of Sociology. New York: Free Press.

1972b   Dialectical sociology: An exemplar for the 1970's. Social Forces 50 (June):447–55.

1972c   Dialectical sociology: Toward a resolution of the current "crisis" in Western sociology. British Journal of Sociology 13 (Mar.): 263–73.

Garfinkel, Harold

1967   Studies in Ethnomethodology. Englewood Cliffs, N.J.: Prentice-Hall.

1974   The origins of the term "ethnomethodology." Pp. 15–18 in Ethnomethodology, edited by Roy Turner. Baltimore: Penguin Books.

Garfinkel, Harold and Harvey Sacks

1970   On formal structures of practical actions. Pp. 337–66 in Theoretical Sociology, edited by John C. McKinney and Edward Tiryakian. New York: Appleton-Century-Crofts.

Gerth, Hans and C. Wright Mills

1946   From Max Weber: Essays in Sociology. New York: Oxford University Press.

Gibbs, Jack

1972   Sociological Theory Construction. Hinsdale, Ill.: Dryden Press.

Gidlow, Bob

1972   Ethnomethodology—A new name for an old practice. British Journal of Sociology 23:39–405.

Goffman, Erving

1974   Frame Analysis. New York: Harper & Row, Colophon Books.

Gouldner, Alvin

1970   The Coming Crisis in Western Sociology. New York: Basic Books.

1976   The Dialectic of Ideology and Technology. New York: Seabury.

Habermas, Juergen

1970a   Technology and science as "ideology." Pp. 81–122 in Habermas 1970b.

1970b   Toward a Rational Society. Boston: Beacon Press.

1970c   Toward a theory of communicative competence. Pp. 115–48 in Recent Sociology, No. 2, edited by H. P. Dreitzel. New York: Macmillan.

1970d   Summation and response. Continuum 8:123–33.

1970e   Zur Logik der Sozialwissenschaften. Frankfurt: Suhrkamp.

1971a   [1968] Knowledge and Human Interests. Boston: Beacon Press.

1971b   Why more philosophy? Social Research 38, no. 4:633–54.

1971a   Vorbereitende Bemerkungen zu einer Theorie der kommunikativen Kompetenz. Pp. 101–44 in Theorie der Gesellschaft oder Sozialtechnologie by J. Habermas and N. Luhmann. Frankfurt: Suhrkamp.

1973a   A postscript to Knowledge and Human Interests. Philosophy of the Social Sciences 3:157–89.

1973b   [1963] Theory and Practice. Boston: Beacon Press.

1973c   Wahrheitstheorien. In Festschrift für Walter Schultz. Neske.

1974a   On social identity. Telos 19:91–103.

1974b Habermas talking: An interview. Theory and Society 1, no. 1: 37–59.

1974c [1964] Rationalism divided in two. Pp. 195–223 in Positivism and Sociology, edited by Anthony Giddens. London: Heinemann.

1975a Legitimation Crisis. Boston: Beacon Press.

1975b Moral development and ego identity. Telos 24:41–55.

1975c Toward a reconstruction of historical materialism. Theory and Society 2, no. 3:287–300.

1976 Some distinctions in universal pragmatics. Theory and Society 3, no. 2 (Summer):155–67.

Heap, James and P. Roth

1973 On phenomenological sociology. American Sociological Review 38, no. 3 (June):354–66.

Heidegger, Martin

1969 Identity and Difference. New York: Harper & Row, Torchbooks.

Holton, Gerald

1965 Introduction. Pp. vii–xxxiii in Science and Culture, edited by G. Holton. Boston: Houghton Mifflin.

Homans, George

1941 English Villagers in the Thirteenth Century. Cambridge: Harvard University Press.

1951 The Human Group. London: Routledge & Kegan Paul.

1958 Social behavior as exchange. American Journal of Sociology 63:597–606.

1961 Social Behavior: Its Elementary Forms. New York: Harcourt, Brace & World.

1962 Sentiments and Activities. Glencoe: Free Press.

1964a Contemporary theory in sociology. Pp. 951–77 in Handbook of Modern Sociology, edited by R. E. L. Faris. Chicago: Rand McNally.

1964b Bringing men back in. American Sociological Review 29 (Dec.): 809–18.

1967 The Nature of Social Science. New York: Harcourt, Brace & World.

1969 A life of Synthesis. Pp. 13–34 in Sociological Self-Images, edited by I. L. Horowitz. Beverly Hills: Sage.

1971 Reply to Blain. Sociological Inquiry 41 (Winter):23–30.

Horkheimer, Max

1972 Critical Theory. New York: Seabury Press.

Jameson, Fredric

1972 The Prison-House of Language. Princeton: Princeton University Press.

Jay Martin

1973 The Dialectical Imagination: A History of the Frankfurt School and the Institute of Social Research, 1923–1950. Boston: Little, Brown.

1974 Some recent developments in critical theory. Berkeley Journal of Sociology 18:27–44.

Kristeva, Julia
1974 La révolution du langage poétique. Paris: Seuil.

Kuhn, Manford
1964 Major trends in symbolic interaction theory in the past twenty-five years. Sociological Quarterly 5, no. 1:61–84.

Kuhn, Thomas S.
1962 The Structure of Scientific Revolutions. Chicago: University of Chicago Press, Phoenix Books.
1969 Postscript—1969. In The Structure of Scientific Revolutions. Second enlarged edition. International Encyclopedia of Unified Science. Chicago: University of Chicago Press.

Lazarsfeld, Paul
1970 The place of empirical social research in the map of contemporary sociology. Pp. 301–18 in McKinney and Tiryakian 1970.

Lecourt, Dominique
1974 Marxism and Epistemology: Bachelard, Canguilhem, and Foucault. London: New Left Books.

Lemert, Charles
1974 Sociological theory and the relativistic paradigm. Sociological Inquiry 44, no. 2:93–104.
1978 [In Press] Ethnomethodology and structuralism: Linguicity and the decentering of core values. Theory and Society.

Lemert, Charles and Garth Gillan
1977 The new alternative in critical sociology: Foucault's discursive analysis. Cultural Hermeneutics 4:309–20.

Lepschy, Giulio
1970 A Survey of Structural Linguistics. London: Faber.

Lévi-Strauss, Claude
1966 The Savage Mind. Chicago: University of Chicago Press.

Luckmann, Thomas
1967 The Invisible Religion. New York: Doubleday.

McCarthy, T. A.
1973 A theory of communicative competence. Philosophy of the Social Sciences 3:135–56.
1975 Translator's introduction. In Habermas 1975a.

McKinney, John C. and Edward A. Tiryakian (eds.)
1970 Theoretical Sociology: Perspectives and Developments. New York: Appleton-Century-Crofts.

Macksey, Richard and Eugenio Donato (eds.)
1970 The Structuralist Controversy. Baltimore: Johns Hopkins University Press.

Masterman, Margaret
1970 The nature of a paradigm. Pp. 59–90 in Criticism and Growth of

Knowledge, edited by Imre Lakatos and Alan Musgrave. Cambridge: Cambridge University Press.

Mead, George Herbert

1962 [1934] Mind, Self and Society. Chicago: University of Chicago Press.

Mehan, Hugh and Houston Wood

1975 The Reality of Ethnomethodology. New York: Wiley.

Meltzer, Bernard N. and John W. Petras

1970 The Chicago and Iowa schools of symbolic interactionism. Pp. 3–17 in Human Nature and Collective Behavior, edited by Tamotsu Shibutani. Englewood Cliffs, N.J.: Prentice-Hall.

Mills, C. Wright

1959 The Sociological Imagination. New York: Grove Press.

Mueller, Claus

1973 The Politics of Communication. New York: Oxford University Press.

Mullins, Nicholas C.

1971 The Art of Theory: Construction and Use. New York: Harper & Row.

1973 Theories and Theory Groups in Contemporary American Sociology. New York: Harper & Row.

Namboodiri, N. Krishnan and Lewis F. Carter and Hubert M. Blalock

1975 Applied Multivariate Analysis and Experimental Designs. New York: McGraw-Hill.

Northrop, F. S. C.

1947 The Logic of the Sciences and the Humanities. New York: Macmillan.

O'Neill, John

1972 Sociology as a Skin Trade: Essays Toward a Reflexive Sociology. New York: Harper & Row.

Parsons, Talcott

1934–35 The place of ultimate values in sociological theory. International Journal of Ethics 45:282–316.

1937 The Structure of Social Action. New York: Free Press.

1949 Essays in Sociological Theory: Pure and Applied. Glencoe: Free Press.

1951a The Social System. New York: Free Press.

1951b Toward a General Theory of Action. New York: Free Press.

1953 Working Papers in Theory of Action. With Robert Bales and Edward Shils. New York: Free Press.

1954 Essays in Sociological Theory. Revised. New York: Free Press.

1955 Family, Socialization and Interaction Process. With Robert Bales. New York: Free Press.

1959 Psychological theory in terms of theory of action. Pp. 612–711 in Psychology a Study of Science, vol. 3, edited by Sigmund Koch. New York: McGraw-Hill.

1961 Theories of Society. Glencoe: Free Press.

1965 Full citizenship for the American Negro? Daedalus 94, no. 4 (Fall):1009–54.

1967 Sociological Theory and Modern Society. New York: Free Press.

1970a Theory in the humanities and sociology. Daedalus 99 (Spring):495–523.

1970b On building social system theory: a personal history. Daedalus 99 (Fall):826–81.

1970c Some problems in general theory in sociology. Pp. 27–68 in McKinney and Tiryakian 1970.

1971 The System of Modern Societies. Englewood Cliffs, N.J.: Prentice-Hall.

1974 Comment on current folklore in the criticism of Parsonian action theory. Sociological Inquiry 44, no. 1:55–58.

Rex, John

1974 Sociology and the Demystification of the Modern World. London: Routledge & Kegan Paul.

Reynolds, Paul D.

1971 A Primer in Theory Construction. Indianapolis: Bobbs-Merrill.

Ritzer, George

1975 Sociology: A Multiple Paradigm Science. Boston: Allyn and Bacon.

Roethlisberger, F. J. and W. J. Dickson

1939 Management and the Worker. Cambridge: Harvard University Press.

Rose, Arnold

1962 A systematic summary of symbolic interaction theory. Pp. 3–19 in Human Behavior and Social Processes, edited by Arnold M. Rose. Boston: Houghton Mifflin.

Said, Edward

1975 Beginnings: Intention and Method. New York: Basic Books.

Saussure, Ferdinand de

1959 Course in General Linguistics. New York: The Philosophical Library.

Schroyer, Trent

1971 The critical theory of late capitalism. Pp. 297–321 in The Revival of American Socialism, edited by G. Fischer. London: Oxford University Press.

1972 The dialectical foundations of critical theory: Jürgen Habermas' metatheoretical investigations. Telos 12:93–114.

1973 The Critique of Domination. New York: Braziller.

Schutz, Alfred

1962 Collected Papers, vol. 1. The Hague: Martinus Nijhoff.

1964 Collected Papers, vol. 2. The Hague: Martinus Nijhoff.

1967 The Phenomenology of the Social World. Evanston: Northwestern University Press.

Schutz, Alfred and Thomas Luckmann
1973 Structures of the Life-World. Evanston: Northwestern University Press.
Scott, John Finley
1963 The changing foundations of the Parsonian action scheme. American Sociological Review 28 (Oct.):716–35.
1974 Interpreting Parsons' work: a problem in method. Sociological Inquiry 44, no. 1:58–61.
Searle, J. R.
1969 Speech Acts: An Essay in the Philosophy of Language. Cambridge: Cambridge University Press.
Shapiro, Jeremy
1970 From Marcuse to Habermas. Continuum 8, no. 1:65–75.
Shibutani, Tamotsu
1970 Foreword. Pp. v–viii in Human Nature and Collective Behavior, edited by Tamotsu Shibutani. Englewood Cliffs, N.J.: Prentice-Hall.
Shils, Edward
1970 Tradition, ecology, and institution in the history of sociology. Daedalus 99 (Fall):760–825.
Simon, Herbert
1957 Models of Man: Social and Rational. New York: Wiley.
Slater, Phil
1977 Origin and Significance of the Frankfurt School. London: Routledge & Kegan Paul.
Smith, Dusky Lee
1971 The sunshine boys: toward a sociology of happiness. Pp. 28–44 in Colfax and Roach 1971.
Stinchcombe, Arthur
1968 Constructing Social Theories. New York: Harcourt, Brace & World.
Sudnow, David (ed.)
1972 Studies in Social Interaction. New York: Free Press
Therborn, Goeren
1970 The Frankfurt school. New Left Review 63:65–96.
Tiryakian, Edward
1965 Existential phenomenology and the sociological tradition. American Sociological Review 30 (Oct.):674–88.
Turner, Jonathan
1974 The Structure of Sociological Theory. Homewood, Ill.: Dorsey Press.
Turner, Jonathan H. and Leonard Beeghley
1974 Current Folklore in the Criticisms of Parsonian Action Theory. Sociological Inquiry 44, no. 1:47–63.
van den Berghe, Pierre
1963 Dialectic and functionalism: Toward a theoretical synthesis.

American Sociological Review 28, no. 5 (Oct.):695–705.

Wagner, Helmut

1963 Types of sociological theory. American Sociological Review 28 (Oct.):735–42.

1970 Introduction. Pp. 1–50 in Alfred Schutz: On Phenomenology and Social Relations, edited by Helmut R. Wagner. Evanston: Northwestern University Press.

Walsh, George

1967 Introduction. Pp. xv–xxix in Phenomenology of the Social World, by Alfred Schutz. Evanston: Northwestern University Press.

Warshay, Leon

1975 The Current State of Sociological Theory. New York: McKay.

Weber, Max

1949 Max Weber on the Methodology of the Social Sciences. Glencoe: Free Press.

1964 The Theory of Social and Economic Organization. New York: Free Press.

Wellmer, Albrecht

1974a Critical Theory of Society. New York: Seabury Press.

1974b Communication and emancipation: Reflections on the "linguistic turn" in critical theory. Philosophy and Social Theory. Stony Brook Studies in Philosophy, vol. 1:74–120.

Wilson, T.

1970 Normative and interpretative paradigms in sociology. Pp. 57–70 in Understanding Everyday Life, edited by J. Douglas. Chicago: Aldine.

Wünderlich, Dieter

1971 Pragmatic, Sprechsituation und Diexis. In Beitraege zur Literaturwissenschaft und Linguistic. Bad Homburg.

1972 Linguistiche Pragmatik. Frankfurt: Athanäum.

Zetterberg, Hans

1963 On Theory Verification in Sociology. Totowa, N.J.: The Bedminster Press.

Zimmerman, Don and Melvin Pollner

1970 The everyday world as a phenomenon. Pp. 30–103 in Douglas 1970.

Zimmerman, Don and D. L. Wieder

1970 Ethnomethodology and the problem of order: Comment on Denzin. Pp. 285–95 in Douglas 1970.

Index